ARE YOU THE CHRIST? THE TRIAL NARRATIVE
IN THE GOSPEL OF MARK

ARE YOU THE CHRIST? THE TRIAL NARRATIVE
IN THE GOSPEL OF MARK

by

John R. Donahue, S.J.

Published by

SOCIETY OF BIBLICAL LITERATURE

for

The Seminar on Mark

DISSERTATION SERIES, NUMBER TEN

1973

ARE YOU THE CHRIST? THE TRIAL NARRATIVE

IN THE GOSPEL OF MARK

by

John R. Donahue, S.J.
Woodstock College
475 Riverside Dr.
New York, New York 10027

Ph.D. 1972
University of Chicago

Advisor:
Norman Perrin

Copyright © 1973

by

SOCIETY OF BIBLICAL LITERATURE

ISBN 0-89130-165-8   (previously ISBN 0-99414-021-0)
Library of Congress Catalog Card Number: 73-81373

Printed in the United States of America

To My Parents

TABLE OF CONTENTS

	Page
ABBREVIATIONS	ix-x
ACKNOWLEDGMENTS	xi
INTRODUCTION	1

Chapter

I. TRIAL NARRATIVE AND PASSION NARRATIVE 5

    Introduction
    Survey of Research
    Methodological Considerations
    Conclusion

II. TRADITION AND REDACTION IN THE MARCAN TRIAL NARRATIVE 53

    Introduction
    The Trial Scene as Marcan
    Tradition and Redaction in the Trial Narrative
    Conclusion

III. THE TEMPLE SAYING OF THE TRIAL NARRATIVE 103

    Introduction
    Tradition and Redaction of the Temple Saying
    The Anti-Temple Theme in Mark
    Conclusion

IV. THE CHRISTOLOGY OF THE TRIAL NARRATIVE 139

    Introduction
    Future Son of Man Sayings and the Christology
      of the Trial Narrative
    Mark's Use of Future Son of Man Sayings
    Son of Man and the Other Titles of the
      Trial Scene
    Conclusion

V. THE TRIAL NARRATIVE IN THE GOSPEL OF MARK 189

    Introduction
    Trial Narrative and Crucifixion Narrative
      (15:20b-41)
    The Trial Narrative and the Marcan Community
    The Trial Narrative as Narrative
    Conclusion

CONCLUSION	237
APPENDIX: THE MARCAN INSERTIONS	241
BIBLIOGRAPHY	245
INDEX OF SCRIPTURAL CITATIONS	261

ABBREVIATIONS

BJRL	Bulletin of the John Rylands Library
BZ	Biblische Zeitschrift
BZAW	Beihefte zur Zeitschrift für die alttestamentliche Wissenschaft
BZNW	Beihefte zur Zeitschrift für die neutestamentliche Wissenschaft
CBQ	Catholic Biblical Quarterly
EvT	Evangelische Theologie
ExpT	Expository Times
FRLANT	Forschungen zur Religion und Literatur des Alten und Neuen Testaments
JBL	Journal of Biblical Literature
JR	Journal of Religion
JTS	Journal of Theological Studies
LXX	The Septuagint Version of the Old Testament
NovT	Novum Testamentum
NTS	New Testament Studies
RB	Revue Biblique
RGG	Religion in Geschichte und Gegenwart
RHPR	Revue d'histoire et de philosophie religieuses
SBL	Society of Biblical Literature
StANT	Studien zum Alten und Neuen Testament
TDNT	Theological Dictionary of the New Testament
ThRu	Theologische Rundschau

ABBREVIATIONS--Continued

TLZ	Theologische Literaturzeitung
USQR	Union Seminary Quarterly Review
WMANT	Wissenschaftliche Monographien zum Alten und Neuen Testament
ZAW	Zeitschrift für die alttestamentliche Wissenschaft
ZNW	Zeitschrift für die neutestamentliche Wissenschaft
ZTK	Zeitschrift für Theologie und Kirche

The system of transliteration of Greek and Hebrew follows that adopted by the Catholic Biblical Quarterly and the Journal of Biblical Literature, with the exception that the initial rough breathing is transliterated as "h."

ACKNOWLEDGMENTS

In the course of completing this study of the trial narrative of the gospel of Mark, two individuals became very much part of my life for over two years. The evangelist, Mark, spoke to me through his text out of the distant past. Prof. Norman Perrin spoke out of a vital presence. To him I owe profound appreciation and gratitude. His own creative research was the impetus to begin this work. He was ever available for help, criticism and encouragement. I am proud to have worked with him. I would also like to thank Prof. Jonathan Z. Smith and Prof. Jay A. Wilcoxen who kindly read the dissertation, and who, in classes and discussion, taught me much about the world of the Ancient Near East and Hellenism. To Prof. Joseph A. Fitzmyer, S.J., I am ever indebted for introducing me to the excitement of New Testament scholarship and encouraging me to pursue research in this area. I owe also a special debt of gratitude to Joseph M. Kitagawa, Dean of the Divinity School of the University of Chicago, who, along with Prof. Perrin, was instrumental in appointing me as Research Associate so that I could finish the dissertation with care and gain experience in teaching.

I owe a special debt of gratitude to my fellow Jesuits at Hopkins Hall in Chicago and to Rev. Thomas Fitzgerald, Pastor, the other priests and the people of St. Thomas the Apostle parish who lived through with me the times of doubt and the times of joy which characterize the writing of a dissertation. Their support and the support and encouragement of many other good friends in Chicago are as close to me as anything I have written.

INTRODUCTION

Progress in the scientific study of any area of human concern is due, usually, to one of two factors: the discovery of new data or the emergence of a new methodology. The discovery, publication and interpretation of both the Qumran scrolls and the texts from Nag Hammadi provide a dramatic illustration of the contribution of new data to the present excitement of New Testament research. Equally influential is the emergence and practice of the new methodology of redaction criticism. Since the mid-fifties this method has given scholars a new way of asking questions of the synoptic gospels, and a way of finding new answers to old questions. Basically redaction criticism argues from the literary activity of one of the evangelists to his theological concerns. In the case of both the Qumran scrolls and the Nag Hammadi texts as well as in the case of redaction criticism, scholarship works in continuity with the past. The discoveries emerging from Qumran and Nag Hammadi build on the previous studies of sectarian Judaism and Gnosticism in the early part of this century. So too, redaction criticism builds on the literary analysis of the synoptic gospels, in its concrete forms of source and form criticism, which has occupied scholars in the past century.

In this light the present work arises as an attempt to apply a new methodology to the Marcan narrative of the trial before the Sanhedrin (Mk 14:53-65)--a section of Mark which has not been studied before from this viewpoint. The concern of the initial chapter of the work is therefore twofold: to survey the problems of this narrative which have eluded the solution of earlier approaches and to outline in detail the various aspects of redaction criticism as they bear on a solution to the problem of the narrative. Redaction criticism involves two major operations: literary analysis to uncover what an author does with his material, and an act of judgment on why he does what he does, or, in other words, on his religious and theological intent. The second chapter of the present work consists of an extensive literary analysis of the trial narrative in order to discover Mark's literary activity--his redaction and composition in this narrative.

The literary analysis of the second chapter will reveal that there are two major areas of concern in the trial narrative, the temple saying of 14:58 and the Christological material of 14:61-62. The task of Chapters III and IV will be to make a judgment of why Mark has integrated these concerns into the trial narrative. Here also the method will consist of literary analysis and theological judgment. Here, also, our analysis will carry beyond the confines of the trial narrative in attempting to show the relation of the temple material and the Christological confession to similar material in other parts of the gospel. A necessary presupposition to redaction criticism is that the final product, the gospel, is a product of one hand, and that any individual part must be considered in relation to the whole.

The final chapter will represent an attempt to pull together loose ends or to answer questions posed by the methodology which have not been answered in previous chapters. The subject matter of the last chapter is, therefore, dictated by the demands of the method. Here, we will seek the relation of the trial narrative as a whole to the gospel as a whole, suggest a contact between the trial narrative and the concerns of the community for whom the gospel was written, and finally discuss the nature of the trial narrative precisely as narrative.

A growing hesitancy about the conclusions of redaction criticism, expressed by some contemporary authors, is that it presupposes a too high degree of literary sophistication on the part of the gospel authors. In approaching the gospels with the heritage and influence of form criticism, many authors find it difficult to view Mark as anyone more than a collector of pre-existing traditions. The study of complex structures, of at times subtle literary techniques and of well worked-out theological views makes some contemporary critics ask: could Mark have intended this? The present work moves in opposition to the above views by studying what Mark actually did, not what he could or could not have done. The great amount of detailed literary analysis in the present work is an attempt to show that Mark's literary work can be detected and that he exercises a creative influence on the traditions he receives and does not simply take them over. The question of conscious intent is a misleading one since not every evidence of literary activity presupposes conscious intent. Modern literary criticism has long seen that the final literary product of an author moves beyond what the author may have consciously intended. Elements of style, evidence of concerns which arise from the author's personal history and cultural situation--all become part of the final product in a way which escapes at times even the author's stated intent. The Mark who is of interest to us in the present work is the Mark who emerges from the text which bears his name. Presuppositions about what a first century Christian author could have intended must yield before judgments about what he actually achieved.

The present stage of redaction criticism carries with it an inherent problem. While the theology of any individual pericope must be judged in light of the theology of the gospel as a whole, there is and cannot be any consensus at the present time on such a theology. An analogy from another discipline may illustrate this problem. Modern psychotherapy has realized that the problems of an individual must be solved in the context of the social group he encounters. Individual analysis is yielding to contextual and group therapy. So too, the "problems" of an individual pericope, must be solved in terms of the larger context of the pericope. In the case of the trial narrative this context is twofold, the context of the Passion narrative and the context of the whole gospel. Since redaction-critical work on the Passion narrative is less developed than work on the other parts of the gospel, and since there is no definite statement on the relation of the Passion narrative to the whole gospel, the present work must represent a small contribution to some future synthetic work on the theology of the Passion narrative and the whole gospel. The results of the research undertaken here are as much a beginning as an end of a detailed study of the trial narrative of Mark.

CHAPTER I

TRIAL NARRATIVE AND PASSION NARRATIVE

Introduction

The fifteen years since the first edition of Willi Marxsen's, Der Evangelist Markus, have seen the emergence of Redaktionsgeschichte as the dominant methodology in the study of Mark.[1] Redaction criticism is an umbrella concept which studies the "theological motivation of an author as this is revealed in the collection, arrangement, editing and modification of traditional material or the creation of new forms within the traditions of early Christianity."[2] In contrast to the earlier methodologies of source and form criticism which posed the question of the origin of material and its function in the pre-Marcan setting, and which viewed the evangelist primarily as a Sammler, redaction criticism asks the question of purpose and affirms that any given material has a definite role and function within the total meaning of the gospel, and is not present simply as a relic of undigested tradition. In terms of

---

[1] Willi Marxsen, Der Evangelist Markus (FRLANT, N.F. Vol. LXVII; Göttingen: Vandenhoeck und Ruprecht, 1956); English translation, Mark the Evangelist by James Boyce (Nashville: Abingdon Press, 1969). A survey of redaction-critical work on Mark can be found in the following authors: J. Delorme, "Aspects doctrinaux du second Évangile. Études récentes de la redaction de Marc," De Jesus aux Évangiles, ed. I. de la Potterie (Bibliotheca Ephemeridum Theologicarum Lovaniensium, Vol. XLIII; Gembloux: J. Duculot, 1967), pp. 42-74; Hans Dieter Knigge, "The Meaning of Mark," Interpretation, XXII (1968), 53-70; F. J. Matera, "Interpreting Mark--Some Recent Theories of Redaction Criticism," Louvain Studies, II (1968), 113-131; Joachim Rohde, Rediscovering the Teaching of the Evangelist, trans. Dorothea M. Barton (Philadelphia: Westminster Press, 1969), pp. 113-149.

[2] N. Perrin, What is Redaction Criticism? (Philadelphia: Fortress Press, 1969), p. 1.

technique redaction criticism has a twofold aspect. One aspect, which builds on form-critical and tradition-historical studies, concentrates on the difference between the received tradition and the author's modification of this tradition in order to discover evidence of the author's theological motivation in his reworking of the tradition.[1] The other aspect does not focus as much on the author's reworking of tradition, but stresses his creative activity as this emerges in the composition of new material and in his arrangement of his material in definite patterns and structures which show his concerns.[2]

Though redaction-critical studies have been extensive in respect to the first thirteen chapters of Mark, little attention has been given to the Passion narrative.[3] This lacuna is explicable on two grounds: (a) form criticism, the parent and often the presupposition to redaction criticism, has not been applied extensively to the Passion narrative,[4] and (b) the long

---

[1]This aspect of redaction criticism has been especially successful in studies of Matthew's and Luke's adaptation of Mark. See G. Bornkamm, G. Barth, and H. J. Held, Tradition and Interpretation in Matthew, trans. Percy Scott (Philadelphia: Westminster Press, 1963); H. Conzelmann, The Theology of St. Luke, trans. G. Buswell (New York: Harper and Row, 1961).

[2]E. Best, The Temptation and Passion: The Markan Soteriology (Society for New Testament Studies, Monograph Series, Vol. II; Cambridge: University Press, 1965); Perrin, Redaction Criticism, pp. 40-63, analyzes patterns and structures, and also see his "The Christology of Mark: A Study in Methodology," JR, LI (1971), 174-176. P. Vielhauer, "Erwägungen zur Christologie des Markusevangeliums," Aufsätze zum Neuen Testament (Theologische Bücherei, Vol. XXI; Munich: Kaiser Verlag, 1965), pp. 199-214.

[3]The only full-scale study of the Passion narrative from a redaction-critical viewpoint is J. Schreiber, Die Theologie des Vertrauens (Hamburg: Furche Verlag, 1969), pp. 1-86, treat of the crucifixion accounts.

[4]Though the "founders" of form criticism, Dibelius and Bultmann treat the Passion narrative, their successors have not concentrated as much on this section of the gospels as on the other sections.

standing opinion that the Passion narrative is the largest block of traditional material taken over by the evangelists, so that there is reluctance to attempt to distinguish tradition and redaction in that section of the gospel which is considered mostly as tradition. This latter view rests mainly on the authority of Dibelius and Kähler. Dibelius, the form critic, who has written most extensively on the Passion narrative, remarks that ". . . exactly what differentiates the Passion story from the Gospel tradition [is] its early-composition as a connected narrative."[1] This view is correlative to Kähler's position, articulated ten years earlier, that the gospels are Passion narratives with extended introductions.[2] Thus, the consensus emerges that there is little activity of the evangelist in the Passion narrative. He is thought to have received it as a "given" and added to it material from the traditions about the life of Jesus, so that the creative activity of the evangelist is to be sought outside the Passion narrative.

Recent studies within the scope of the work of Dibelius himself, and the implications of his work have suggested that this view must be modified.[3] The work of Jeremias on the Eucharistic words of Jesus, of Kuhn on the Gethsemane pericope, of Klein on the denial of Peter, and of Schreiber on the crucifixion narrative, suggest that each of these narratives went through a stage of development and that the evangelist himself

---

[1] Martin Dibelius, From Tradition to Gospel, trans. Bertram Woolf (The Scribner Library; New York: Charles Scribner's Sons, n.d.), p. 180.

[2] Martin Kähler, The So-Called Historical Jesus and the Historic Biblical Christ, trans. Carl Braaten (Philadelphia: Fortress Press, 1966), p. 80, n. 11.

[3] Though Dibelius holds to an early connected narrative, his own work in distinguishing primary and secondary elements in the present narrative provided the starting point for a questioning of his position.

was active in the final form of the narrative.¹ In a recently published and exhaustive form-critical study of each pericope of the Passion narrative, Eta Linnemann has shown that every pericope shows traces of a development, and she attempts to describe Mark's activity in the final product.² At the conclusion of her research she writes:

> Alle redaktionsgeschichtliche Arbeit am Markusevangelium, die bisher geleistet wurde, ging von der Voraussetzung aus, dass dem Evangelisten bereits eine zusammenhängende Passionsgeschichte vorgelegen hat. Diese Voraussetzung ist--wie wir zeigen konnten--nicht gegeben. Die redaktionsgeschichtliche Erforschung des Markusevangeliums hat deshalb noch einmal neu anzusetzen und der Tatsache Rechnung zu tragen, dass der Evangelist ebenso wie das übrige Evangelium auch die Passionsgeschichte aus Einzeltraditionen gebildet hat.³

Despite the comparative paucity of form and redaction-critical work on the Passion narrative, there is, therefore, a growing opinion that within the Passion narrative it is possible to distinguish between tradition and redaction, and, hence, to detect the redactional and compositional activity of the evangelist in that narrative.

Faced with the growing opinion that the monolithic view of the Passion narrative is breaking down, and yet, at the same time, faced with a lack of any detailed work on, or agreement on, the theology of the Passion narrative as a whole, the contemporary researcher must content himself with study of individual parts of the Passion story in order to prepare the way for further and more comprehensive studies. In this light

---

[1] Joachim Jeremias, The Eucharistic Words of Jesus, trans. N. Perrin (3rd rev. ed.; London: S. C. M. Press, 1966); K. G. Kuhn, "Jesus in Gethsemane," EvT, XII (1952-53), 260-285; Günther Klein, "Die Verleugnung des Petrus: Eine Traditionsgeschichtliche Untersuchung," ZTK, LVIII (1961), 286-328.

[2] Eta Linnemann, Studien zur Passionsgeschichte (FRLANT, Vol. CII; Göttingen: Vandenhoeck und Ruprecht, 1970).

[3] Studien, pp. 174-175.

the trial narrative, the hearing before the Sanhedrin in Mark 14:53-65, assumes a very real importance.[1] First of all, the subsequent review of the discussion of the trial narrative will show that there is a consensus among authors of many different viewpoints that, in terms of tradition history, the trial narrative is secondary to whatever was the original Passion narrative.[2] Secondly, the narrative itself is replete with apparent literary inconsistencies and difficulties of content which should be adequately resolved if the narrative is to make sense. Some of these may be listed as follows:

1. Why is the narrative intercalated within the story of the denial of Peter (14:54, 66-72)?
2. Why is there a double introduction to the narrative (14:53, 55)?
3. Why is there the excessive repetition of the inadequacy and of the falseness of the witnesses (14:55, 56a, 56b, 57, 59)?
4. Why is the saying about the destruction of the temple put on the lips of these witnesses, and what is the meaning of the saying?
5. Why is the material which comprises the substance of the charge in 14:55-61a, i.e., the temple material, not taken up again in the question of the high priest?

---

[1]By the use of the term "trial narrative" in the present discussion we make no judgment on whether the actual historical event was a formal trial or an informal hearing. The term is used simply as a standard way of designating the pericope.

[2]The term "secondary" here means that, in terms of what various authors will designate as the earliest literary traditions of the Passion narrative, there are parts which are additions to or later than this early tradition. Again the question of historicity is not the direct object of concern in the present discussion.

6. In 14:61b and 62 the major Christological titles of Mark's gospel reappear and we find in Jesus' answer, egō eimi, the first public acceptance by Jesus of a messianic title, without a command to secrecy. How is this to be explained?[1]

7. Why is it that the exaltation and parousia of Jesus are joined together in 14:62 and not in any other passage?[2]

The review of the discussion of the trial narrative, which will occupy the greater part of this chapter, will illustrate how various scholars have touched on the above problems. However, there has of yet been no attempt to show how all the elements of the trial narrative fit together in a consistent narrative. The prevailing tendency has been to attribute the complexities to poor Marcan composition. The tensions are thought to exist because Mark has taken over traditional material and does not attempt to resolve the inconsistencies within the material.[3] The presupposition of redaction

---

[1] Christian Maurer, "Das Messiasgeheimnis des Markusevangeliums," NTS, XIV (1967-68), 519: "Mark. xiv. 62 ist die einzige Stelle im ganzen Evangelium, an der Jesus offen ausspricht, wer und was er ist."

[2] Eduard Schweizer, The Good News According to Mark, trans. Donald H. Madvig (Richmond: John Knox Press, 1970), p. 326.

[3] Since the famous quote of Papias that Mark did not set things down in order (ou mentoi taxei), the primitive and unartistic quality of Mark in contrast to the other evangelists has been overemphasized. See Vincent Taylor, The Gospel According to St. Mark (2nd ed.; London: Macmillan, 1966), p. 2. One of the legacies of the Marcan hypothesis of the nineteenth century was to affirm the primitive quality of Mark, W. G. Kümmel, Das Neue Testament: Geschichte der Erforschung seiner Probleme (2nd rev. ed.; Munich: Verlag Karl Alber, 1970), pp. 180-191; Albert Schweitzer, The Quest of the Historical Jesus, trans. W. Montgomery (New York: Macmillan, 1961), pp. 121-137. As late as 1959 X. Léon-DuFour writes: "Mc. n'est pas un styliste, pas meme un conteur de talent il apparait comme un rapporteur fidèle, naïf. Cela découle du caractère stéréotypé des récits comme de l'indigence de son vocabulaire, et des traits dont il parsème son oeuvre," Introduction à la Bible, ed. A. Robert and A. Feuillet (Paris: Desclee, 1959), II, 205.

criticism, on the other hand, is that an author works with his material with conscious artistry and purpose, so that a major aim of the present study will be to show that the elements of the trial narrative which have caused so much difficulty in the past are indices of Marcan theological concerns, and that the narrative is a deliberate and well worked-out mixture of various motifs and concerns of the evangelist Mark.[1]

The numerous contacts of the trial narrative with other parts of Mark suggest that it should be considered as an entree to a study of his total theological purpose. The first and third passion predictions (8:31; 10:33) show contact with this narrative in the mention of the handing over of Jesus to the Jewish officials and the condemnation to death.[2] The lack of faith and the misunderstanding of the disciples, which permeates 8:27-10:52, culminates in the flight of the disciples (14:50) and the denial by Peter (14:54, 66ff.). As was mentioned, the main Christological titles of the gospel are recapitulated in 14:61-62, and the veil of the Messianic Secret is lifted here. The preoccupation of Jesus with Jerusalem and the temple which begins in ch. 11 reaches its culmination in the temple saying of 14:58.[3] Such considerations indicate that the trial narrative merits discussion not only in order to resolve the difficulties intrinsic to the narrative, but also in order to further understand the whole gospel.

---

[1] The results of redaction-critical work done on Mark confirm that this is not a groundless presupposition, but that Mark is master of his material.

[2] Georg Strecker, "The Passion- and Resurrection Predictions in Mark's Gospel," *Interpretation*, XXII (1968), 421-442.

[3] Lloyd Gaston, No Stone on Another (Supplements to Novum Testamentum, Vol. XXIII; Leiden: E. J. Brill, 1970); Ernst Lohmeyer, Lord of the Temple: A Study of the Relation between Cult and Gospel, trans. Stewart Todd (Edinburgh and London: Oliver and Boyd, 1961).

The purpose of the present treatment is, therefore, to examine the trial narrative from a redaction-critical point of view. As necessary prerequisites to this discussion two things must be done. First of all, it is necessary to survey the previous discussions of the trial narrative in order to see how various commentators have isolated problems connected with it and how they view the status of the material in it. For the most part this research has been indirect, that is, as part of a larger study of the whole Passion narrative, so that it will be necessary to examine how various authors see the trial narrative in the context of the whole Passion narrative. Upon completion of this whole survey not only will the main problems of the trial narrative clearly emerge, but only then can the second prerequisite to a study of the narrative be discussed. This prerequisite will consist in a detailed statement on the methodology of redaction criticism and its mode of application to the present task. The function of the present chapter is, therefore, to delimit carefully the subject matter of the present study, to examine the successes and inadequacies of previous treatments, and to suggest a methodology which will move the present discussion beyond previous treatments.

Survey of Research

Martin Dibelius

Of all the studies done in the past fifty years on the Passion narrative, Dibelius' work is significant, not only because it is first, but also because, in many ways, his insights remain unsurpassed, though often undeveloped.[1] From his

---

[1] Though we will disagree with Dibelius when he posits an early connected narrative, we follow his observations about the secondary quality of the trial narrative, and his seminal remarks about the theological importance of the trial narrative provide the starting point for the present research.

earliest works on the Passion narrative in 1915 until his latest in 1939, Dibelius examined the forces at work in the formation of the narrative, its theological and religious concerns, and the stages of its formation.[1] Dibelius is, of course, well known as one of the founders of the formgeschichtliche method, and it is this method which explains his view of the formation of the Passion narrative in its pre-literary tradition. In contrast to the later work of Bultmann, Dibelius does not begin with the text of the New Testament and analyze the forms of literature found there in order to find their function and setting, but he begins with some situation in the early church and discusses what form is proper to this situation.[2] The situation *par excellence* which explains the origin of the Passion narrative is early Christian preaching which, in Dibelius' view, demanded a connected story of the events at a very early stage.[3] Despite the expectation of the imminent

---

[1] In chronological order the works of Dibelius on the Passion Narrative are: "Herodes und Pilatus," ZNW, XVI (1915), 113-126; "Die alttestamentlichen Motive in der Leidensgeschichte des Petrus-und Johannes-Evangeliums," BZAW, XXXIII (1918), 125-150; Die Formgeschichte des Evangeliums (Tübingen: J. C. B. Mohr [Paul Siebeck], 1919); "Das historische Problem der Leidensgeschichte," ZNW, XXX (1931), 193-201; "La signification religieuse des récits évangéliques de la Passion," RHPR, XIII (1933), 30-45; "Gethsemane," The Crozer Quarterly, XII (1935), 254-265; "Judas und der Judaskuss," Deutsches Pfarrerblatt, 1939, pp. 727-731. With the exception of "La signification," the articles of Dibelius on the Passion narrative have been collected in Botschaft und Geschichte: Gesammelte Aufsätze von Martin Dibelius, Vol. I: Zur Evangelienforschung, ed. Günther Bornkamm (Tübingen: J. C. B. Mohr [Paul Siebeck], 1953). References will be to the collection.

[2] For a discussion of the differences in the method see Rudolf Bultmann, History of the Synoptic Tradition, trans. John Marsh (rev. ed.; New York: Harper and Row, 1968), pp. 5-6; M. Dibelius, "Zur Formgeschichte der Evangelien," ThRu, N.F. I (1929), 185-216.

[3] In his earliest work on the Passion narrative Dibelius sets up the principle that the Passion, in contrast to the other stories about Jesus, required a connected narrative because salvation was seen in the events themselves, while the other stories served only an exemplary function, "Herodes und Pilatus," Botschaft und Geschichte, I, 278.

return of the Lord, the early Christian communities were driven by a missionary desire to proclaim the message of salvation through Jesus. This preaching normally took the form of a statement of the kerygma, proofs from scripture and an exhortation to repentance.[1]

The observation that the primitive preaching is filled out by the use of Old Testament quotes and allusions becomes very important to Dibelius' thought. In the year before his famous **Formgeschichte des Evangeliums**, Dibelius published an article on the use of Old Testament motifs in the gospel of John and the apocryphal gospel of Peter.[2] In noting that the oldest kerygmatic reference to the Passion claims that the death of Jesus was "according to the scriptures," Dibelius says:

> Längst ehe es Evangelienbücher und ehe es die erste zusammenhängende Leidensgeschichte gab, hatten die Lehrer der Gemeinde diese Quellen erschlossen und die Prediger diese 'Texte' behandelt.[3]

The Old Testament texts served a double function. On the one hand, they provided an apology for the death of Jesus; on the other, they exerted a formative influence on the tradition, since whole pericopes were composed to illustrate an Old Testament text, rather than recount an historical event. What is at work here is not simply a matter of allusions to some Old Testament text, but the creation of whole narratives to illustrate the text. The only detailed example which Dibelius gives of this process is the reference in Jn 19:13 to Jesus being brought before the bēma of Pilate.[4] By a complex series of arguments and by reference to the way in which Isa 58:2-3 is used in the **Gospel of Peter** and the **Apology of Justin**, Dibelius is able to show that Jn 19:13 represents a historicization of an

---

[1] "Die alttestamentliche Motive," Botschaft und Geschichte, I, 221.

[2] Ibid. [3] Ibid., I, 223. [4] Ibid., I, 224-235.

Old Testament text for Christological and apologetic purposes.[1]

The importance of the work of Dibelius in this area is not so much the validity of his examination of the relation of Isa 58:2 to Jn 19:13, but his insight about the formative power of Old Testament texts. Contemporary studies of the *pesher* and midrashic use of Old Testament texts in the New by scholars such as Barnabas Lindars and Lars Hartmann have shown that whole narratives are simply historicizations of the Old Testament.[2] They have also shown that in every case it is not necessary to have an explicit Old Testament allusion, since, at times, the contact with the Old Testament is hidden behind layers of tradition. In the present treatment this initial insight of Dibelius about the influence of the Old Testament on the Passion narrative and the way this insight has been used by other scholars will provide the key to the problem of the false witnesses in the trial narrative, and contribute to an understanding of the formation of the Christological traditions in the narrative.

The third major characterization of the pre-Marcan Passion narrative, in addition to its setting in the preaching of the church and its growth by the use of Old Testament texts, is its eschatological dimension. Dibelius pictures a community which lives in expectation of the imminent return of the Lord, and which saw in his death and resurrection the eschatological event which brought history to a conclusion, and offered to men

---

[1] *Ibid.*, I, 235. In his *From Tradition to Gospel*, Dibelius summarizes this process: ". . . and thus these motives which had been at home in the Old Testament came into the text of the Passion. This took place, without citing the Old Testament words, simply in the form of narrative" (p. 185).

[2] Lars Hartmann, *Prophecy Interpreted: The Formation of Some Jewish Apocalyptic Texts and of the Eschatological Discourse Mark 13 par.* (Lund: G. W. K. Gleerup, 1966); Barnabas Lindars, *New Testament Apologetic* (Philadelphia: The Westminster Press, 1961); N. Perrin, "Mark XIV.62: The End Product of a Christian Tradition?" NTS, XII (1965-66), 150-155.

the promise of salvation.¹ This community was driven by an intense desire to spread this message of salvation, so that Dibelius writes: "missionary purpose was the cause and preaching the means of spreading abroad that which the disciples of Jesus possessed as recollection."² The primary content of this preaching was the Passion of Jesus which, in contrast to other blocks of unconnected material and sayings of Jesus, was narrated in connected form, because, in the case of the Passion, the events themselves were the kerygma, while the other material which circulated was illustrative of the kerygma.³

Thus, initial observation of Dibelius' studies on the pre-Marcan Passion tradition reveals his conception of the forces at work in the formation of this tradition. The primary force was the mission preaching of the Church. This preaching used Old Testament texts which themselves were formative of other traditions. Finally, the preaching had a definite slant--the eschatological message of salvation revealed in the events surrounding the death of Jesus.

Since the Marcan Passion narrative is present to us in the form of literature, Dibelius applies to it literary and stylistic criteria in order to find if there is an older, connected account at the basis of the present narrative--a postulate that Dibelius finds necessary from the use of this account in preaching. We will indicate the reasons why Dibelius postulates an older account, and, at the same time, try to evaluate the relationship of the trial narrative to this older account.

---

[1] "Die Passion ist der Anfang der Endeschichte," "Das historische Problem," Botschaft und Geschichte, I, 249.

[2] From Tradition to Gospel, p. 32.

[3] Supra, p. 13, n. 3. "Das historische Problem," Botschaft und Geschichte, I, 250, and Erich Fascher, Die Formgeschichtliche Methode (BZNW, Vol. II; Giessen: A Töpelmann, 1924), p. 55.

Two arguments are basic to his view that, prior to Mark, there was an older literary account of the Passion narrative: (a) the present account is relatively self-enclosed and (b) there is significant agreement between John and the Synoptics only in this section of the gospels.[1] While skeptical about being able to isolate exactly any Grundschrift to the Marcan account, Dibelius does attempt to distinguish primary and secondary elements in the narrative, discusses the status of individual units which are considered secondary, and comments on the author's motivation in the final account.

The first bit of literary evidence which Dibelius finds as a way of distinguishing accounts are the two chronological indications of Mk 14:1 and 14:10.[2] According to these indications the arrest took place before the feast, but this stands in tension with the Marcan view that Jesus ate a Passover meal with the disciples. The second literary evidence is the remark in 14:28 that Jesus would "go before" the disciples in Galilee which presupposes appearances of the risen Lord in Galilee, and thus a different ending is demanded for the Passion narrative than that of the empty tomb in 16:8.[3] Finally, in the present account Dibelius finds evidence of expansions and insertions. The anointing at Bethany interrupts the flow of the narrative from 14:2-10; the introduction to the last supper, 14:12-16, is a later addition which serves to make the supper into a Passover meal; the Gethsemane scene, 14:32-42, is linked artificially to the narrative and has a tradition history of its own;[4] finally, the trial narrative seems simply to be an expansion of a saying

---

[1] From Tradition to Gospel, pp. 23, 178.

[2] Ibid., p. 180.   [3] Ibid., pp. 181-182.

[4] Ibid., p. 182; "Gethsemane," Botschaft und Geschichte, I, 258-271.

of Jesus against the temple.[1]

Thus, the older account did not contain the anointing, the Passover meal, Gethsemane or the trial before the Sanhedrin. This account had one purpose--to describe the meaning of the events on which the Easter faith was founded.[2] The apologetic motif is strong in attempting to show not only that Christ now lives with the Father, but that the horror and ignominy of the Passion was willed by God, and to show that the catastrophe of the crucifixion was nothing more than the prelude to the coming in majesty of the risen Lord whom the community worshipped.[3] Dibelius then makes the evocative remark that by comparing the older account with the Marcan additions, we can arrive at some notion of the purpose of Mark. The significance of this observation is that it anticipates one very important facet of redaction criticism, the discovery of an author's motivation from the way in which he alters traditional accounts.[4]

Dibelius' treatment of the trial narrative, though not extensive, can now be seen in the light of his view of the Passion narrative as a whole. The secondary quality of the trial narrative is indicated first of all by its position as an insertion into the story of Peter's denial, which is part of the older account.[5] The narrative itself is an expansion of a single utterance of Jesus, his saying against the temple in 14:58.[6] It may be that the trial before the Sanhedrin was

---

[1] *From Tradition to Gospel*, pp. 182-183. In another place Dibelius holds that the mocking by the Sanhedrin is a historicization of Isa 50:6, "Die alttestamentliche Motive," *Botschaft und Geschichte*, I, 241.

[2] *From Tradition to Gospel*, p. 184.

[3] "Das historische Problem," *Botschaft und Geschichte*, I, 249.

[4] *From Tradition to Gospel*, p. 189.

[5] *Ibid.*, pp. 183, 193.   [6] *Ibid.*, p. 182.

completely lacking in the older account, so that the only mention of the Sanhedrin was in 15:1.[1] The chief Marcan concern of the trial scene is "the motive which is decisive in the whole narrative, the confession of Jesus as the Messiah." Dibelius also writes:

> What Mark means to describe in 14:61-63 is that a supernatural majesty flamed in the midst of all the shame of Jesus and while the criminal was dying his heavenly future was announced to the world.[2]

Such a view of the Christology of the trial scene is in harmony with Dibelius' general view of the gospel of Mark as the book of "secret epiphanies," so that the trial scene is, in effect, the epiphany, no longer secret.[3]

As indicated, the remarks of Dibelius on the trial scene are more evocative than satisfying since he adduces little evidence to support his view that it grows out of an expansion of the temple saying, and since he does not develop the implications of the statements he makes. For our purposes the following things are of special significance. He clearly sees the trial scene as secondary to whatever was the original Passion account, and sees Mark at work in it for theological reasons. He notes the tension between the temple saying of 14:58 and the Christological material of 14:61ff. He alludes to the influence of the Old Testament on the formation of the whole scene, especially to the mocking section (14:65). Finally, he remarks that, along with the trial scene, Mark makes the crucifixion narrative into the second "high point" of the Passion narrative. He thus raises the question of the relation of the trial scene to this narrative, and to the Passion narrative as a whole.[4]

---

[1]Ibid. [2]Ibid., pp. 192-193.
[3]Ibid., p. 230. [4]Ibid., pp. 192-193.

Rudolf Bultmann

In contrast to the constructive and deductive method of Dibelius, Bultmann's method is analytic and inductive.[1] He begins with the text rather than an early Church situation (preaching), and, by careful literary analysis of the forms found and the laws of the development of tradition, argues to a situation which produced or transmitted the materials. In this vein, he treats the Passion narrative in the section on narrative traditions, under the rubric of historical stories and legends.[2]

Bultmann begins with the observation that the Passion narrative, as found in Mark, cannot be considered an organic unity.[3] Some of the stories (e.g., the anointing) are isolated units and do not depend on their context for their intelligibility; others have all the earmarks of supplementary embellishments of elements found in the stories themselves.[4] Bultmann does hold that, prior to Mark, there was a connected and coherent narrative, as comparison with the Johannine account and the Marcan Passion predictions would suggest. He then postulates a four stage development of the Passion narrative: (a) the kerygmatic tradition of the Passion and death of Jesus, (b) a short historical narrative of the arrest, condemnation and execution of Jesus, (c) the addition of unconnected stories such as the anointing and Gethsemane, and (d) supplementary embellishments.[5]

Bultmann characterizes the trial narrative as one of the supplementary embellishments which represents an expansion of an individual moment in an earlier account, represented by the mere

---

[1] Bultmann, Synoptic Tradition, p. 5.
[2] Ibid., pp. 262-287.   [3] Ibid., p. 265.
[4] Ibid., p. 275.   [5] Ibid.

mention of the gathering of the priests as found in Mk 15:1 and Lk 22:66.[1] Various motifs influence the formation of the trial narrative. The mocking in 14:65 is a development of Isa 50:6, and is put by Mark in a "peculiarly unfortunate place."[2] The narrative arises from the theological motivation to show that Jesus was put to death as the Messiah, so that 14:60-62 represents the nucleus of the first stage in the expansion of the narrative.[3] The material of the false witnesses in 14:57-59 is an insertion and the temple saying of 14:58 represents an insertion within an insertion and has its original setting in the prophetic and apocalyptic tradition.[4] In this latter view Bultmann stands in opposition to the earlier position of Welhausen and Dibelius who asserted that the temple saying was the nucleus of the original trial narrative.[5] Beyond these brief indications that a complex tradition history lies behind the trial narrative, Bultmann does not add detailed discussion or suggest how the various elements are related in the final form of the narrative. One valuable aspect of his treatment is that he has called attention to the problem of the relation of the temple saying of 14:58 to the Christological material of 14:61-62.

Eta Linnemann

Linnemann's recent work represents the first full scale form-critical study of the Passion narrative since Dibelius and

---

[1] Ibid., p. 270.　　[2] Ibid., pp. 281, 275.

[3] Ibid., pp. 275, 269-270.

[4] Ibid., p. 270. Bultmann holds also that the trial before the Sanhedrin is a doublet of the trial before Pilate (15:1-5).

[5] Julius Wellhausen, Das Evangelium Marci (Berlin: Georg Reimer, 1909), pp. 123-124. Dibelius, From Tradition to Gospel, p. 182.

Bultmann. From an analysis of each pericope she attempts to show that the hypothesis of a pre-Marcan connected narrative is no longer tenable. Her major purpose is to show that the things which make the Passion narrative a connected narrative are Marcan, that the major pericopes have a complex tradition history of their own, and that individual pericopes have existed as isolated units in some context other than the Passion narrative.[1] Her method is that of literary analysis (Sprachgestalt) and the isolation of different motifs at work in the formation of the narrative.[2] Since her work is so recent and reviews and criticisms are still lacking, and since the purpose of the present treatment is not a full discussion of the Passion narrative, we will limit our comments to her view of the trial narrative.

Linnemann begins her study of the trial narrative by comparing Mark 14:53-65 with 15:1-5.[3] Both narratives are alike in stressing the silence of Jesus before his accusers which represents a leitmotif taken from the Old Testament (Isa 53:7; Ps 38:13-16). This motif is clear in the trial before Pilate in 15:4 where the silence of Jesus confounds his accusers. In the trial before the Sanhedrin this motif becomes obscured by the answer of Jesus in 14:62, which is precipitated by the question of the high priest in 14:60. Linnemann then proceeds to a

---

[1] In Studien, pp. 170-178, Linnemann summarizes her results.

[2] By the method of Sprachgestalt Linnemann means the analysis of inconsistencies within the flow of the narrative which then suggest to her that pre-existing blocks are put together. In form and content her method resembles the earlier studies of Emanuel Hirsch, Frühgeschichte des Evangeliums, Vol. I, Das Werden des Markusevangeliums (2nd rev. ed.; Tübingen: J. C. B. Mohr [Paul Siebeck], 1951), and Emil Wending, Die Entstehung des Marcus-Evangeliums (Tübingen: J. C. B. Mohr [Paul Siebeck], 1908).

[3] Studien, pp. 110, 134-135.

literary analysis of the trial scene to find out what verses best fit in with this motif of silence.

If the motif of silence is to be effective, the indication of the falseness of the witnesses in 14:59 is superfluous, since it would preclude the anticipation of a response on the part of Jesus.[1] The following verses are confused for Linnemann and she attempts a reconstruction.[2] The question of the high priest in 14:60b, "Have you no answer to make?" is the logical response of the high priest to the temple charge. However, for the sake of the smooth flow of the narrative Linnemann postulates that the second question of the high priest, 14:61b, "Again the high priest asked him," should go before 60b, and the pericope on silence would conclude with the notation of 14:61a, "But he was silent and made no answer," so that in form and structure, Linnemann's reconstructed pericope on silence would be like 15:1-5. Linnemann thus ends up with a pre-Marcan pericope which consists of 14:55, an introduction to the pericope, and the narrative of the silence of Jesus, 14:57, 58, 61b, 60b, 61a, in that sequence. She then notes that the remaining verses also form a consistent narrative, but with a different motif. These tell of the messianic claim of Jesus and emphasize the Christian viewpoint that Jesus was put to death simply because he was the Messiah.

Linnemann finds different motifs at work in the formation of the pericope on the silence of Jesus.[3] The first motif is from the Old Testament where Jesus is portrayed as the innocent lamb who is led to slaughter in silence.[4] The temple saying and

---

[1]Ibid., p. 128.   [2]Ibid., pp. 128-129.
[3]Ibid., pp. 130-131.

[4]The Old Testament texts which Linnemann finds at work on the formation of the perciope are: Isa 53:7; Ps 38:13-16, on

its presence on the lips of false witnesses causes her special difficulty. The saying arises from a legendary motif (<u>marchenhaft</u>) that a man exhibits a certain boldness in the face of his accusers, so that it becomes necessary for God to perform a miracle to implement the bold claim of the man. It is put on the lips of false witnesses because of an apologetic desire to make the claim so absurd that it could not have been truly said by Jesus. Thus, the legend was used in the tradition as an attack against Jesus. Its presence on the lips of false witnesses and Jesus' silence in the face of the charge is a Christian answer to the charge.

Linnemann, thus, postulates two independent pre-Marcan pericopes at the basis of the trial scene: pericope "A" the silence of Jesus, and pericope "B" the narration of the messianic claim. Mark unites these in the trial narrative which he constructs in imitation of 15:1-5. In the course of the present study, we will have occasion to suggest a tradition history for the trial narrative, different from the one she postulates, so detailed discussion is not demanded at this point.[1] At present certain general criticisms can be made. Despite her claim to be basing her analysis on Marcan <u>Sprachgestalt</u>, she shows little awareness of Marcan compositional techniques and stylistic devices as they are found throughout the gospel. The most basic defect of her treatment is that it never really moves beyond the realm of form criticism and the evangelist Mark is reduced to a rather poor collector of two independent pericopes which he puts together in a rather unskilled way. Linnemann makes no attempt, then, to suggest what is the meaning of the trial narrative,

---

the silence of Jesus; on the innocence of Jesus before false witnesses, Pss 27:12, 109:2, <u>Studien</u>, p. 131.

[1]<u>Infra</u>, Chap. II, pp. 63-102.

once these two original pericopes are joined or how they relate to each other in the final product. Therefore, her work still leaves the way open for a redaction-critical analysis of the scene.

Vincent Taylor

The authors treated thus far approach the trial narrative from a form critical point of view and represent a "radical" approach traditionally associated with German scholarship. The views of Vincent Taylor on the trial narrative will be briefly discussed since he approaches the narrative from a source analysis point of view and represents in general a more conservative view of the tradition. Taylor attempts to isolate two independent narratives at the basis of the Marcan Passion narrative.[1] By using the criteria of the sequence of the narrative and the presence or absence of Semitisms, Taylor finds that certain narratives, such as "the Anointing, the story of Gethsemane, the Trial before the Priests, the Denial, and the Mockery by the soldiers (15:16-20)," are intercalated into the narrative, and, at the same time, contain a large number of Semitisms. Taylor calls these pericopes part of an older Passion account, B, which, he says, is based on the recollections of Peter. This account has been integrated into the straightforward narrative of the suffering of Jesus, account A, which was written by Mark to provide an apology for the suffering and death of Jesus, to be used by the Roman community.

The most problematic part of Taylor's reconstruction is the trial before the Sanhedrin. As an intercalation, it seems that it should be assigned to the B account, but there are not many Semitisms in it, and its theology is more in accord with

---

[1] Mark, pp. 653-671.

A.[1] Taylor cautiously assigns it to A, but for him it is still basically an historical narrative, and shows little evidence of Marcan redaction. The problem of the false witnesses Taylor calls almost insoluble, and the mocking of 14:65 is "manifestly a separate item of tradition."[2] Taylor's work is valuable in calling attention to the problematic nature of the trial narrative, even in terms of his own criteria, and to its position as an intercalation, which suggests that Mark is here using a literary device evident in other parts of his gospel.[3]

Cult-Historical Considerations

Although we are not concerned to discuss in any detail the religionsgeschichtlich background to the trial narrative, we may here indicate certain directions which that discussion has taken, since investigations from this viewpoint also suggest that it is secondary to the earlier Passion traditions and that cultic and credal influences are at work in its formation.

A pioneer form critic who directed particular attention to the Passion narrative is Georg Bertram.[4] For Bertram the Passion narrative arose not out of apologetic or dogmatic concerns, but out of the cultic worship of the community.[5] Cult for Bertram has a rather psychologized connotation; it is the inner relation of the believer to the cult hero.[6] A cultic

---

[1] Ibid., pp. 658-659.   [2] Ibid., p. 570.

[3] Taylor's work has been followed by Wilfred Knox, The Sources of the Synoptic Gospels, Vol. I: St. Mark (Cambridge: University Press, 1953), and Ivor Buse, "St. John and the Marcan Passion Narrative," NTS, IV (1957-58), 215-219.

[4] Georg Bertram, Die Leidensgeschichte Jesu und der Christuskult (FRLANT, N.F. Vol. XXII; Gottingen: Vandenhoeck und Ruprecht, 1922).

[5] Ibid., p. 6.

[6] Dibelius, "Zur Formgeschichte der Evangelien," ThRu, N.F. I (1929), 196, criticizes Bertram's notion of the cult as "psychologistic."

motif arises when the cult participant historicizes some element of his religious experience.[1] In the case of the Passion narrative the believer's experience of the risen Lord makes him view the Passion of Jesus as the way to the victory of the risen Lord. Such a motif arises within the worship of the community, and the pericopes of the Passion narrative in its final form mirror the cultic convictions of the community.[2]

In his analysis of the trial scenes (before the Sanhedrin and before Pilate), Bertram notes a certain recession of cultic motifs in the face of their apologetic intent.[3] The narratives serve to encourage a community undergoing trials and persecutions, and urge the community to be courageous as they follow Jesus in standing trial before pagans and Jews. The motif of imitation of the person Jesus directs the believer's attention to him and it is here that the cultic dimension returns. In the secular trial before Pilate the verb thaumazein (Mc 15:5) expresses the religious awe of Pilate before the divine majesty of Jesus. The scene does not recount history, but tells of the religious awe the Christian should have before the Lord. The trial before the Sanhedrin arises from a conjunction of two cultic motifs. In the temple saying (14:58), especially by the Marcan addition of "not made with hands," the community expresses it consciousness of itself as the new temple. The use of egō eimi in 14:61 and the Son of Man saying of 14:62 make the trial into an Epiphaniegeschichte, so that historical considerations of the genuinity of the saying are not important here.

Bertram's work is valuable in the present discussion, not because his conclusions about the origin of the trial narrative

---

[1] Leidensgeschichte, p. 5.   [2] Ibid., pp. 97-102.

[3] Ibid., pp. 55-61 (the trial before the Sanhedrin); pp. 65-71 (the trial before Pilate).

are valid, but because he has pointed out a dimension which must be considered in any treatment of the narrative. His emphasis on the religious function of the narrative and its relation to the experience of a definite community is a counterbalance to an excessively literary consideration of the trial narrative. As we will indicate in the final chapter of the present discussion, it is necessary to suggest not only how the trial narrative is important to the structure and meaning of Mark's gospel, but also how the theology contained in it is related to the experience of the people for whom Mark wrote his gospel. Bertram's work thus represents an anticipation of an aspect of the redaction-critical treatment of the trial narrative which will evolve in the course of the present discussion.[1]

Summary of Survey of Research

The authors discussed thus far were selected because they illustrate the main problems which have arisen in connection with the trial narrative, and the different methods used in approaching the problems. Since the main purpose of the present discussion is a literary analysis of the trial scene by the method of redaction criticism, those authors such as Lietzmann, Burkill, and Winter who combine historical and literary criticism in their analysis of the trial scene have not been discussed. However, their analyses support the position that the trial narrative is secondary to the earliest Passion traditions, and the objections they bring against its historicity suggest

---

[1] Work on the possible cultic setting of the Passion narrative has been continued by Hans-Werner Bartsch, "Historische Erwägungen zur Leidensgeschichte," EvT, XXII (1962), 444-459; "Early Christian Eschatology in the Synoptic Gospels," NTS, XI (1964-65), 387-397, and Gottfried Schille, "Das Leiden des Herrn: Die evangelische Passionstradition und ihr Sitz im Leben," ZTK, LII (1955), 161-205; "Bemerkungen zur Formgeschichte des Evangeliums," NTS, IV (1957-58), 1-31.

that some motivation other than historical reminiscence was at work in its origin and composition.[1]

Those authors discussed, even though they approach the trial narrative from different viewpoints regarding the synoptic tradition, conservative in the case of Taylor, radical in the case of Bultmann, or with different methodologies, form criticism or source criticism, all agree on the secondary quality of the trial narrative in relation to other parts of the Passion narrative. The chief reasons which lead them to this conclusion are that it appears to be a doublet of 15:1-5 and that it interrupts the flow of the narrative. There is also a consensus on the internal difficulties of the narrative. The relation of the temple saying of 14:58 to the Christological material of 14:61-62 causes continual problems of interpretation. The solutions offered usually affirm that one or the other was part of

---

[1] The historical difficulties with the trial narrative have long been noted: (1) the discrepancies between the gospel accounts and the Mishnaic regulations (the trial at night, Sanhedrin 4:1; the judges take part in seeking witnesses, thereby disqualifying themselves as judges, Tosephta, Sanhedrin 7:5; verdict and trial take place on same day as they should not, Sanhedrin 4:1; (2) the question as to whether Jesus' answer (Mk 14:62) fulfills the technical requirements for blasphemy (Sanhedrin 7:5); (3) the dispute over whether the Jews had the power to execute at the time of Jesus. If they did, the trial would be unhistorical since not the Jews but the Romans executed Jesus. Josef Blinzer, Der Prozess Jesu (4th rev. ed.; Regensburg: Pustet, 1969), pp. 1-38, has an exhaustive survey of the various opinions on these questions. There is a growing consensus among authors who combine historical research with literary analysis that the trial narrative, as well as being secondary in terms of tradition history is also nonhistorical: T. Alec Burkill, "The Trial of Jesus," Vigiliae Christianae, XII (1958), 1-18; Ernst Haenchen, Der Weg Jesu (2d rev. ed.; Berlin: Walter de Gruyter, 1968), pp. 504-516; Paul Winter, "Marginal Notes on the Trial of Jesus," ZNW, LIII (1962), 260-263; On the Trial of Jesus (Studia Judaica; Berlin: Walter de Gruyter, 1961); "The Marcan Account of Jesus' Trial by the Sanhedrin," JTS, N.S., XIV (1963), 94-102. Though the present treatment does not enter directly into the debate about the historicity of the trial, by showing that Mark composed the scene for theological reasons pertinent to his gospel, it suggests that the Marcan account must be used with great caution in any attempt at historical reconstruction.

an earlier tradition to which a later tradition was added. These solutions say nothing about the relation of the two blocks of material in the final narrative.

Therefore, three major problem areas emerge in the consideration of the trial narrative. If the narrative is secondary, how is the secondary quality to be explained? Is it a product of early church tradition or did Mark himself produce it? If Mark produced the trial narrative, what evidence is there for his creative activity? What traditions were available to him and how did he use them? The first major problem is, therefore, to define as exactly as possible Mark's redactional and compositional activity in the trial narrative.[1] The second major problem is twofold and it concerns the temple saying (14:58) and the Christological material (14:61-62). Here the origin and function of the material of these verses must first be discussed, and then its use by Mark in the trial narrative. The third major problem is the function of the trial narrative in the Passion narrative and in the gospel as a whole. One of the observations which in the past led to a recognition of the problematic character of the trial narrative was that it did not fit in with the smooth flow of the narrative. If we wish to affirm serious authorial intent on the part of Mark in the trial narrative, we must try to show how it fits in with the final form of Mark's gospel.

---

[1] Because of the difficulty in exactly determining what is Mark and what the tradition he worked with, a hard and fast distinction cannot be maintained between "redactional activity" and "compositional activity." In the present work "redactional activity" is used with the nuance that Mark is working with tradition while "compositional activity" is used with the nuance on his own creative work. The general term "Marcan literary activity" will be used to describe the activity of Mark in both areas.

Methodological Considerations

Any methodology is only as strong as its ability to answer questions which have been impervious to previous methodologies. In this light, the complete methodological statement has been delayed until the problems of the trial narrative have been delineated. In our initial statement we mentioned that redaction criticism is an umbrella concept which involves many different approaches to a gospel, and many different ways of finding the author's intent. The purpose of the present section is to spell out in detail what these approaches are. First of all, we will make some statement about the relation of redaction criticism to other methodologies. Secondly, we will review the ways in which redaction criticism has been applied to Mark in recent years. Finally, we will attempt to show how the various aspects of redaction criticism come to bear on the problems of the present discussion.

Relation to Other Methodologies

Literary criticism of the synoptic gospels in the first fifty years of this century developed in two main directions. On the one hand there is the continued interest in source criticism which asked the question of the larger "documents" or blocks of material which underlie our present gospels.[1] The

---

[1] The general acceptance of the two source theory today is the heritage of the nineteenth century. Marxsen, Introduction to the New Testament, trans. G. Buswell (Philadelphia: Fortress Press, 1968), suggests that "theory" is too weak a term to describe the consensus on the priority of Mark and Q. The following works indicate the continued interest in this aspect of synoptic studies: Kendrick Grobel, Formgeschichte und Synoptische Quellenanalyse (FRLANT, N.F. Vol. XXV; Göttingen: Vandenhoeck und Ruprecht, 1937), pp. 67-123, discuss English and American source criticism from 1912-1936; Owen E. Evans, "Synoptic Criticism since Streeter," ExpT, LXXII (1961), 295-299. The most recent attempt to question the two source theory, W. R. Farmer, The Synoptic Problem: A Critical Analysis (New York: Macmillan, 1964), has not met wide acceptance.

prime emphasis of this criticism was to isolate the sources the evangelists used; it did not attempt to discuss in detail how they used the sources except to raise the question of how the sources were put together.[1] The second major direction literary criticism of the gospels took was form criticism.[2] Strictly speaking, it is literary criticism in an extended sense since it sought to find the pre-literary forms in which the gospel material was handed down, to classify these forms and discuss the ways in which the material was modified in its transmission. Unlike source criticism, form criticism had a directly historical interest in that it not only attempted to discuss the forms of the literature, but tried to show what historical situation or Sitz-im-Leben was responsible for the production or transmission of the forms.

In contrast to these earlier methodologies, redaction criticism does not concentrate directly upon the status of the material prior to its incorporation in a gospel. It rather asks the question what the author does with the material he receives and how this is an index of his religious or theological concerns.[3] Redaction criticism, however, does build on source and form criticism since one index of the author's intent is the way in which he alters or adapts traditional material, so it is

_____

[1] Paul Feine, Johannes Behm, and Werner Georg Kümmel, Introduction to the New Testament, trans. A. J. Mattil, Jr. (Nashville: Abingdon Press, 1966), pp. 35-61.

[2] Martin Dibelius, "Zur Formgeschichte der Evangelien," ThRu, N.F. I (1929), 185-216; "Zur Formgeschichte des Neuen Testaments (ausserhalb der Evangelien)," ThRu, N.F. III (1931), 207-242. Gerhard Iber, "Neuere Literatur zur Formgeschichte," appended to Martin Dibelius, Die Formgeschichte des Evangeliums, ed. G. Bornhamm (3d ed.: Tübingen: J. C. B. Mohr [Paul Siebeck], 1963), pp. 302-312.

[3] Though all redaction critics speak of the "theology" of the evangelists, the term is not used in the technical sense of a systematic exposition or reflection, but as a generic term for his teaching or religious message.

important to isolate what traditions were available to him. Thus, a major facet of redaction criticism is the presupposition of conscious artistry on the part of the author. Too often in the past, the evangelists were seen as collectors of unharmonized material and the theologies of their gospels only as the expression of community belief.[1] However, in taking seriously conscious artistry on the part of the author, the redaction critic must try to find if there is a purpose or reason why the material in the gospel has the form it has, and whether the apparent difficulties and inconsistencies may not be purposeful.[2] The caution must still be observed that the evangelists are not authors in the modern sense, but composed their gospels by using material handed down to them, so that the mode of interpretation is still determined by the mode of composition. This position, however, must be the end product of a careful investigation, not its starting point.

To take the evangelist seriously as an author, is to use with reservation certain methods which have become normative in New Testament research. In the concrete, the method which must be used with caution is that of "background analysis," whether the background be the historical background or the

---

[1] In this sense F. C. Grant includes in his book a chapter on "The Theology of Mark," and, at the same time, writes: "Hence, his 'theology,' so far as he has a theology, is not his own, but merely the theological interpretation--as far as it had gone in his day--of the tradition held by the contemporary church." The Earliest Gospel (Nashville: Abingdon-Cokesbury, 1943), p. 148.

[2] In contrast to the view of the evangelists as unsophisticated reporters, Ulrich Simon cautions: "We return to them [the evangelists] with the thesis that the writers of the Gospels knew what they were doing. They were competing with the Rabbis and the sectarian writers. They told a story like Josephus. They were using it like Philo before them." "The Problem of Biblical Narrative," Theology, LXXII (1969), 250. H. Weiss, "History and a Gospel," NovT, X (1968), 81-94, compares the gospel to the secular writer Lucan, confirming conscious artistry on the part of the evangelist.

religionsgeschichtlich background. Since our research will
touch often on the religious meaning of Mark, we must say something briefly about the use of this latter methodology in the
thesis. As it has evolved in this century the history of reli-
gions research seeks to interpret motifs or themes in the gospel
in terms of some religious institution or theme contemporary
with or prior to the evangelist.[1] We will see later that this
has especially been the case with the temple saying of Mk 14:58.
It was thought that, once a parallel in Judaism or Hellenism was
found to a Marcan statement, the explanation of Mark was complete. Mark is seen simply as incorporating a contemporary
motif. However, in terms of a redaction-critical analysis, this
should be the last, not the first step. It is necessary, first
of all, to find how Mark treats a certain theme in any one place
and throughout his gospel. For example, the role of the temple
and of Jerusalem in Mark can be studied independent of any re-
course to religionsgeschichtliche antecedents. Only when the
Marcan treatment is complete, should the question of contact
with parallel themes be raised. Analysis of such contacts
represents a valid field of inquiry, but it is not directly the
redaction-critical field of inquiry, since it goes beyond the
literary product, the gospel.[2]

---

[1]Wilhelm Bousset, "Die Religionsgeschichte und das Neue Testament," ThRu, VII (1904), 265-277, 311-318; XV (1912), 251-278. C. Clemen, Religionsgeschichtliche Erklärung des Neuen Testaments (Giessen: Alfred Töpelmann, 1924). Carsten Colpe, Die religionsgeschichtliche Schule (FRLANT, N.F. Vol. LXXVIII; Göttingen: Vandenhoeck und Ruprecht, 1961). J. Hempel, "Religionsgeschichtliche Schule," RGG, 3d ed., V, 991-994. Kümmel, Das Neue Testament, pp. 310-358, 439-466.

[2]Modern literary criticism would reject such an approach as seeking the meaning of a literary work outside the internal dynamics of the work. See W. K. Wimsatt, Jr., The Verbal Icon (New York: Noonday Press, 1953).

Evolution of a Method

The contemporary practice of redaction criticism is to a certain extent anticipated in the work of Wrede and Wellhausen, of the early form critics, and of the American, B. W. Bacon in the twenties, since all discussed various aspects of the theologies of the evangelists.[1] The work of Lohmeyer and Lightfoot in the thirties stands closer to the present concerns of redaction criticism, since they saw elements of Mark's gospel such as geography and structure, not simply as part of the received tradition, but as an entree to his creative theology.[2] The rise of the redaction criticism of Mark, in its modern understanding, is traceable to the publication in 1956 of Willi Marxsen's four studies on the gospel of Mark.[3] In two of these studies, the one on John the Baptist and in his study of Mark 13, Marxsen works with the distinction between tradition and redaction, and shows how Mark altered the traditions he received

---

[1] William Wrede, Das Messiasgeheimnis in den Evangelien (Göttingen: Vandenhoeck und Ruprecht, 1901), discusses the theological use of the Messianic Secret, and writes: "Man betrachte Markus durch ein starkes Vergrosserungsglas, und man hat etwa eine Schriftstellerei, wie sie Johannes zeigt" (p. 145). Wellhausen gives special attention to Mark's use of traditional material: "Markus nahm auf was die Tradition ihm bot. Die Sammlung und Ordnung des Stoffes ist sein Werk." Julius Wellhausen, Einleitung in die Drei Ersten Evangelien (2d ed.; Berlin: Verlag Georg Reimer, 1911), p. 45. Dibelius, as noted, finds the theological interest of Mark by comparing the older Passion account with the Marcan additions. Bultmann discusses the way in which the different evangelists alter traditional material. Synoptic Tradition, pp. 322-368. Bacon argues for a dating of Mark after A.D. 70 on the basis of Marcan additions to ch. 13. Benjamin W. Bacon, The Gospel of Mark: Its Composition and Date (New Haven: Yale University Press, 1925), pp. 319-320.

[2] Ernst Lohmeyer, Galiläa und Jerusalem (FRLANT, N.F. Vol. XXXIV; Göttingen: Vandenhoeck und Ruprecht, 1936). Robert Henry Lightfoot, History and Interpretation in the Gospels (New York: Harper and Brothers, 1934); Locality and Doctrine in the Gospels (Ibid., 1938).

[3] Supra, p. 5, n. 1. The German edition of Conzelmann's work on Luke which uses the method but not the name redaction criticism was published in 1953, so the modern use of the method dates from his work on Luke.

in terms of his theological purpose. In a third study, he
analyzes the geography of Mark and finds that its intent is
theological, rather than topological, and, in the fourth study,
he attempts to find what Mark intended by writing a "gospel" and
how gospel represents the creation of a new literary form in
early Christianity. Marxsen's work is important, not only because it opened up new vistas, but also because he anticipated
the major directions redaction criticism would take: (a) the
use of the distinction between tradition and redaction, (b) the
study of Marcan compositional techniques evident in the arrangement of material, and (c) the study of Marcan concerns and major
motifs as they permeate the whole gospel. It is to these different aspects of redaction criticism that we now turn.

Aspects of a Method

Tradition and Redaction

The first major aspect of redaction criticism is the use
of the distinction between tradition and redaction.[1] Tradition
is the generic term for the material received by the evangelist;
redaction, in this context, means the alterations the evangelist
makes in this material. In using this distinction redaction
criticism seeks the author's intent in the alterations he makes.
The success of this aspect of redaction criticism has been most
notable in the case of Matthew and Luke, where the Vorlage of
Mark and Q provide a base of traditional material, and the
Matthean and Lucan alterations can be rather easily found.[2] In
the case of Mark, without any discernible Vorlage, the

---

[1] Robert H. Stein, "What is Redaktionsgeschichte?" JBL, LXXXVIII (1969), 45-56; "The 'Redaktionsgeschichtlich' Investigation of a Markan Seam (Mc 1:21f.)," ZNW, LXI (1970), 70-94.

[2] Supra, p. 6, n. 1.

distinguishing of tradition and redaction is more difficult and the results more problematic. The use of the insights of form criticism, which can determine the status of some material in its pre-Marcan form, provides one way to find traditional material. For example, Bultmann is enabled to discern the melding of different traditions in the story of the healing of the paralytic (Mk 2:1-13) where "a miracle story from the tradition is used as a frame for the saying about the right to forgive sins."[1] The saying about forgiveness and the reaction of the opponents (2:5b-10) interrupts the flow of the narrative and represents for Bultmann an expansion of the miracle story by the early church which roots its power to forgive sins in the tradition of Jesus' exousia over illness.[2] In instance after instance Bultmann shows that different narratives are a blend of different traditions, and, in the final section of his work, he gives stylistic criteria by which we can determine how Mark deals with traditional material.[3] In conjunction with Bultmann's work must be considered the work of K. L. Schmidt who was able to isolate Marcan literary activity in the linking together of separate bodies of tradition, and in the creation of the Sammelberichte.[4]

In addition to the work of the form critics in isolating the smaller sections of traditional material, there is the work

---

[1] Synoptic Tradition, p. 331.   [2] Ibid., pp. 14-15.

[3] Thematic ordering and linking by catchword; linking in succession by spatial temporal connection; insertion of apothegms; schematizing scenes; creating summaries and temporal links. Synoptic Tradition, pp. 322-334.

[4] Karl Ludwig Schmidt, Der Rahmen der Geschichte Jesu (Berlin: Trowitzsch und Sohn, 1919). The Sammelberichte are found in Mark 1:14-15; 1:39; 2:13; 3:7-12; 5:21; 6:6b; 6:12-13; 6:30-33; 6:53-56; 10:1. Schmidt also shows that it was in effect Mark who created the framework of the ministry of Jesus.

of those who have attempted to isolate larger blocks of traditional material behind Mark. The survey of research on the Passion narrative is the prime example of this, but it seems, also, that the material of ch. 4 (the parable discourse) and ch. 13 (the apocalyptic discourse) existed as a larger block, prior to Mark.[1] Recent studies by Keck and Achtemeier have suggested that, prior to Mark, there existed different catenae of miracle stories which Mark took over, and that by his use and arrangement of them, he indicated definite concerns of his theology.[2] Finally, the work of Lindars, Hartmann and Perrin on the isolation of the New Testament use of Old Testament traditions, provides a way of finding early Christian exegetical traditions which were available to Mark.[3]

---

[1] On the parable discourse see: G. H. Boobyer, "The Redaction of Mark IV, 1-34," NTS, VIII (1961-62), 59-70; W. Marxsen, "Redaktionsgeschichtliche Erklärung der sogennanten Parabeltheorie des Markus," ZTK, LII (1955), 255-271; Ernst Lohmeyer, Das Evangelium des Markus (Kritisch-exegetischer Kommentar über das Neue Testament, Vol. II; 17th ed.; Göttingen: Vandenhoeck und Ruprecht, 1967), pp. 82-93; D. E. Nineham, The Gospel of St. Mark (Pelican Gospel Commentary; Baltimore: Penguin Books, 1967), p. 125. On the various attempts to reconstruct the pre-history of the eschatological discourse of ch. 13 see the comprehensive survey by George R. Beasley-Murray, Jesus and the Future (London: Macmillan and Co., 1954), pp. 1-112; Rudolph Pesch, Naherwartungen: Tradition und Redaktion in Mk 13 (Düsseldorf: Patmos Verlag, 1968), pp. 19-47. Pesch brings Beasley-Murray's survey up to the year of the publication of his work. H.-W. Kuhn, Ältere Sammlungen im Markusevangelium (Studien zur Umwelt des Neuen Testaments, Vol. VIII; Göttingen: Vandenhoeck und Ruprecht, 1971), attempts to isolate certain blocks of pre-Marcan tradition and discuss their Sitz-im-Leben. He discusses the following groups of texts: Mk 2:1-3:6; 4:1-34; 10:1-45; 4:35-6:52.

[2] Leander E. Keck, "Mark 3:7-12 and Mark's Christology," JBL, LXXXIV (1965), 341-358, shows that Mark in 3:7-12 introduces a cycle of miracle stories in which Jesus is portrayed as a divine man. Paul J. Achtemeier, "Toward the Isolation of Pre-Markan Miracle Catenae," JBL, LXXXIX (1970), 265-291, and "The Origin and Function of the Pre-Markan Miracle Catenae," JBL, XCI (1972), 198-221.

[3] Supra, p. 15, n. 2.

While the above means help us to discover parts of Mark which are traditional, they do not tell us exactly where the Marcan reworking or redaction of these traditions can be found. Different techniques have been evolved to discover the specifically Marcan literary activity. The Sammelberichte have already been noted, and allied to these would be the Marcan "seams," introductions, and transitional sentences.[1] The existence of Marcan summaries and introductions raises the problem of the use of vocabulary, grammar and style as a means of finding Marcan redaction. Due to the painstaking research of men like Lagrange, Swete, Hawkins and Turner in the early years of this century, we now have a fairly accurate picture of the kind of Greek Mark wrote and of his literary style.[2] A difficulty is that criteria based on style and language do not become an absolute way of distinguishing tradition from redaction, since the same style is found both when Mark is rewriting traditional material as when he is composing new material. However, in recent years there has been a conjunction of the use of criteria based on language and style with other criteria of Marcan redaction, which enables us to isolate the language and style Mark uses in those sections in which he is especially active as author. If, for example, one takes a section, which, on grounds

---

[1] See Taylor, Mark, pp. 82-86, for a list of such devices.

[2] M.-J. Lagrange, Évangile selon Saint Marc (Paris: Librarie Victor Lecoffre, 1920), pp. lxiv-xcix; Henry B. Swete, The Gospel According to St. Mark (London: Macmillan and Co., 1908), pp. xliv-l; John C. Hawkins, Horae Synopticae (Grand Rapids: Baker Book House, 1968; first published in 1899 by the Clarendon Press, Oxford). C. H. Turner, "Marcan Usage: Notes, Critical and Exegetical, on the Second Gospel," JTS, XXV (1924), 377-386; XXVI (1925), 12-20; 145-156; 225-240; XXVII (1926), 58-62; XXVIII (1927), 9-30; 349-362; XXIX (1928), 275-289; 346-361. Modern studies on Mark's language and style include: John C. Doudna, The Greek of the Gospel of Mark (Journal of Biblical Literature, Monograph Series, Vol. XII; Philadelphia: Society of Biblical Literature, 1961), and Max Zerwick, Untersuchungen zum Markus-Stil (Rome: Pontifical Biblical Institute, 1937).

other than language and style alone, is seen as Marcan such as a Sammelbericht, a Messianic Secret text, or a geographical or topological indication, he can, by analysis of the vocabulary and style of these sections, construct, in effect, a redactional grammar and lexicon of Mark.[1] It was by such a method that E. Schweizer was able to evolve his view on the didactic nature of Mark and the importance of discipleship in Mark.[2] Also, as Grobel has pointed out, statistically, the highest portion of distinctive Marcan vocabulary and style appears in the transitional and introductory sentences, so here, also, we are able to find how Mark writes Greek when he is composing his own material, rather than when he is taking over traditional sections.[3]

In the second chapter of the present study criteria of language, style and compositional techniques will be used to find evidence of Marcan activity in the trial scene. In contrast to the work of Linnemann and others who attempt to separate tradition and redaction with a mathematical precision extending to verses and half verses, we will renounce any attempt to define the exact status of the tradition prior to Mark. The nature of the tradition itself precludes this. As form criticism has definitively shown, the material existed in a fluid state prior to its fixation by writing in a gospel text so that it is impossible to delineate exactly the form and content

---

[1] Though Wrede thought that the Messianic Secret was a pre-Marcan motif which Mark employed, the work of Bultmann and Conzelmann show that these sections are Marcan productions; see Knigge, "The Meaning of Mark," pp. 57-59, for a full discussion of the problem.

[2] E. Schweizer, "Anmerkungen zur Theologie des Markus," Neotestamentica (Zürich: Zwingli Verlag, 1963), pp. 93-104; "Die theologische Leistung des Markus," EvT, XXIV (1964), 337-355.

[3] Kendrick Grobel, "Idiosyncracies of the Synoptists in Their Pericopae--Introductions," JBL, LIX (1940), 405-410.

of traditional material.[1] What can be said is that in a certain place Mark is working with a tradition, his redactional activity can be seen, and some general statements about the form of pre-Marcan material can be made. Therefore the distinction between tradition and redaction becomes a valuable, but limited entree to the total theological enterprise of Mark.

Composition Criticism

The second way in which redaction criticism has developed does not stress the distinction between tradition and redaction, but concentrates on modes of composition, literary devices, and the discovery of patterns and structures, all of which serve as an index to Mark's thought. This has often been called composition criticism and its model is the way in which any literary critic would approach a text.[2] The emphasis is on the final product as an integral self-contained work of the author and the previous stages of the work and outside influences are not critical for interpretation. This type of redaction criticism uses two sets of categories: one, taken from an analysis of the gospel itself to discover compositional techniques which the evangelist uses; the other consists in the application of modes of interpretation taken from classical and contemporary literary

---

[1] One of the insights gained from Käsemann's, "Sentences of Holy Law in the New Testament," New Testament Questions Today, trans. W. J. Montague (Philadelphia: Fortress Press, 1969), pp. 66-81, is that certain forms retain a fluid character prior to their use by a specific evangelist. Also Tödt's work on the Q Son of Man sayings cautions against seeing the "sources" or tradition prior to the gospels as rigid and fixed, Heinz E. Tödt, The Son of Man in the Synoptic Tradition, trans. Dorothea M. Barton (Philadelphia: Westminster Press, 1965).

[2] The term "composition criticism" in the title of this section may be ambiguous. Haenchen, Der Weg Jesu, p. 24, has proposed this title for all aspects of redaction criticism, and Perrin, What is Redaction Criticism? agrees with him on this. Often the term is used simply to designate that aspect of Marcan literary activity which can be discerned, independently of whether he is reworking traditional material or composing material of his own.

criticism to the text of Mark.[1]

One of the ways in which Mark composes his material is the often noted method of intercalation. By this technique Mark interrupts a narrative by the insertion of another narrative and then returns to the original narrative.[2] In the trial scene this is most evident where the introduction to the story of Peter's denial (14:54) is interrupted by the trial itself, and the story of Peter resumes in 14:66. Von Dobschütz, in studying this device, sees it only as a literary technique to heighten suspense or to create the illusion of passing time.[3] More recent studies have suggested that there is an added dimension to these intercalations, and they may be an index of Mark's theological concerns.[4] There is a dialectical relationship between the inserted material and its framework whereby the stories serve to interpret each other. For example, the cleansing of the temple, intercalated within the cursing of the fig tree (11:12-25), shows that the cursing is an eschatological judgment against Israel symbolizing the end of its cult and institutions.[5] In our discussion of the trial scene we will allude to the significance of its intercalation within the story of

---

[1] William A. Beardslee, *Literary Criticism of the New Testament* (Philadelphia: Fortress Press, 1970), and Amos Wilder, *The Language of the Gospel* (New York: Harper and Row, 1964), apply categories taken from modern literary criticism to the gospel material.

[2] The Marcan intercalations are found in the following places: 3:20-21 [22-30] 31-35; 5:21-24 [25-34] 35-43; 6:7-13 [14-29] 30-32; 11:12-14 [15-19] 20-26; 14:1-2 [3-9] 10-11; 14:12-16 [17-21] 22-25; 14:54 [55-65] 66-72.

[3] E. von Dobschütz, "Zur Erzählungskunst des Markus," *ZNW*, XXVII (1928), 193-198.

[4] Nineham, *St. Mark*, p. 112, pursues the theological meaning of these intercalations.

[5] *Ibid.*, p. 299: "The manner and place of its insertion strongly suggests that the story was intended to make a didactic point, the fate of the fig tree symbolizes the fate that awaited Jerusalem and the Jewish people and religion."

Peter's denial. We will also attempt to show that in the scene there is another definite Marcan composition technique, a Marcan insertion technique, which permeates his whole gospel and is significant for an understanding of the scene.[1]

The second major compositional activity of Mark is found in analysis of his use of structures and patterns. Not only has debate ranged about the structure of the whole gospel, but the theological meaning of these structures has been debated.[2] In the middle section of Mark, 8:27-10:52, the use of patterns has become a key way for an understanding of this section.[3] In every case after the Passion predictions, 8:31, 9:31, 10:33, there is a misunderstanding of the disciples about the necessity of suffering, followed by teaching of Jesus to correct this misunderstanding. Since much of the material in this section is non-contextual, that is, material which circulated independently and was brought to its present position by Mark, its position and location in a definite structure becomes an index of Mark's concern to show the necessity of instruction for the Christian disciple if he is to follow Jesus on the *hodos* to the cross.[4] Therefore, throughout the gospel, questions of ordering, patterns and location of material become a way of finding Marcan concerns. In the present treatment especially in our claim that the trial scene is the culmination of a carefully

---

[1] *Infra*, Chap. II, pp. 77-84.

[2] For a comprehensive survey of the various structures proposed, see Pesch, *Naherwartungen*, pp. 50-73; Feine, Behm, and Kümmel, *Introduction*, pp. 63-66, say the structure of Mark is geographical-theological.

[3] Perrin, *Redaction Criticism*, pp. 40-63. Edward J. Mally, "The Gospel of Mark," *Jerome Biblical Commentary*, ed. Raymond Brown, Joseph Fitzmyer, and Roland Murphy (Englewood Cliffs, N.J.: Prentice Hall, 1968), II, 40-41, shows that the structure of this section shows that it is the "hinge" section between the two major parts of Mark's gospel.

[4] Perrin, *Redaction Criticism*, p. 45.

articulated pattern of opposition to Jesus, and in our view that the Christological material of 14:61-62 exists in a definite pattern which enlightens its meaning, we utilize structural considerations as an index to Mark's thought.[1]

Not only are structures, patterns and compositional techniques a key to finding Marcan concerns, but the ways in which he indicates contacts between key parts of his gospel must be observed. R. H. Lightfoot has shown that there are numerous contacts between ch. 13 and the Passion narrative which indicate that Mark wants to bring these two sections into close relationship.[2] Such a procedure is necessary to avoid the atomistic exegesis of any one passage. In the present treatment it will be necessary, to study not only the interrelation of the various elements within the trial narrative, but also the contacts the trial narrative has with other parts of the gospel.

Finally, as mentioned, redaction criticism is moving in the direction of the application of criteria taken from secular literary criticism to the gospel of Mark. The difficulty here is that such analysis is present more in promise than in production.[3] In terms of classical literary criticism questions can be asked about who the protagonist is, the roles of the secondary characters, the question of the turning point in the gospel and the relation of the hearers to the text.[4] The work of a modern critic like Sheldon Sacks which poses the problem of a careful delineation of the form of a given work as a

---

[1] *Infra*, Chaps. II, III, IV.

[2] Robert H. Lightfoot, *The Gospel Message of St. Mark* (London: Oxford University Press, 1962), pp. 48-59; Francis Dewar, "Chapter 13 and the Passion Narrative in St. Mark," *Theology*, LXIV (1961), 99-107.

[3] *Supra*, p. 42, n. 1; Perrin, "The Christology of Mark," p. 176.

[4] Such questions would be to examine Mark in categories taken from Aristotle's *Poetics*.

prerequisite to the understanding of content, suggests that a similar question must be asked of Mark.[1] This has immediate contact with recent studies on the meaning of euaggelion by Mark, and how he understands and uses this form which he has created.[2] Therefore, the question of the form used and how this form functions provides another way to arrive at Mark's intention. The use of this methodology is not dominant in the present discussion, but would rather represent a way in which further questions could be posed on the basis of the Marcan activity we find in the trial scene.

The Study of Themes and Motifs

The third major way in which redaction criticism has been done is by the study of peculiar Marcan concerns which permeate his gospel. The first major breakthrough in this area came with the work of Lohmeyer who saw the geography of Mark as "theological." Galilee is the land of the mission to the gentiles, and hence, in the gospel is the place where the success of Jesus takes place. Jerusalem is the place of opposition to Jesus and the center of the people who reject the gospel in Mark's time, so that Mark shows in the location of material in his gospel distinct theological concerns.[3] Such research was continued by Evans and Boobyer, and Schreiber has extended observation on geographical concerns to observations on topological designations by showing that the location of a pericope in places such

---

[1] Sheldon Sacks, Fiction and the Shape of Belief (Berkeley: University of California Press, 1967). Sacks does not discuss the biblical material. What he does show is that constant misinterpretations of literature arise when individual parts of a work are not interpreted in terms of the form of the total work.

[2] Marxsen, Mark, pp. 117-150. Perrin, "The Literary Gattung 'Gospel'--Some Observations," ExpT, LXXXII (1970), 4-7.

[3] Lohmeyer, Galiläa und Jerusalem. Johannes Schreiber, Theologie des Vertrauens, pp. 17-190.

as a house, on a mountain or by the sea, shows often a theological motif at work.[1]

Along with geographical and topological concerns, authors have isolated "ideological" or theological motifs of Mark. Though the work of Robinson on Mark's concept of history and Best on the Marcan soteriology are not redaction-critical works in the strict sense, they do raise the question of the total import of Mark's theology.[2] Since Wrede, the Marcan use of the Messianic Secret has provided a constant impetus to the study of Mark as a theologian.[3] The study of Mark's Christology has also

---

[1] G. H. Boobyer, "Galilee and Galileans in St. Mark's Gospel," BJRL, XXXV (1953), 334-348; C. F. Evans, "I Will Go before You into Galilee," JTS, N.S. V (1954), 3-18. Schreiber discusses the topological indications in Theologie, pp. 158-210.

[2] James M. Robinson, The Problem of History in Mark (Studies in Biblical Theology, Vol. XXI; London: S. C. M. Press, 1957); "The Problem of History in Mark, Reconsidered," USQR, XXX (1965), 131-147. Best, The Temptation and Passion. In his article, Robinson addresses himself to Köster's criticism (p. 133) that his original book is not redaction-critical since he makes no attempt to distinguish tradition and redaction. Best's work is called not strictly redaction-critical because, although he discusses Marcan compositional and redactional techniques, the theology which emerges from his discussion arises from an extrinsic pattern, the suffering servant motif, imposed on Mark.

[3] Coming to terms with Mark's use of the Messianic Secret has become almost a hermeneutical persupposition for making any statement about the theology of Mark as a whole. In the present treatment, the importance of the secret will emerge in the discussion of the Christology of the trial scene. For a survey of various understandings of the secret since Wrede, see: G. H. Boobyer, "The Secrecy Motif in Mark's Gospel," NTS, VI (1959-60), 225-235; H. Minette de Tillesse, Le Secret messianique dans l'Évangile de Marc (Lectio Divina, Vol. XLVII; Paris: Cerf, 1968). Not only has the whole gospel been approached from this viewpoint, but various aspects of the gospel are interpreted under this rubric. For conceptions of the whole gospel see: T. A. Burkill, Mysterious Revelation (Ithaca, N.Y.: Cornell University Press, 1963) and Jürgen Roloff, "Das Markusevangelium als Geschichtsdarstellung," EvT, XXIX (1969), 73-93. For various aspects see (a) Christology: T. A. Burkill, "The Hidden Son of Man in St. Mark's Gospel," ZNW, LII (1961), 189-213; Ulrich Luz, "Das Geheimnismotiv und die Markinische Christologie," ZNW, LVI (1965), 45-74; Christian Maurer, "Das Messiasgeheimnis des Markusevangeliums," NTS, XIV (1967-68), 515-528; Georg Strecker, "Zur Messiasgeheimnistheorie im Markusevangelium," Studia Evangelica, Vol. II (Texte und Untersuchungen, Vol. LXXXVII, ed. F. L. Cross; Berlin: Akademie Verlag,

been a major entree to his theology. Research on Christology has developed in two major directions. One aspect has focused on the titular Christology of Mark and how Mark uses and adapts the traditional Christological titles of the early church. Hahn's work in this area represents a necessary propaedeutic to a study of Mark, and the professed aim of his work was to study the pre-Marcan traditions, rather than Mark's use of them.[1] The second aspect of Marcan Christology is represented by the work of Vielhauer on Son of God and Perrin on Son of Man, since both authors show how Mark adapts the traditional titles to his own purposes, creates new Christological traditions, using the material and imagery of the older traditions, and uses the titles in dynamic interrelation rather than in isolation.[2] Since a major portion of our present study will be devoted to the Christology of the trial scene, we will draw on these previous researches, while at the same time suggesting that Mark is creative in certain aspects of his Christology which were thought to be traditional, and that this creativity is most evident in the trial scene.

In our discussion of form criticism we noted that it has a literary and historical dimension, the delineation of the forms and their development, as well as the discovery of the setting and function of these forms in early communities. A

1964), pp. 87-104; (b) discipleship: Alfred Kuby, "Zur Konzeption des Markus-Evangelium," ZNW, XLIX (1958), 52-64; (c) the use of the parables: T. A. Burkill, "The Cryptology of the Parables in St. Mark's Gospel," NovT, I (1956), 246-262.

[1] Ferdinand Hahn, The Titles of Jesus in Christology, trans. H. Knight and G. Ogg (London: Lutterworth Press, 1969).

[2] Vielhauer, "Erwägungen," (supra, p. 6, n. 2). Norman Perrin, "The Son of Man in the Synoptic Tradition," Biblical Research, XIII (1968), 1-23; "The Creative Use of the Son of Man Traditions by Mark," USQR, XXIII (1968), 357-365; "The Christology of Mark" (supra, p. 6, n. 2).

similar observation can be made about redaction criticism. In addition to discovering how any section of the gospel is related to the whole gospel, the literary-theological question, redaction criticism can also ask the question about the historical setting of the gospel as a whole. Questions about the audience to whom the gospel was directed, the apologetic intent or opponents encountered, and the outside influences which are mirrored in the gospel, can be raised, once the meaning of the gospel is ascertained by internal criticism. In this light, Pesch has suggested that Mark was written after A.D. 70, in response to false eschatological expectations occasioned by the destruction of Jerusalem,[1] and Weeden sees the gospel as an answer to groups in the community who professed a false Son of God Christology and a false view of discipleship.[2] The delineation of the historical situation which best corresponds to the theology of the trial scene, as it evolves in the present discussion, is not our prime purpose. However, in the final chapter, we will suggest that certain aspects of the dating of Mark and the historical setting can be clarified on the basis of our discussion. Redaction criticism, thus, provides a valuable adjunct to the continued historical research on early Christianity.

Conclusion

The survey of research on the trial narrative indicates the major problems surrounding the literary history and theological meaning of the trial narrative. The figure of Martin Dibelius looms large over all the authors treated; however, in a rather paradoxical way. His view that the Passion narrative was

---

[1] Pesch, Naherwartungen, esp. pp. 224-226.

[2] Theodore J. Weeden, "The Heresy that Necessitated Mark's Gospel," ZNW, LIX (1968), 145-158, and Mark: Traditions in Conflict (Philadelphia: Fortress Press, 1971).

the longest block of connected narrative prior to the gospels made subsequent authors shy away from form-critical and tradition-history investigations of this section. At the same time, his insights that the trial narrative is secondary, is the high point of the Passion narrative, and that it is of high theological significance, provide the starting point for the present discussion. What we attempt is, in effect, a full-scale presentation of the implications of Dibelius' work.

The statement on method suggests that redaction criticism provides a way to solve certain of the old problems surrounding the trial narrative and ask new questions of it. In general terms, previous research has simply not shown what function this narrative has in the gospel of Mark, nor how the parts of the narrative are related to each other. Form-critical and tradition-history studies agree that the narrative is secondary to the earliest traditions of the Passion narrative. It is also significant that in none of the references to the Passion of Jesus outside of Mark is the <u>night trial</u> before the Sanhedrin mentioned.[1] However, the exact origin of the trial narrative

---

[1]Luke structures his material so that the "hearing" takes place in the day. Also Luke has neither the elements which in Mark give the scene its character of trial (the calling of witnesses, the formal condemnation) nor the most problematic elements of the Marcan scene (the temple saying, the combination of Dan 7:13 and Ps. 110:1). In the references to the Passion outside of the gospels the mention of the trial before the Sanhedrin is completely lacking. (See X. Léon-Dufour, <u>DBS</u>, VI, 1423, for complete list.) Therefore the trial scene is unique to Mark, and Matthew who follows him very closely here. It is still sharply debated whether Luke is following Mark in his version of the trial or working with an independent <u>Vorlage</u>. Bultmann, <u>Synoptic Tradition</u>, p. 440, and Conzelmann, <u>Theology of St. Luke</u>, p. 200, hold that Luke has no source other than Mark for his Passion narrative. In a recent study Gerhard Schneider argues for independent Lucan sources: <u>Verleugnung, Verspottung und Verhör Jesu nach Lukas 22. 54-71</u> (StANT, Vol. XXII; Munich: Kösel Verlag, 1970); "Gab es eine vorsynoptische Szene 'Jesus vor dem Synedrium?'" <u>NovT</u>, XII (1970), 35-36; "Jesus vor dem Synedrium," <u>Bibel und Leben</u>, XI (1970), 1-15. Independently of the resolution of this question, we can still affirm that it is Mark who creates the real problems surrounding

has not been specified. Does it mirror the theology of some
early Christian tradition, or is it a Marcan composition? The
one recent major tradition history of the trial narrative, that
of Linnemann, underscores the inadequacy of previous solutions.
Her conclusions leave little room for the study of Marcan redactional activity since Mark is seen as combining, in a rather
awkward way, two originally independent pericopes. She makes no
attempt to show why Mark has done this or how the trial narrative relates to other parts of his gospel.

Granted that a full appreciation of the ability of redaction criticism to solve the problems of the trial narrative will
emerge only when the redactional work of Mark is seen in detail,
the method itself offers the best line of approach. The continued success of the method over the years in leading to an understanding of other parts of the gospel bodes equal success
when applied to the trial narrative. In the present study, the
second chapter will be devoted to a careful literary analysis of
the trial narrative in order to find in it evidence of Marcan
redaction and composition. We will attempt to show that it is
Mark who created the trial narrative out of the disparate traditions available to him. In the trial narrative Mark is active
in two major areas: (a) he has "inserted" the temple saying of
14:58 into an earlier tradition about Jesus' innocence before
his accusers (14:56, 59), and (b) he has made 14:61-62 into a
Christological tableau which becomes the major Christological
statement of his gospel. The third chapter, therefore, will be
devoted to a study of the temple saying of Mk 14:58, and the
fourth to the Christological material. In each chapter a
similar method will be employed. The traditions available to

---

the trial narrative. If Luke is following Mark he omits them;
if he has his own source, it did not contain them.

Mark will be isolated and his use and adaptation of these traditions in the trial narrative will be studied. Secondly, the relation of both the temple saying and the Christological material to corresponding material earlier in the gospel will be examined, so that an atomistic exegesis of the trial narrative is avoided. In the final chapter we will concentrate on those aspects of redaction criticism not stressed in the previous chapters. Three things will be attempted. First of all, we will suggest how the trial narrative functions in relation to the Passion narrative and the rest of the gospel. Secondly, we will suggest a setting in the life of the Marcan community for the trial narrative. And, finally, we will attempt to suggest ways in which contemporary thinking on the function of narrative as narrative leads to a deeper understanding of the trial. In this way all the aspects of the methodology of redaction criticism as it has evolved in recent years come to bear on a solution to the problems posed by the narrative.

CHAPTER II

TRADITION AND REDACTION IN THE MARCAN TRIAL NARRATIVE

Introduction

The consensus among scholars that the trial narrative is secondary to the earliest traditions of the Passion narrative, leaves unanswered the problem of the relation of the evangelist, Mark, to this narrative. Did he take it over *en bloc* as a narrative which he found in the tradition and which he altered little in taking it over? Did he compose it himself, and, if so, how? Or, is it rather midway between these two polarities, and a combination of traditional material and Marcan redaction and composition? In our presentation we will accept the third of these possibilities. The argument must, therefore, proceed in two stages. In the first stage we will attempt to show that, on the basis of language, style, and a definite compositional technique (intercalation), the form and location of the narrative is due to the evangelist Mark. At this stage of the argument all that can be affirmed is that, in the broadest sense, the trial narrative is Marcan. The way in which it is Marcan still remains unspecified. Therefore, the second stage of the argument will consist in a detailed analysis of the pericope in order to discern as exactly as possible the Marcan literary activity. We will see that in some instances he is working with traditional material, especially in his use of Old Testament traditions, originally associated by early Christians with the Passion of Jesus, but not necessarily with the trial narrative. In other instances he composes material which, in effect, makes the narrative a "trial." We will also note the presence of definite

Marcan compositional techniques which he uses to indicate what is of special importance to him in the narrative. Finally, at the conclusion of the analysis we will attempt to suggest an outline for the development of the tradition of the trial narrative.

The Trial Scene as Marcan

In the present section our aim will be to discuss certain familiar and distinctive Marcan constructions found throughout his gospel and in the trial scene. The purpose here, it must be repeated, is to show that, in terms of grammar, language and style, the trial scene is from the same hand as the rest of the gospel. Prior to the full analysis of the scene in the second part of the chapter, the work is incomplete here, and the conclusions negative in showing that it is Mark and not some other who is author of the trial scene.[1]

Historical Present

Characteristic of the Marcan style is the use of the historical present, i.e., the use of the present tense in a narrative in place of the aorist.[2] Mark uses this construction 151 times in contrast to Matthew's 78 times, and Luke's 6 times in

---

[1] In the present work the terms author, evangelist, and Mark are used interchangeably. We do not touch on the question of the identity of the Mark to whom tradition assigns the authorship of the gospel.

[2] F. Blass and A. Debrunner, A Greek Grammar of the New Testament and Other Early Christian Literature, trans. and rev. Robert Funk (Chicago: University of Chicago Press, 1961), p. 167, No. 167. The older authors use the term "historic present" to describe this phenomenon, while more recent authors use the term "historical present." The edition of the Greek New Testament followed throughout is The Greek New Testament, ed. Kurt Aland, Matthew Black, Bruce Metzger, and Allen Wikgren (New York: United Bible Societies, 1966). All direct quotes in English follow the R.S.V.

his gospel and 13 times in Acts.[1] The historical present is used throughout the gospel in both narrative and discourse material. In the trial narrative the historical present is found in 14:53, synerchontai; 14:61, 63, legei. It is also found in two sentences which stand in close connection with the trial scene, 14:51, kratousin and 14:66, erchetai. Therefore, in terms of this usage, the trial scene mirrors the hand of Mark.

Kai Parataxis

One of the more noticeable characteristics of Mark's style is the frequent and almost monotonous use of kai parataxis. Continually pericopes (80 of 89 in Mark) begin with kai, and sentences are joined in simple coordination by kai, rather than by subordinate clauses or the use of participles.[2] Matthew and Luke consistently rework this aspect of Mark's text.[3] In the trial scene Mark uses the particle kai 23 times. Of these 23 usages, 10 can be called kai parataxis: 14:53, kai apēgagon; 14:53, kai synerchontai; 14:54, kai ho petros; 14:54b, kai ēn sygkathēmenos; 14:57, kai tines; 14:59, kai oude isē; 14:60, kai anastas; 14:65, kai ērxato and kai hoi hypēretai. Thus, in the short span of 13 verses, this characteristic Marcan trait occurs 10 times which argues for a Marcan writing of the trial scene. In contrast to Mark, Matthew who in all other respects follows Mark closely in the trial scene uses kai only 8 times, and he rewrites all but one of the instances of kai parataxis listed above.[4] Therefore on the basis of this usage it is clear that

___

[1] Hawkins, Horae Synopticae, pp. 144-149; Taylor, Mark, pp. 48-49.

[2] Zerwick, Untersuchungen, p. 1, notes that 80 of 89 pericopes in Mark begin with kai.

[3] Ibid.

[4] Mt 27:57-68. Only 14:60 is not altered by Matthew.

Mark is as active here as in other sections of the gospel and did not find the narrative as a piece of traditional material.

Minor Stylistic Devices

In addition to these major stylistic devices there are in the trial scene numerous other usages which characterize the Greek of Mark. The double negative, ouk apekrinato ouden in 14:60, 61, is a frequent Marcan usage.[1] Pleonasms or the use of redundant or apparently redundant phrases occur frequently in Mark and are found in 14:54 apo makrothen and in 14:61, esiōpa kai apekrinato ouden.[2] Also characteristic of Mark is the use of archesthai as an auxiliary verb, 14:65, ērxato emptyein, which is found in Mark 26 times in contrast to Matthew's 13 usages and Luke's 14.[3] Allied to this usage is the periphrastic einai with the participle as found in 14:54, ēn sygkathēmenos.[4] Asyndeton, the absence of a connective which according to Turner is found between 14:63b and 14:64, is found 38 times in Mark.[5] These minor stylistic devices which are found both in the trial narrative and throughout the gospel support the view that Mark was no less active in writing the trial narrative than in other parts of the gospel.

---

[1] See Mark 1:44; 2:2; 3:20; 27; 5:3; 37; 6:5; 7:12; 9:8; 11:14; 12:14; 14:25; 60, 61; 15:4, 5; 16:8, and Taylor, Mark, p. 46.

[2] 1:28, 32, 35, 38, 42, 45; 2:25; 3:26; 4:2; 5:15; 7:15, 21, 33; 9:2; 14:1, 43, 54, 61; Taylor, Mark, pp. 50-51.

[3] 1:45; 2:23; 4:1; 5:17, 20; 6:2, 7, 34, 55; 8:11, 31, 32; 10:28, 32, 41, 47; 11:15; 12:1; 13:5; 14:19, 33, 65, 69, 71; 15:8, 18; Turner, "Marcan Usage," JTS, XXVIII (1927), 352-353.

[4] 1:6, 13, 22, 33, 39; 2:6, 18; 4:38; 5:5, 11; 6:52; 9:4; 10:32 (2); 14:4, 40, 48, 54; 15:7, 26, 40, 43, 46. This usage is rare in Matthew, though frequent in Luke, see Turner, "Marcan Usage," pp. 349-351.

[5] Ibid., pp. 15-18. Turner lists 38 occurrences which are not found in the Matthean or Lucan parallels.

Vocabulary

In addition to observations about the Greek style of Mark, the presence or absence of language, typically Marcan, may indicate Marcan literary activity. Among the words which according to the lists given by Swete, Lagrange, and Hawkins occur with great frequency in Mark, there occur in the trial scene: eperōtān (14:60, 61) favored by Mark over the usual erōtān; preference for compounds of erchesthai; 14:53, synerchontai; the use of palin (14:61); siōpa (14:61), and the verb akolouthein (14:54).[1] E. Schweizer has also noted that pas (pantes hoi archiereis, 14:53) and holos (holon to synedrion) appear frequently in Mark, especially in the redactional sections.[2]

In this connection it should be noted that there are also a series of words which are unfamiliar to Mark and also rare in other parts of the New Testament. Among these are: sygkathēmenos (14:54)--Mark usually prefers the uncompounded root kathesthai;[3] thermainomenos (14:54)[4], the use of thanatōsai in 14:55 in place of the more usual Marcan words for "killing";[5] the use of tou eulogētou as a substantive;[6] chitonas (14:63) in the plural; the use of phainetai (14:64) in place of the more normal

_____

[1] Hawkins, Horae Synopticae, pp. 10-15; Lagrange, Marc, pp. lxv-lxvi; Swete, St. Mark, pp. xliv-xlvii.

[2] Schweizer, "Anmerkungen," p. 97.

[3] 2:6, 14; 3:22, 34; 4:1; 5:15; 10:46; 12:36; 13:3; 14:62; 16:5.

[4] Cf. Jn 18:18, 25.

[5] For "kill" Mark uses apokteinein in 3:4; 6:19; 8:31; 9:31, and 10:34 (the last three are in the Passion predictions); 12:5, 7, 8; 14:1 and apolesai in 1:24; 3:6; 4:38; 9:22; 11:18; 12:9; thanatoun is used only here and in 13:12.

[6] This is used six times in the New Testament, but nowhere else as a substantive; see Lk 1:6; Rom 1:25; 9:5; 2 Cor 1:3; 11:31; Eph 1:3; 1 Pet 1:3.

dokei.[1] Of themselves rare or unfamiliar words are not an index of tradition or redaction, but, as will be seen later, when taken in conjunction with other criteria, they can serve to uncover Marcan literary activity.[2]

Therefore, in terms of language and style, the trial scene is from the same hand as the rest of the gospel of Mark; it is not simply a piece of unredacted tradition taken over by Mark with little editorial activity. The same activity he uses in other parts of the gospel when he deals with traditional material or composes new material is present, in general terms, in the trial scene. In addition to the observations on style and language which touch on the internal make-up of the narrative, there is one significant compositional device which shows a particular and distinctive Marcan interest in the trial scene and which also brings it into close contact with other parts of the gospel. This is the already mentioned technique of intercalation whereby Mark breaks the flow of a narrative by inserting a new pericope after the beginning of an initial story. Though we have alluded to this technique before, it is now necessary to examine it in more detail in order to see what light its use throws on Marcan literary activity in the trial scene.[3] The Marcan intercalations are found in the following places:

1. 3:20-21 [22-30] 31-35. Beelzebub controversy and saying about sin against the Spirit are inserted into narratives about relations between Jesus, disciples, and relatives.

---

[1] Mt 26:66 alters the phrase to ti hymin dokei.

[2] Cf. infra, pp. 67-71, 85-86.

[3] See supra, pp. 42-43, for initial observations on intercalations.

2. 5:21-24 [25-34] 35-43. Story of woman who touched Jesus' garment is inserted into the cure of the daughter of Jairus.

3. 6:7-13 [14-29] 30-32. Story of death of John the Baptist is inserted between mission and return of the twelve.

4. 11:12-14 [15-19] 20-26. Story of temple cleansing is inserted into the narrative about the fig tree.

5. 14:1-2 [3-9] 10-11. The anointing at Bethany is inserted into the two plans to kill Jesus.

6. 14:10-11 [12-16] 17-21 [22-25]. The material is complex for, as Best has noted, there is a "double sandwich" here.[1] On the one hand, the indications of the betrayal (14:10-11, 17-21) frame the supper material; on the other, this material (14:12-16, 22-25) frames the second mention of the betrayal.

7. 14:54 [55-65] 66-72. The trial narrative is framed by the denial of Peter.[2]

Examination of the sections framing the intercalated material reveals that, with the exception of intercalation 2, the framing verses are concerned in some way with Jesus' teaching on discipleship or with the reaction of the disciples to Jesus.[3] In the first intercalation the intimates of Jesus

---

[1] Best, *Temptation and Passion*, p. 91.

[2] Though not usually listed among the Marcan intercalations, it is interesting to note that Mark frames the whole central portion of his gospel, 8:27-10:45, by two stories on the healing of blind men, 8:22-26; 10:45-52.

[3] The second intercalation does not fit the pattern of the Marcan use of the technique which will be described in subsequent pages. K. L. Schmidt holds that "Es ist kein Zweifel dass Mk diesen Zusammenhang schon vorgefunden hat," *Rahmen*, p. 148. It may well be that Mark found this technique as part of the tradition available to him, and modified it for his own purposes. It is in accord with the technique of *inclusio* which is frequent in both classical and biblical literature, see, Charles

(hoi par' autou) think he is "beside himself," and in 3:35, Jesus responds to the presence of his mother and brothers with the saying on doing the will of God. In the third intercalation the sending and return of the twelve frame the material on the Baptist. In 11:12-26 instruction on the meaning of the fig tree frames the cleansing of the temple. The anointing, 14:3-9, is surrounded by the plan to kill Jesus and the participation of Judas in this plan, and, as noted, the trial scene is framed by the denial of the chief disciple, Peter.

Thus, Mark uses the technique of intercalation, not simply as a literary device to create the illusion of passing time, but in terms of a theological interest in relating the disciples to the work and fate of Jesus. Therefore, the presence of the trial scene intercalated within the story of Peter's denial shows that Marcan literary activity in the structuring and ordering of material is no less in evidence in the trial narrative, than in other parts of the gospel.

A brief survey of the content of the intercalated material shows that it is not simply some general relation of the disciples to Jesus that Mark portrays by using this technique. He uses it to cast over the whole gospel the shadow of the cross, and all the intercalations contain some allusion to the suffering and death of Jesus. In the first intercalation, the charge which Jesus answers is brought by "scribes from Jerusalem" who appear out of place in this Galilean setting of the ministry. As Lohmeyer remarks, "Jerusalem ist der Ort der heftigsten Feindschaft gegen Jesus," and, in Mark, the scribes are always hostile to Jesus.[1] In this pericope, very early in

---

Lohr, "Oral Techniques in the Gospel of Matthew," CBQ, XXIII (1961), 409-410. Our interest is primarily in the Marcan use of this technique.

[1] Lohmeyer, Markus, p. 77.

the gospel the agents as well as the location of the final fate of Jesus are put before the reader.

The content of the third intercalation, 6:14-29, is complex, including a statement of Herod's fears and his question of Jesus' identity (6:14-16), with an appended story on the death of the Baptist. The arrangement of the material is curious here. Herod's question that Jesus may be John, risen from the dead, presupposes that the narrative of vss. 17-29 should precede the question.[1] The narrative itself, 17-29, the only story in Mark which is not directly about Jesus, in terms of language and style is non-Marcan.[2] Bultmann has classed it as a Christian legend of Hellenistic origin concerning John.[3] Why then has Mark introduced it at this point? Marxsen has pointed out that, in Mark, stories about John serve to bring the fate of John and Jesus into close parallel.[4] Jesus begins his ministry after the "handing over" (paradothēnai) of John (1:14), so that John is the precursor of Jesus, not simply temporally, but also topically. Therefore, in the present context the introduction of the story about John, after a question about Jesus, serves to indicate to the reader that the future fate of Jesus is anticipated in the present fate of John.[5]

In the fourth intercalation the reaction of the priests

---

[1] Ibid., p. 117.

[2] Taylor, Mark, p. 310; Lohmeyer, Markus, p. 119. Non-Marcan elements include the absence of the historical present and the introduction of sentences by participles.

[3] Bultmann, Synoptic Tradition, p. 302.

[4] Mark, pp. 42-43.

[5] Such a view is confirmed by the similarity of the answer given Herod in 6:14b-15: "Some said, 'John the Baptizer has been raised from the dead'; . . . but others said, 'it is Elijah. And others said, 'It is a prophet like one of the prophets of old,'" and the response given Jesus in 8:28: "John the Baptist, Elijah, one of the prophets," which is then followed by the confession of Peter and the first Passion prediction.

and the scribes to Jesus' cleansing of the temple is their plan to seek a way to kill him (11:18). The three intercalations in the Passion narrative bring this theme of opposition and suffering to its fullest development. The anointing is done <u>eis ton entaphiasmon</u> (14:8), in anticipation of Jesus' death. In the intercalated sections connected with the supper, the meal concludes with the solemn prediction that Jesus will drink wine with the disciples only in the kingdom of God (14:25), pointing beyond his death to the parousia. In the final intercalation, the trial, the culmination of the mortal opposition to Jesus is met in the assembling of the Sanhedrin to kill him and their ratification of this plan. At Jerusalem (cf. 3:22) in the presence of the scribes, the chief priests and the priests, the final sentence is passed.

Therefore in Mark the framing sections and intercalated material make up a carefully articulated dialogue, where sections leading to the suffering and death of Jesus are framed by discipleship material. Thus, Mark uses the technique of intercalation to underscore two major themes of his gospel, the way of suffering of Jesus, and the necessity of the disciple to follow Jesus on this way.[1] Since the trial scene, which is the culmination of the opposition to Jesus, is intercalated within the story of the denial of Peter who functions after 8:27 as the typical disciple, we have strong literary evidence that Mark used the device of intercalation in terms of his theological purpose. He did not simply find the material in this order, but actively arranged the material to bring to culmination motifs at work in the earlier framing verses and intercalated material.

---

[1]Johannes Schreiber, Theologie des Vertrauens (Hamburg: Furche Verlag, 1967), p. 166: "Die Gemeinschaft mit dem erhöhten Gottessohn ist nur in der Bejahung seiner Leiden und der ganz persönlichen Übernahme des Kreuzes durch die Mission möglich." Schweizer, Mark, pp. 385-386.

Peter, the leader of the disciples, denies his Lord at that very moment when the opposition to Jesus reaches its pinnacle in the sentence of death.

In the first section of this chapter we noted that by the criteria of language and style, it is Mark who gave us the final version of the trial scene, so that he did not simply take it over as a bit of unredacted tradition. The survey of the intercalations is a further bit of literary evidence that Mark has been active in the trial scene. He composes the trial scene in a pattern he uses elsewhere and to express theological themes which exist throughout his gospel in a similar compositional pattern. The question still remains unanswered, however, as to how active Mark is in the trial scene. We have seen that the narrative is not simply unredacted tradition. We have yet to specify what is traditional material, what is Mark's reworking of tradition, and what is due to Mark's own composition. It is therefore necessary to embark on a close analysis of the individual parts of the narrative, in order to delineate more exactly Mark's literary activity in the trial scene.

Tradition and Redaction in the Trial Narrative

The Introductory Verses: 14:53-55

Mark 14:53

Kai apēgagon ton Iēsoun pros ton archierea kai synerchontai pantes hoi archiereis kai hoi presbyteroi kai hoi grammateis.

This verse affirms two things: (a) the leading away of Jesus to the high priest, 14:53a, and (b) the gathering of the Sanhedrin, 14:53b. Certain elements of the verse suggest that the first half is a Marcan redaction of a traditional allusion to the arrest of Jesus, while the second half seems to be a Marcan composition. Elements suggesting Marcan redaction in the first half of the verse are: (a) the Marcan custom of indicating a new stage in the dramatic action by noting a change of place,[1] (b) the introduction of a new section by the use of the third person impersonal plural,[2] and (c) the use of kai parataxis.[3] The mention by name of Jesus as the object of the verb (apēgagon) betrays the common Marcan redactional technique of naming Jesus in introductory sentences.[4] Other indications suggest traditional material. In the Koine of the period, apagein, has become a terminus technicus for the leading away of a prisoner for judgment, and Mark rarely uses agein or its compounds in the sense of lead, but prefers pherein.[5] The mention of the high priest in the singular stands in tension with the indications of the three groups who make up the Sanhedrin in the second half of the verse. In all other places in Mark when reference is made to the Passion or handing over of Jesus, the reference is to the archiereis (pl) who, along with the presbyteroi and grammateis, become, after 8:31, the agents of Jesus' death.[6]

---

[1] Examples are found in 1:9, 12, 14, 16, 21, 29, 35; 2:1, 13; 3:1, 7, 13, 20; 4:1, 10; 5:1, 21; 6:1, 6b, 45, 53; 7:24, 31; 8:22, 27; 9:2, 30, 33; 10:1, 32, 46; 11:1, 15, 27; 13:1; 14:3, 32; 15:1.

[2] See examples cited in previous note and Turner, "Marcan Usage," JTS, XXV (1924), 373-386, and Taylor, Mark, p. 47.

[3] Hawkins, Horae Synopticae, pp. 150-152.

[4] 1:9, 14; 3:7; 6:30; 8:27; 9:2; 10:23, 32; 12:35; 13:2, 14:27; 15:1, 24. Pesch, Naherwartungen, p. 59, n. 79, writes: "Die Nennung Jesu in einführenden Sätzen zu Beginn eines Abschnittes ist ein deutliches kompositorisches Stilmittel bei Mark."

[5] On apagein see William F. Arndt and F. Wilbur Gingrich, A Greek-English Lexicon of the New Testament and Other Early Christian Literature (4th rev. ed.; Chicago: University of Chicago Press, 1952), p. 78, and on the use of pherein, Turner, "Marcan Usage," JTS, XXVI (1925), 19-20.

[6] The terms are found in the plural in 8:31; 10:33; 11:18, 27; 14:1, 10, 43, 55; 15:3, 11, 15, 31.

The mention of the leading away of Jesus to the high priest and the gathering of the Sanhedrin must be compared with a similar reference in 15:1 where "The chief priests, with the elders and scribes, and the whole council held a consultation; and they bound Jesus and led him away to Pilate." Debate has ranged over the literary relationship of this verse to 14:53, centering on whether 15:1 is an older tradition with 14:53 an expansion of it, or whether 14:53 is the older tradition, or whether both represent independent traditions.[1] While the solution of the above dispute is beyond the scope of the present discussion, we can note that in 15:1 there are two key words which are used in connection with the Passion. They lead Jesus away (apēnegkan) and they hand him over (paredōkan) to Pilate. The use of paradidonai in connection with the Passion argues for an early pre-Marcan tradition, as Perrin has conclusively shown.[2] With this observation in mind, we would suggest that both 14:53 and 15:1 represent relics of an older tradition, the substance of which was the simple indication of the leading away of Jesus and his being handed over to his adversaries. On this basis and on the basis of the evidence of Marcan redaction discussed in the previous paragraphs we suggest that 14:53a represents a Marcan reworking of an earlier tradition on the "handing over" of Jesus.[3]

---

[1] On 15:1 as the older tradition see Bultmann, Synoptic Tradition, p. 279; Haenchen, Weg Jesu, p. 509; Nineham, St. Mark, p. 410; on 14:53ff as the older tradition see, Schneider, "Gab es eine vorsynoptische Szene," pp. 27-29, and Lohmeyer, Markus, p. 334. George Braumann, "Mk 15,2-5 und Mk 14,55-64," ZNW, LII (1961), 273-278, holds the independence of the two pericopes.

[2] N. Perrin, "The Use of (para)didonai in Connection the Passion of Jesus in the New Testament," in Der Ruf Jesu und die Antwort der Gemeinde, Festschrift für Joachim Jeremias zum 70 Geburtstag, ed. Eduard Lohse (Göttingen: Vandenhoeck und Ruprecht, 1970), pp. 204-212.

[3] Both Luke (22:66) and John (18:13) repeat this notation of the "leading away" of Jesus.

In contrast to the first half of the verse, the second half evidences strong Marcan compositional activity. The introduction by <u>kai</u> parataxis (<u>kai synerchontai</u>) is Marcan, as is the historical present of the main verb.[1] The verb itself reveals the Marcan fondness for compounds of <u>erchesthai</u>, and the compound <u>synerchontai</u>, is found only in the redactional introduction at 3:20 and in the <u>Sammelbericht</u> of 6:33.[2] In describing the gathering of the Sanhedrin, only Mark mentions that all (<u>pantes</u>) the chief priests, elders and scribes assemble. E. Schweizer has already noted a fondness for the use of <u>pas</u> in Marcan redactional sections.[3] Closer analysis of the places in Mark with parallels in the other synoptics where he uses <u>pas</u> indicates a fondness for "universalizing" scenes--a tendency which Matthew and Luke continually modify in their reworking of Marcan material. A few examples will illustrate this:[4]

> Mk 1:32; Mt 8:16; Lk 4:40: Only in Mark do they bring Jesus <u>all</u> the sick and demoniacs.
>
> Mk 2:12; Mt 9:7; Lk 5:25: In Mark the man sick of palsy appears before <u>all</u> the people; while in Mt and Lk he returns home.
>
> Mk 2:13; Mt 9:9; Lk 5:27: Only in Mark does the introduction to Levi's call begin with the notation that the <u>whole</u> crowd comes to Jesus.
>
> Mk 6:33; Mt 14:13; Lk 9:11: (A <u>Sammelbericht</u>) In Mark the crowds follow Jesus from <u>all</u> the cities.
>
> Mk 9:15; Mt 17:14; Lk 9:37: Only in Mark, after the Transfiguration, does the <u>whole</u> crowd become amazed.
>
> Mk 11:17; Mt 21:13; Lk 19:46: Only Mark includes the complete quote from Isa 56:7 which makes the temple a house of prayer for <u>all</u> nations (<u>pasin tois ethnesin</u>).

---

[1] Hawkins, <u>Horae Synopticae</u>, pp. 150-151, 143-150.

[2] <u>Erchesthai</u> is one of the words listed as preferred by Mark, <u>supra</u>, p. 57, n.1 ; cf. also Taylor, <u>Mark</u>, p. 235.

[3] "Anmerkungen," p. 97.

[4] This phenomenon is found in the following places in Mark: 1:15, 32, 37; 2:12, 13; 4:1; 5:20; 6:33, 41, 50; 7:3; 9:15; 11:17, 18b; 13:10, 23, 37; 14:53, 64.

This "universalizing" tendency of Mark shown in the fondness for pas appears in those sections which most betray the hand of Mark--in introductions to sections of the narrative, and in editorial comments on them and conclusions to them.[1] While it is difficult to assign a definite meaning to this usage, it is consistent with Mark's portrayal of the ministry of Jesus as a series of epiphanies, which, even if the people do not recognize, they are exposed to.[2] In the trial scene it is only Mark who implies that the whole Sanhedrin assembles (14:53b), concurs in the plan to assemble the witnesses (14:55), and participates in the condemnation (14:64).

Therefore the introductory verse to the trial scene shows considerable Marcan redactional activity. He takes over a traditional allusion to the "leading away" and by the introduction of the members of the Sanhedrin required for a formal trial, he, in effect, makes it into a trial scene rather than a simple hearing. The language of 14:53b which gives the scene this formality is the most strongly Marcan part of the verse.

Mark 14:54

> Kai ho Petros apo makrothen ēkolouthēsen autō heōs esō eis tēn aulēn tou archiereōs, kai ēn sygkathēmenos meta tōn hyperetōn kai thermainomenos pros to phōs.

In contrast to 14:53, the following verse shows strong traditional and non-Marcan terminology. Sygkathēmi and pros to phōs are hapax legomena in Mark, and only Mark and John (18:18, 25) mention that Peter was "warming himself" at the fire. Mark tends to use the imperfect of akolouthein in redactional

---

[1] Introductions: 1:5; 2:13; 4:7; 7:3; 9:15; Comments and Conclusions: 2:12; 5:20; 6:33 (Sammelbericht); 6:50; 13:37.

[2] Schweizer, "Anmerkungen," p. 97, holds the use of pas and holos is to connote "die universale Wirkung des Kerygmas."

sections and leaves the aorist in traditional verses.[1] The verse exists in a certain tension with the surrounding verses. In 14:50 it is mentioned that all flee, yet the reappearance of Peter in 14:54 is not explained. Finally the preferred Marcan sentence structure of verb followed by subject (synerchontai pantes, 14:53) is replaced by the less familiar order of subject (ho Petros) verb (ēkolouthēsen).[2] In light of these considerations of language and style, we may consider 14:54 as a traditional introduction to the story of Peter's denial, which Mark has severed from its original context (14:66) in order to intercalate the trial scene within the story of the denial.

Mark 14:55

> hoi de archiereis kai holon to synedrion ezētoun kata tou Iesou martyrian eis to thanatōsai auton, kai ouk hēuriskon.

In content this verse serves a double function. On the one hand it is a secondary introduction to the trial scene after the mention of Peter's following in 14:54; on the other, it is a summary of the next four verses in denying that testimony was found against Jesus. In terms of language and style it betrays strong Marcan redaction. In contrast to the usual Marcan use of kai parataxis, the verse begins with hoi de. Such a style is better Greek than the monotonous kai and has led Wohleb to suggest that the verse is an insertion of a later redactor.[3]

---

[1] The aorist, ēkolouthēsen, seems strange here since Peter's action stretches over a long period of time. The imperfect is found in 2:15 which Bultmann, Synoptic Tradition, p. 331, calls a Marcan formulation; in 5:24b, a Marcan introduction and transitional verse; in 10:52 which shows Marcan interest in the use of pistis, and especially in the allusion to the following en tē hodō. The only place where the aorist is found in an apparently redactional section is the Sammelbericht of 3:7, but K. L. Schmidt suggests that 3:7a "bis einschliesslich ēkolouthēsen . . . zum ursprüglichen Bestand dieses Stückes gehört haben kann." Rahmen, p. 107. The aorist is also found in 1:18, 2:14; 3:7.

[2] Zerwick, Untersuchungen, p. 75.

[3] "Beobachtungen zum Erzählungsstil des Markus

However, as Zerwick has shown, it is rather a conscious technique used by Mark either for (a) emphasis, (b) to engage the reader or (c) to increase the pace of the narrative.[1] Initially, then, this verse calls attention to the first important issue of the trial scene, the matter of the false witnesses against Jesus, and the use of hoi de underlies this.

The verse recounts that the chief priests and the whole Sanhedrin sought testimony against Jesus, eis to thanatōsai auton. This combination of the plan of Jesus' opponents, usually expressed by the verb zētein, with the object of the plan, the death of Jesus, occurs at four other crucial places in Mark's gospel.

> 3:6 kai exēlthontes hoi pharisaioi euthys meta tōn Hērodianōn symboulion edidoun kat' autou hopōs auton apolesōsin.
>
> 11:18 kai ēkousan hoi archiereis kai hoi grammateis, kai ezētoun pōs auton apolesōsin.
>
> 12:12 kai ezētoun auton kratēsai.
>
> 14:1 kai ezētoun hoi archiereis kai hoi grammateis pōs auton en dolō kratēsontes apokteinōsin.

Schweizer and Gaston have seen in this sequence a definite Marcan pattern whereby the whole gospel is written from the viewpoint of the death of Jesus.[2] In 14:55 the form of this plan differs from the previous indications in that the aim is no longer the "how" of the plan but its definite execution. The term used for "killing" is interesting. The three Passion predictions (8:31; 9:31; 10:33) use the verb apokteinein, which, along with apolesai, is Mark's usual word for "kill."[3] In

---

Evangeliums," Rom. Quart.-Schr., XXXVI (1928), 185-196, cited in Zerwick, Untersuchungen, p. 3.

[1] Untersuchungen, p. 12.

[2] Schweizer, Mark, p. 242, and Gaston, No Stone, pp. 473-474, note the Marcan use of these indications.

[3] Supra, p. 57, n. 5.

contrast to this, thanatoun is rare in Mark, occurring only here and in 13:12, and is also infrequent in the New Testament, and never used in the credal formulae concerning the death of Jesus.

The object of the quest of the Sanhedrin, martyrian, is also infrequent. Though found often in John (13 times), it is found in the synoptics only in Mark (14:55, 56, 59) and in Luke once (22:71). The more frequent usage is the concrete martyrion or some form of the verb.[1] The imperfect of heuriskein is also unfamiliar in Mark who uses the aorist form seven times and the imperfect nowhere else.[2] A final phrase which must be considered is the addition of kai holon to synedrion. As was noted, Schweizer has shown that the use of pas and holos with a definite substantive is characteristic of Mark.[3] In the present verse such a definite Marcan characteristic seems strange since the latter half of the verse contains much unfamiliar Marcan terminology. However, if the phrase represents a Marcan addition to the simple statement that the high priests and scribes sought evidence against Jesus to kill him, then it is Mark who has brought this indication of the plan to kill Jesus into the context of the trial scene. Therefore the Marcan redaction of 14:55 emerges in the following pattern. He has taken a traditional allusion to the plan of the chief priests to kill Jesus, which, as its presence in other contexts of the gospel shows, is not necessarily localized in the trial scene. Mark has created this localization by making the whole verse an introduction to the trial scene proper which begins with the false witnesses in 14:56. By putting the fifth and final indication of the plan to

---

[1] Martyrion is used in 1:44; 6:11; 13:9.

[2] The aorist is found in 1:37; 7:30; 11:4, 13; 13:36; 14:16; 14:40.

[3] "Anmerkungen," p. 97.

kill Jesus here, Mark lets the reader know that the opposition to Jesus, begun in 3:6 has reached its high point. Also, by adding the phrase "and the whole Sanhedrin" Mark now gives the plan the sanction of the Sanhedrin, which is further evidence that it is Mark who creates that particular aspect of the narrative whereby it can be called a trial before the Sanhedrin.

The False Witnesses and the Temple Saying

Mark 14:56-59

56 polloi gar epseudomartyroun kat' autou, kai isai hai martyriai ouk ēsan.

57 kai tines anastantes epseudomartyroun kat' autou legontes.

58 hoti hēmeis ēkousamen autou legontos hoti egō katalysō ton naon touton ton cheiropoiēton kai dia triōn hēmerōn allon acheiropoiēton oikodomēso.

59 kai oude houtōs isē ēn hē martyria autōn.

After the three introductory verses which give the setting to the scene, the trial itself begins and involves three distinct events: (a) the charge of the false witnesses about the temple saying of 14:58, (b) the examination conducted by the high priest on the identity of Jesus, and the reaction of the Sanhedrin to Jesus' answer (14:60-64), and (c) the mocking of 14:65.[1] Within the scene itself the most complex problems arise from the material concerned with the false witnesses and the temple saying. In such a short narrative of twelve verses, four are devoted to material which has no apparent relevance to the rest of the narrative, since the charge about the temple is not taken up again in 14:60. There is a burdensome repetition of the falseness or inadequacy of the witnesses (14:55, 56a, 56b, 57, 59). Coupled with this is the problem of the presence on the lips of false witnesses of a threat of Jesus against the

---

[1] Following Lohmeyer's suggestion, Markus, p. 326.

temple which Mark, in other places, does not record as false (13:2; 15:29), and which, in other traditions, is recorded as a true saying of Jesus.[1]

Various suggestions have been proposed to solve the problem of the temple saying and the false witnesses. Taylor and Schmid see in the attribution of the statement to false witnesses the desire of early Christians to disassociate themselves from opposition to the temple.[2] Haenchen sees the use of the false witnesses as a device to ascribe a distorted tradition to the opponents of Jesus,[3] and Bertram suggests that they are false, not because they utter an untruth, but because they attack Jesus.[4] Schweizer sees in the false witnesses a theological device to heighten the malice of men and the gravity of the suffering of Jesus.[5] The defect of these often opposing solutions is that they focus simply on harmonization of content and take little cognizance of Mark's purpose in allowing such a problem to exist in the final redaction. In the following pages we will suggest a solution to the problem posed by these verses by attempting to show that the false witnesses arise from a pre-Marcan apologetic tradition, based on the use of Old Testament texts and which originally had nothing to do with the temple saying of 14:58. We will then suggest that Mark alters this tradition of false witnesses to "witnesses not in agreement,"

---

[1] The saying against the temple in 13:2 uses different language, but is recorded as a true saying of Jesus against the temple. In 15:29 the saying is on the lips of mockers, but is not said explicitly to be false. John records it as a true saying of Jesus (2:19-22). Matthew (26:60-61) arranges the Marcan material so that the statement is not directly attributed to false witnesses.

[2] Taylor, Mark, p. 566; Josef Schmid, The Gospel According to Mark, The Regensburg New Testament, trans. Kevin Condon (Staten Island, N.Y.: Alba House, 1968), p. 281.

[3] Weg Jesu, p. 510.

[4] Die Leidensgechichte, p. 56.   [5] Mark, p. 190.

and by the use of a literary technique which we call "Marcan insertions," Mark "inserts" the temple saying between 14:56 and 14:59. The ultimate meaning of the temple saying and its importance to the trial scene will occupy a later chapter.

The influence of the Old Testament on the formation of the Passion traditions has long been recognized.[1] Within the trial narrative the mocking of 14:65, which Taylor calls a manifest piece of separate tradition, is influenced by Isa 50:5-6.[2] Jeremias and Maurer have seen a "suffering servant" motif at work in the earlier traditions surrounding the trial narrative.[3] Thus far, however, there has been no attempt to explain the matter of the false witnesses in terms of the influence of Old Testament texts.

The material concerning the false witnesses is introduced by the phrase, polloi gar epseudomartyroun, which provides the initial key to a solution of the problem of the witnesses. The introduction of a sentence by an unmodified polloi is infrequent in Mark and found in places which, on other grounds, are clearly

───────────

[1]Dibelius, "Die alttestamentlichen Motive"; Tradition, pp. 186-190; C. H. Dodd, According to the Scriptures (New York: Charles Scribner's Sons, 1953); Lindars, New Testament Apologetic, pp. 75-138; A. Rose, "L'influence des psaumes sur les annonces et les récits de la Passion et de la Résurrection dans les Evangiles" (Orientalia et Biblica Lovaniensia, Vol. IV, ed. Robert de Langhe; Louvain: Publications Universitaires, 1962), pp. 297-356; Alfred Suhl, Die Funktion der alttestamentlichen Zitate und Anspielungen im Markusevangelium (Gütersloh: Gerd Mohn, 1965), pp. 26-27.

[2]Mark, p. 510.

[3]Joachim Jeremias and Walther Zimmerli, The Servant of God (Studies in Biblical Theology, Vol. XX; rev. ed.; London: S. C. M. Press, 1965), pp. 99-101; Christian Maurer, "Knecht Gottes und Sohn Gottes im Passionsbericht des Markus," ZTK, L (1953), 1-51, and "Das Messiasgeheimnis," pp. 520-523. Best, Temptation, pp. 150-151, while admitting the influence of Isaiah 53 on the trial narrative, is more reserved about seeing the figure of the servant here.

Marcan compositions.[1] The use of gar is also significant. In an incisive article C. H. Bird explains that in addition to the usual "explanatory" gar, Mark uses a "gar allusive" where one factor in a given situation is emphasized because it is the point of contact with another set of ideas familiar to the reader which elucidates the fuller significance of the whole context.[2] Thus the gar serves to direct the reader to a set of associations or allusions which are not evident from the immediate context. In Bird's examples the other set of ideas alluded to is often veiled Old Testament references. We suggest, then, that the introduction of the sentence by polloi gar is due to Marcan composition, and that Mark warns his readers to be on the lookout for some Old Testament allusion.

The activity of witnesses in vss. 57-58 is twofold: (a) they rise up (anastantes, 14:57; cf. anastas 14:60), and (b) they give false testimony (epseudomartyroun, 14:56, 57). A similar pattern in Pss 27:12 and 35:11 has led A. Rose to postulate allusions to these psalms in 14:56-57.[3] The psalm verses read:[4]

---

[1] 2:15, a Marcan formulation, Bultmann, Synoptic Tradition, p. 331; 6:31, a Sammelbericht.

[2] C. H. Bird, "Some gar clauses in St. Mark's Gospel," JTS, N.S. IV (1953), 171-187. Some examples would be: 1:16b; 1:38d; 2:15c; 4:2b; 6:31c; 9:6b; 11:13c; 16:8c.

[3] Rose, "L'influence," pp. 309-310.

[4] Since Psalm 27 (26):12b presents major problems of text and translation, I have translated literally from the Septuagint. Modern translations of the Massoretic text of this verse render the last phrase, wīpēᵃḥ ḥāmās, as "they breathe forth violence" (RSV, Chicago Bible, Bible of Jerusalem). The Septuagint, epseusato hē adikia heautē, whatever its exact translation, does not translate the Massoretic text. The versions which follow the Septuagint translate 27:12b as "et mentita est iniquitas sibi" (Sixto-Clementine Vulgate) and "iniquity hath lied to itself" (Douay Version). In a recent study Mitchell Dahood has given evidence that the Septuagint and the translations based on it may be closer to the original Hebrew than the Massoretic pointing would suggest, Psalms I (Anchor Bible, Vol. XVI; New York: Doubleday and Co., 1966), p. 169. Dahood shows

Ps 27:12, LXX, 26:12 . . . for unjust witnesses (martyres adikoi) have risen up (epanestēsan) against me, and their injustice is false (epseusato hē adikia heautē).

Ps 35:11, LXX, 34:11 Unjust witnesses rise up (anastantes martyres adikoi), they ask me of things that I know not.

In these psalms we have the lament of the innocent speaker against those who threaten him with false and lying words.[1] In terms then of situation and language we have a parallel to the false charge brought against the innocent Jesus in 14:56ff. The apparent difficulty with this view is that in the psalms the witnesses are not called pseudeis but adikoi, with epseusato providing the verbal contact with the Marcan text. This problem provides the final key to the tradition history of these verses. Behind the martyres adikoi of Ps 27:12 lies the Hebrew 'ēdê šeqer, which, at other places in the Septuagint and especially in the Decalogue, is translated as pseudomartyroun (Ex 20:16) or pseudēs martys (Prov 6:19; 19:5, 9).[2] Therefore Greek translators of the Hebrew exercised freedom with 'edê šeqer, translating it at times as martyres adikoi, and, at other times, using pseudēs and martys. The difference between epanestēsan and anastantes is not significant since they both translate

---

that the Massoretic text vocalizes the Hebrew consonants wyph as if they came from the verb pwh, "wheeze against." Dahood suggests the alternative vocalization, wīpēhē, and derives the form from the Ugaritic root yph, "witness, testifiers." He then translates 27:12b "as well as malicious testifiers," literally, "Testifiers of wrong." The Septuagint would then represent an attempt to capture the meaning of this pre-Massoretic Hebrew.

[1] Sigmund Mowinckel, The Psalms in Israel's Worship, trans. D. R. Ap-Thomas (New York: Abingdon Press, 1967), I, 227-228; II, 6, and Johannes Pedersen, Israel: Its Life and Culture (London: Oxford University Press, 1926), I, 447.

[2] In Ps 35:11 the martyres adikoi translates 'edê hamas which indicates that the Hebrew 'edê šeqer, wīpēhē hāmās and 'edê hāmās are translated freely either by the Greek martyres' adikoi or some form of pseudēs. Psalm 35 (34) has other contacts with the Passion narrative, 35:4 and 14:55, "They sought my life"; 35:7 and 15:32, the mocking; see Nineham, St. Mark, p. 406.

qûm.¹ Therefore, the earliest allusion to the innocence of Jesus before his accusers used Pss 27:12 and 35:11 as part of a Passion apologetic in a circle familiar with the Hebrew text, where the verbal allusion to the psalms would be clear, but the traditions were handed on in a Greek speaking milieu which allowed variant translations of the Hebrew. We suggest that along with the early Christian apologetic which told of Jesus being "handed over" according to the scriptures, there existed a tradition of Jesus before false accusers.² The introduction of the false witnesses in the trial scene, therefore, arises from Mark's adaptation of the tradition affirming the innocence of Jesus. The fact that this tradition exists in narrative form and that the Old Testament allusions are veiled does not militate against this conclusion, since recent studies on the pesher mode of exegesis in early Christianity suggests that historicization of Old Testament texts on the basis of verbal allusions was a common practice in early Christianity.³

---

¹There are no compound verbs in the semitic languages so the differences in the Greek arise from the presence of the Hebrew bᵉ with qûm, cf. Ps 35(34):11; Dt 19:11, 22:26; Jgs 6:31; Ps 3:1, 27(26):3, 44(43):5.

²Perrin, "(para)didonai," shows the influence of the "handing over" tradition.

³The word, pesher, is used here in reference to the biblical commentaries found at Qumran, which often begin with the word, pishro, literally, the interpretation of. Ringgren writes of this method: "The method of interpretation is reminiscent of that which is used in certain late Targums (e.g., to the Song of Songs) and in the Midrashim: the interpretations are based on single words lifted out of their context, on paronomasia, on the assumption of double meaning in certain expressions, and on small emendations of the text to fit the view of the interpreter," The Faith of Qumran (Philadelphia: Fortress Press, 1963), p. 10. Lindars notes that the pesher mode of interpretation involves shift of application and modification of the text (New Testament Apologetic, p. 17). Coupled with this is the tendency already inherent in the Midrashim to put a commentary on the text in the form of narrative. The three elements which make up the pesher mode, (a) freedom with the text, (b) the actualization of the text in terms of the interpreter's own experience, and (c) the tendency to make a narrative of the

The above observations solve the problem of the presence of false witnesses in the trial narrative. They do not indicate how the specific charge about the temple (14:58), which for Mark is a saying of Jesus appears on the lips of these witnesses. In addition to the characterization of these witnesses as "false" there is the comment of vs. 56 (kai isai hai martyriai ouk ēsan) and vs. 59 (oude houtōs isē hē martyria autōn). By calling their testimony "not in agreement" or "inadequate," Mark softens the original tradition of false witnesses and leaves the truth of the charge as an open question.[1] We will suggest that Marcan composition here is evident on the basis of a major Marcan stylistic device, indicated by the similarity of language between vss. 56 and 59. This device which we will call a "Marcan insertion" has not been discussed before as an entree to Mark's compositional activity. In order to see the presence and significance of its use in the trial narrative, we must say something about the nature and use of the technique by Mark.

The Marcan Insertion Technique.--Certain observations about the style of Mark in general must be made before we can discuss the insertions. We have already noted the Marcan fondness for intercalation, the framing of a body of material by two sections similar to each other but different from the intercalated material. Mark also shows a fondness for catchword composition, the linking of sentences together by the repetition of

---

text, are seen now by commentators as explaining the formation of many New Testament narratives.

[1]The RSV translates ouk isai as "did not agree." Both Swete, St. Mark, p. 356, and Taylor, Mark, p. 566, mention the view of Erasmus and Grotius that the phrase can be translated as "inadequate" but prefer as do most modern commentators, "not in agreement" or "not alike."

significant terms,[1] a fondness for parallelism,[2] and for the use of chiasm where the final element in a section refers back to the initial element.[3] In light of these recognized Marcan composition techniques, the repetition of the inadequacy of the witnesses in vss. 56 and 59 calls for further discussion. Three things are characteristic of these verses: (1) stylistically the two allusions are tautological, especially in a context where the inadequacy of the witnesses is patent, (2) there is a close verbal correspondence between the two statements, and (3) Matthew, in his reworking of the material (27:60-61) omits the two references.

Close reading of the text of Mark reveals that there are at least 45 places where a phrase or sentence is repeated soon after its initial statement. Some scattered examples, the significance of which will be treated later, illustrate the point.

2:6	dialogizomenoi en tais kardiais autōn
2:8b	dialogizesthe en tais kardiais hymōn
3:7	kai poly plēthos
3:8	plēthos poly
10:23b	pōs dyskolōs hoi ta chremata echontes eis tēn basileian tou theou eiseleusontai
10:24b	pōs dyskolon estin eis tēn basileian tou theou eiselthein.

---

[1] Both Bultmann, Synoptic Tradition, p. 325, and Taylor, Mark, pp. 408-409, note the Marcan fondness for catchword composition and list as the clearest example 9:37-50.

[2] In addition to the parallelism within sentence structure noted by Black, An Aramaic Approach to the Gospels and Acts (3d rev. ed.; Oxford: Clarendon Press, 1967), pp. 143-149, and Taylor, Mark, p. 57, Mark shows a fondness for parallelism in language and style in recounting similar narratives, cf. 1:25-27 with 4:31-34; 7:32-36 with 8:22-26, and 11:1-6 with 14:13-16.

[3] Chiasms can be noted in 2:27; 13:1-2; 14:58, and in the structure of 2:13-3:8. See Nils W. Lund, Chiasmus in the New Testament (Chapel Hill, N.C.: University of North Carolina Press, 1942), pp. 32, 303.

This is the exact verbal pattern we find in 14:56 and 59. However, in 20 of the 46 instances of the repetition of phrases or sentences, there is a closer similarity to 14:56 and 59. In these 20 cases there emerges the pattern that: (a) the second repeated phrase is superfluous--it could be omitted without harming the sense of the passage in which it is found, (b) the verbal correspondence is exact or very close, and (c) the other synoptic writers change the tautology.[1] Some examples of Mark's

---

[1] The identification of and study of the function of the Marcan insertions has not been made before. The following considerations have led to their identification. A. Robert and A. Feuillet in their *Introduction to the New Testament*, trans. Patrick Skehan et al. (New York: Desclee and Co., 1965), p. 195, remark, "A skilled narrator gives his hearers time to remember what he has said; the same sentence is repeated by different speakers" (italics mine). During the convention of the Catholic Biblical Association in the summer of 1969, Quentin Quesnell pointed out that, among the many characteristics of Mark's style is his fondness for repeating phrases. The Marcan technique of intercalating pericopes suggests that Mark is fond of enclosing significant material within two sections of similar content. These considerations led me to make a complete study of the Greek text of Mark to see if such techniques existed on the smaller scale of verses as well as pericopes. The result was the identification of the verses listed in the appendix and described below. The criteria evolved for distinguishing between a true insertion and simple repetition are an attempt to find Marcan composition and deliberate intent at work in the use of the technique. The first two are evident from an analysis of the text. The criterion of synoptic alteration has been used by J. Schreiber in an attempt to find Marcan redaction in other spheres. He writes: "Where Matthew or Luke or indeed both alter the text of Mark at a given point, especially if this is carried through the whole gospel, we very probably have to do with a theological statement which they reject." *ZTK*, LVIII (1961), 154-155. Schreiber's criteria for a Marcan redaction are translated by J. M. Robinson in "The Problem of History in Mark, Reconsidered," *USQR*, XX (1964), 134. What Schreiber says regarding a theological statement is also true of an aspect of Mark's style. The study of the content of the inserted material confirms that we have a Marcan redactional technique here, since the material inserted is important to Mark's theology. In a recent meeting (April, 1971) of the Chicago Society for Biblical Research, Quesnell presented further observations on his research, done in independence of the present work. In his presentation he did not discuss criteria for identifying these as Marcan redaction, nor did he discuss the function of the technique as an entree to Mark's theology. Three recent helpful and important studies on the phenomenon of repetition in Mark are F. Neirynck, "Mark in Greek," *Ephemerides Theologicae Lovanienses*, XLVII (1971), 144-198, "Duality in Mark," *Ibid.*, 394-463 and "Duplicate Expressions in the Gospel of Mark," *Ibid.*, XLVIII (1972), 150-209.

use of this technique confirm the above observations.[1]

1. 3:7   kai poly plēthos
    3:8b   plēthos poly

    Comment: Marcan editorial work is evident in this Sammelbericht.[2] The second reference to the "large crowd" is unnecessary and some Western manuscripts omit it. Matthew (4:23-25) omits both references to the plēthos poly and Luke (6:17-20) omits the second reference.

2. 10:23b pōs dyskolōs, etc.
    10:24b pōs dyskolon, etc.

    Comment: The double saying on the difficulty of entering is superfluous in such a short compass as the present verses. Both Matthew (19:23-25) and Luke (18:24-26) have the first saying and the metaphor of the camel (Mk 10:25), but omit the second saying.

3. 13:35   grēgoreite
    13:37   grēgoreite

    Comment: The second grēgoreite is definitely pleonastic as well as a Marcan composition.[3] Neither Matthew nor Luke follows Mark here. The inserted verses denote the times at which the master of the house may return, and themselves are Marcan compositions which serve to anticipate the time sequence which Mark will follow in the Passion narrative.[4]

These examples confirm the existence of the Marcan insertion

---

[1]See Appendix for a complete listing of the insertions.

[2]Schmidt, Rahmen, p. 105.

[3]Pesch, Naherwartungen, p. 200.

[4]R. H. Lightfoot, The Gospel Message of St. Mark (London: Oxford University Press, 1962), p. 53.

technique. Whether Mark found such a stylistic device in the tradition can never be determined. The frequency of the usage and the fact that the other synoptics consistently alter it, are strong evidence, however, that the use of the technique is an element of Mark's composition. Mark uses this technique to call attention to certain verses throughout his gospel much in the same fashion that a modern writer would use italics or an asterisk. Thus far we have merely established the existence of the use of framing verses to call attention to inserted material. Certain observations must be added about the content and function of the <u>inserted material</u> in order to appreciate the full significance of this technique.

A general survey of the inserted material indicates that it contains much material which is very important to the major themes of Mark's gospel: the <u>exousia</u> of the Son of Man (2:10; 13:34);[1] the role of the disciples and their reaction to Jesus' activity (5:30-34; 3:14b-15; 8:30-9:4; 10:24; 13:36), the suffering and death of Jesus (9:12b-13a; 15:23). This brief survey of the content of the inserted material does not tell us exactly why Mark chose to include such themes within the insertions since he treats similar themes in other parts of his gospel. What exactly does Mark want to tell his readers by including material within the insertions?

The two insertions in Mk 2:1-11 provide a way of answering the above question. In 2:7-8a and in 2:10, we have two insertions in close sequence. In the first the charge of blasphemy is recorded along with the saying on the forgiveness of sin; in the second the power of the Son of Man over sin is affirmed. The tradition history of 2:1-11 is complex, since the

---

[1] N. Perrin, "The Son of Man in the Synoptic Tradition," <u>Biblical Research</u>, XIII (1968), 21.

pericope is a combination of a miracle story, 2:1-5a; 10b-11, and an apophthegem, 2:5b-10a,[1] which is not part of the original miracle story.[2] The material to which Mark calls attention by his use of the two insertions is, therefore, extraneous to the context in which it is found. Also, this inserted material changes the whole tenor of the narrative. In 2:1-11 by the addition of the charge of blasphemy, of the saying on forgiveness and of the statement on the *exousia* of the Son of Man, a *Wundergeschichte* has been refashioned into a pericope of highest significance for Mark's theology.[3] The function of the insertions in Mk 2:1-11 lets us, then, see their function throughout Mark. He uses the insertions (a) to call attention to his use of "free floating" material, that is, material which is not necessarily part of the context in which it is found; and (b) to illumine and give an added dimension to the context in which the inserted material is finally placed.

Though a complete discussion of the function of all the inserted material would detract from our main purpose of studying its importance in the trial scene, a select survey indicates that the type and function of the material in the other insertions conforms to the pattern of 2:1-11. The geographical names in 3:7-8a have been noted by Wellhausen and others as owing their present location to Mark, and they have for Mark a

---

[1] Taylor, *Mark*, p. 191.

[2] Bultmann, *Synoptic Tradition*, p. 331; Haenchen, *Weg Jesu*, pp. 103-105; Nineham, *St. Mark*, p. 91.

[3] Perrin, "Son of Man in Synoptic Tradition," pp. 20-21, shows it is by the saying on the *exousia* of the Son of Man Mark is able to present "a full scale presentation of the authority of Jesus as Son of Man being exercised in his earthly ministry," so that the insertion here is an index of Mark's theological interest in this section.

theological significance.[1] The free floating quality of 3:14b-15 (the function of the twelve) is attested by Schweizer and Taylor, and the verse illumines the context by bringing the role of the disciples into close connection with the role and function of Jesus.[2] In 6:14b-15 the saying on Elijah or one of the prophets is "free floating" as its subsequent use in 8:28 shows. Yet it is precisely this saying which serves to bring the fate of John and that of Jesus into close parallel. The saying of 8:18, "they have eyes, but do not see, and have ears, but do not hear," appears in another context, 4:12. The inserted verse illumines the whole context by showing that the disciples have misunderstood the miracles of the bread (6:30-8:21), just as they have misunderstood the mystery of the kingdom manifest in the parables of ch. 4. Such examples of cases where the inserted material is free floating and where it gives an added dimension to the context in which it is found, could be multiplied for all the insertions.

The presence of the saying about the temple 14:58, "We heard this man say: 'I will destroy,'" etc. which is found within the Marcan insertion of 14:56 and 14:59, provides the first major key to Mark's redactional work in the trial scene. It is Mark who has introduced the saying on the destruction of the temple into the trial narrative. The saying itself, as will be shown in detail in a subsequent chapter, has a tradition history of its own, and is brought to the present context by Mark. Its presence in the trial narrative is strange since the

---

[1] Welhausen, Marci, p. 24; Bultmann, Synoptic Tradition, p. 341; Taylor, Mark, p. 225, agree on the Marcan editorial activity here. Marxsen, Mark, p. 64, holds the names are significant not only because of the religious meaning of Galilee in Mark, but also because there were Christians of Mark's community living in this area. Schreiber, Theologie, pp. 174-175, stresses the theological meaning.

[2] Schweizer, Mark, p. 81; Taylor, Mark, p. 230.

charge is never alluded to in the subsequent part of the narrative and in the trial before Pilate. Yet, we have seen that one function of the Marcan insertion technique is to bring to a pericope an added dimension which serves to illumine the surrounding material. It is "free floating" as the detailed examination of the tradition history will show; it gives an added dimension to the trial narrative by bringing to culmination the concern with the temple which begins in ch. 11 of Mark's gospel.[1]

The Christological Material

Mark 14:60-62

    60   kai anastas ho archiereus eis meson epērotēsen ton Iēsoun legōn, ouk apokrinē ouden; ti houtoi sou katamartyrousin;

    61   ho de esiōpa kai ouk apekrinato ouden. palin ho archiereus epērōta auton kai legei autō, su ei ho Christos ho huios tou eulogētou;

    62   ho de Iēsous eipen, egō eimi, kai opsesthe ton huion tou anthrōpou ek dexiōn kathēmenon tēs dynameōs kai erchōmenon meta tōn nephelōn tou ouranou.

Since Wellhausen first suggested that 14:61b-62 are an interpolation and that the subsequent condemnation of 14:63-64, was in response to the temple saying, commentators have struggled with the relation of the Christological affirmations of 14:62 to the rest of the trial narrative.[2] While contemporary commentators generally agree that the Christological confession of 14:62 is a product of early Christian theological reflection rather than an historical report, these same commentators have not adequately shown why the confession comes at this point in Mark's gospel, nor have they seen Mark as active in the

---

    [1]Detailed proof of this statement will be given in Chap. III.

    [2]Welhausen, <u>Marci</u>, pp. 123-124; Taylor, <u>Mark</u>, p. 568; Nineham, <u>St. Mark</u>, p. 407.

composition of the verses.¹ There are, therefore, two main questions still unanswered about these verses: to what extent was Mark active in their composition, and what is the relation of these verses to the rest of the narrative? In the following pages we hope to give a partial answer to the first of these two questions by showing that it is Mark who is responsible for the piling up of Christological titles in these verses. The response to the second question and the detailed analysis of the way Mark used the traditions available to him will occupy a subsequent chapter.

In content verses 60-61a affirm the silence of Jesus when confronted with the charge about the temple. They also serve to introduce the high priest as the principal protagonist who will pose the decisive question to Jesus in 14:61b. In terms of language and style they show a mixture of clear Marcan usage and usages unfamiliar to Mark. The structure of the first two words, kai anastas, betrays a Marcan fondness for the order kai, verb, subject.² The use of the compound, ep-erōtan, in preference to the uncompounded erōtan is characteristic of Mark.³ Uncharacteristic of Mark is, however, the use of legō with eperotan as well as the use of apokrinein in the middle

---

[1] The following authors represent the leading commentators who see the verse as an early Christian product: Wilhelm Bousset, Kyrios Christos, trans. John E. Steely (5th ed.; Nashville: Abingdon Press, 1970), p. 73, "The account of Mark 14:61b does not move on a historical base but is a creation of Christian dogmatics." Bultmann, Synoptic Tradition, p. 270; Heinz Tödt, The Son of Man in the Synoptic Tradition, trans. Dorothea M. Barton (Philadelphia: Westminster Press, 1965), p. 47; Ferdinand Hahn, The Titles of Jesus in Christology, trans. H. Knight and G. Ogg (London: Butterworth Press, 1969), pp. 130-134, 162, 284-286; Perrin, "Mark XIV. 62: The End Product of a Christian Tradition?" NTS, XII (1965-66), 150-155.

[2] Zerwick, Untersuchungen, p. 75, notes that this order is in contrast to the usual Greek order.

[3] Mark uses eperōtan 25 times; Matthew, 8 times and Luke 17. Mark uses erōtan only 3 times.

voice.¹ In vss. 60-61a, the silence of Jesus is mentioned three times, twice by the use of apokrinesthai and the double negative, and once by the use of siōpan. While apokrinein in the middle is uncharacteristic of Mark, siōpan is one of the verbs which Hawkins has designated as characteristic of Mark.² While this is the only place in which it is used to characterize Jesus, in other places it appears in close relation to some manifestation of Jesus' mysterious power. In 3:4 the opponents of Jesus are silent; in 4:39 the sea is calmed with the command, "be silent"; in 9:34 the disciples are silent in the face of passion prediction and in 10:48 the crowds enjoin silence on the healed Bartimaeus. For Mark, then, the term connotes a religious silence in the face of the presence of Jesus' power. Since it appears tautologically in 14:61 in relation to two other indications of the silence of Jesus, we suggest that it is added here by Mark to prepare the way for the solemn Christological confession of 14:62.

The tautological repetition of the silence of Jesus and comparison of 14:60-61a with 15:4 suggest a tradition history for these verses. In the trial before Pilate we find virtually the same question on the lips of Pilate as on the lips of the high priest:

15:4 ho de Pilatos palin epērota auton legōn, ouk apokrinē ouden;

Noteworthy here is the agreement of unfamiliar usages, the use of legōn with eperōtan and the middle of the verb. A similar allusion to the silence of Jesus with the middle of apokrinein

---

¹Eperōtan and legein are used together only in 5:9, 8:27, 9:11, 12:18, and 14:60. Of the 30 uses of apokrinein in Mark, 27 are in the aorist passive form, and the middle appears only in these verses and in 15:4. Arndt and Gingrich, Lexicon, p. 92, suggest that the middle form implies solemn legal terminology.

²Horae Synopticae, pp. 12-13.

appears in the Lukan account of the trial before Herod where Jesus' reaction is described in the same terminology (Lk 23:9). In John 19:9 the silence of Jesus before Pilate is indicated, but the way of expressing it differs from the synoptics, apokrisin ouk edōken autō. These allusions to the silence of Jesus which occur in different contexts, but which use similar language suggests that the motif of the silence of Jesus before his accusers was in the tradition prior to its incorporation into any definite narrative. While Linnemann and Maurer see a direct reference to Isa 53:7, ". . . yet he opened not his mouth," Jeremias and Best are more reserved about finding a direct allusion to Isaiah since there is no verbal contact between Mark and the Septuagint text.[1] While the question of the exact Old Testament reference remains disputed, it is still probable that the motif of the silence of Jesus before his accusers was in the tradition prior to Mark. Mark then employs this tradition, as Best notes, dramatically, that is, to provide the contrast between Jesus and his accusers, and also structurally, to provide the link between the charge about the temple and the Christological material of 14:61b-62.[2] Mark, in effect, says that the charge about the destruction of the temple merits no complete answer until the solemn confession of Jesus is made in 14:62. These verses also serve the dramatic function of isolating Jesus and the high priest. While the whole Sanhedrin assembles in 14:53 and 55, and while many bring false charges in 14:56, now the protagonist who "rises up" is the supreme representative of Judaism, the high priest, who now confronts Jesus who stands alone, with Peter in the distance (14:54). By

---

[1] The Septuagint reads, ouk anoigei to stoma. Linnemann, Studien, p. 131; Maurer, "Knecht Gottes"; Jeremias, Servant, pp. 99-101; Best, Temptation, pp. 150-151.

[2] Ibid., p. 151.

isolating the characters Mark has made the Christological confession into the dramatic high point of the trial narrative.

14:61b-62: The Christological Confession.--The introduction of the question in 14:61b betrays definite Marcan literary characteristics--the use of palin which is found often in Marcan redactional sections, and the pleonastic, epērota kai legei.[1] The phrasing of the high priest's question merits special consideration. Though from the sense of the passage the formula sy ei ho Christos should be understood as an interrogative, in terms of sheer grammatical structure it is not so unambiguously and could well be interpreted in an ironic sense. Matthew (26:64) and Luke (22:67) make it clearly into a question by putting it in the form of an indirect question. Is there perhaps a deliberate reason why Mark allows this ambiguity to stand? The formulaic use of su ei occurs at the following places in Mark:[2]

1:11   sy ei ho huios mou ho agapētos. The baptism of Jesus where the speaker is the voice from heaven.

3:11   sy ei ho huios tou theou. This occurs in the Sammelbericht and the speaker is a demon.

8:29   sy ei ho Christos. Confession of Peter.

14:61 sy ei ho Christos, ho huios tou eulogētou.

15:2   sy ei ho basileus tōn Ioudaiōn.

Though he uses the formula in an interrogative sense in 14:61, by his close adherence to the verbal correspondence with other occurrences, Mark suggests to the reader the other occurrences

---

[1] Palin is found in 2:13, a Sammelbericht (according to Taylor, Mark, p. 85) and in the Marcan transitional verses: 3:20; 7:14; 7:31; 8:1, and 10:1. Taylor (ibid., p. 192) calls palin a favorite Marcan word.

[2] Eduard Norden, Agnostos Theos (Leipzig: Teubner Verlag, 1913), pp. 183ff., discusses the Old Testament background of the formula (Ps 2:7; Gen 17:1. 28:13; Ex 3:6, 20:2) and makes the interesting observation that it is a correlate to egō eimi (p. 186).

of the formula in his gospel. In the uses of the formula prior to 14:61 a definite pattern is discerned. The title, introduced by the formula, is either not a public proclamation or if it is public, silence is enjoined.[1] Only in 14:61 is the title which is the predicate of the formula accepted by Jesus in a public context. Also, outside of the baptism, the title is put on the lips of those who do not know the full import of its meaning.[2] The object of the sy ei formula in Mark is to express a title which is true of Jesus, but not in the sense understood by those who utter it. We suggest, therefore, that Mark uses the formula here as an initial indication that he is about to make an important Christological statement and that he is about to give meaning and content to the two titles, Son of God, and Christos which have been used earlier in his gospel.

The second half of verse 61 and verse 62 contain a density of Christological titles found nowhere else in the gospel of Mark.[3] While the title Christos appears as a designation of Jesus six times in the gospel of Mark (1:1; 8:29; 9:41; 12:35; 14:61; 15:32), it is applied directly to Jesus as a title prior to 14:61 only in 8:29. In both these latter cases Jesus accepts the title, but in both cases it is qualified--in 8:29 by the saying on the suffering of the Son of Man and in 14:62 by the saying on the coming Son of Man. The second title which follows

---

[1] Though the baptism seems to be the exception to this pattern, there is no mention in the text that anyone heard the phōnē of 1:11. The alterations Matthew makes in the account, the double use of idou (3:16, 17) and the addition of legousa (3:17) show that Matthew makes the baptism into a public proclamation.

[2] 3:11, the demons; 8:29, Peter who misunderstands the meaning; 14:61, the high priest; and 15:2, Pilate.

[3] Hans Conzelmann, "History and Theology in the Passion Narratives of the Synoptic Gospels," Interpretation, XXIV (1970), pp. 190-191, calls the trial narrative a "compendium" of Mark's Christology.

sy ei, huios tou eulogētou, is interpreted by most commentators as a surrogate for Son of God.[1] That title or some paraphrase of it appears seven times in Mark.[2] In the first part of the gospel it is used in connection with Jesus' activity as an exorcist (3:11; 5:7); it appears in the baptism and transfiguration in the form "beloved son," and reappears in the confession of the centurion (15:39). While the meaning of the title in the various contexts is complex and disputed, its presence in the trial narrative suggests that here Mark is about to give definite content to the title.[3] Finally, in 14:62 we have the third

---

[1] Wellhausen, Marci, p. 132; Taylor, Mark, p. 567; Nineham, St. Mark, p. 407. Reginald Fuller, The Foundations of New Testament Christology (New York: Charles Scribner's Sons, 1965), p. 110, sums up the current view of the phrase when he sees it as a "reverential periphrasis" and says that its presence in Mark 14:62 argues for a Palestinian origin to the text. There are however serious objections against this view. Of the eight uses of eulogētos in the New Testament, the usage in Mk 14:61 is the only time the word is found as a substantive. In all other cases it is used as an adjective modifying primarily ho theos (Lk 1:68; Rom 1:25; 9:5; 2 Cor 1:3, 11:31; Eph 1:3; 1 Pet 1:3). Also, in these cases, with the exception of Rom 1:25 the phrase is always used in a doxology or liturgical formula. Ezra P. Gould, The Gospel According to St. Mark (International Critical Commentary, Vol. VII; New York: Charles Scribner's Sons, 1913), p. 278. In the Septuagint, eulogētos is never used as a substantive. In the Massoretic text the phrase ben barūk which would presumably be at the basis of huios tou eulogētou is never found. This lack of the use of the term as a substantive and its presence in liturgical formulae which are addressed in Paul's epistles to a Greek speaking audience militates against the view that the term is a Greek translation of a Palestinian surrogate for the divine name. Of all the authors who treat the phrase, only Klausner suggests that the title is a later addition despite its "semitic appearance." Joseph Klausner, Jesus of Nazareth (London: Allen and Unwin, 1925), p. 342. If this is the case, its presence in Mark 14:61 could be due to Mark's adaptation of a liturgical usage, common in the church, which he puts on the mouth of the high priest to give a semitic flavor to the question, without being aware that he does so in an inaccurate manner.

[2] Huios theou, 1:1, 3:11, 5:7, 15:39; huios agapētos, 1:11, 9:7; huios tou eulogētou, 14:61. To these some authors add, huion agapēton of the parable in 12:6.

[3] Conzelmann, "History and Theology," p. 190; Perrin, "The Creative Use of the Son of Man Traditions by Mark," USQR, XXIII (1968), 357-365, shows that Mark uses Son of Man to give a proper meaning to Son of God.

of the three sayings which deal with the future Son of Man.[1] In a subsequent chapter an attempt will be made to discuss the full implications of the convergence of these titles in 14:61b-62. Here it is sufficient to note that nowhere else do all the titles appear in such close relation. Ernest Best has remarked that in Mark the titles Christos and Son of God "chase" each other through the gospel.[2] In the trial narrative the chase has ended. From a convergence of the titles, from Jesus' acceptance of them and from the meaning which will be given them in this section, it will become clear that in 14:62 the veil of secrecy surrounding Jesus which has dominated Mark's gospel is lifted and that Mark is about to make the definitive Christological statement of his gospel. We ascribe, therefore, the convergence of titles in this section to Marcan composition.

Two other terms in the response of Jesus indicate Marcan redactional activity here, egō eimi and opsesthe. The initial response of Jesus is egō eimi. Debate on this phrase has centered around three questions: (1) is it simply a solemn way of saying "yes," an interpretation favored when the Matthean parallel (26:64) is used to interpret Mark?[3] (2) Is it a formula recalling the Old Testament revelational formula, '^{a}nî hû' (or one of its variations)?[4] (3) Or is it better explained by reference to the Hellenistic formula found in Gnostic

---

[1] See 8:38 and 13:26.   [2] Temptation, p. 95.

[3] Swete, St. Mark, p. 359, lists this as the traditional interpretation.

[4] Heinrich Zimmerman says that in 14:61 the egō eimi recalls the Old Testament usage and functions as a Rekognitionsformel, "Das absolute 'Ich bin' in der Redeweise Jesu," Trierer Theologische Zeitschrift, LXIX (1960), 20. See also his, "Das absolute Egō eimi als die neutestamentliche Offenbarungsformel," BZ, N.F. IV (1960), 24-69. Ethelbert Stauffer, Jesus and His Story, trans. Richard and Clara Winston (New York: Knopf, 1963), pp. 174-193, gives a full list of the Old Testament uses of this phrase.

literature?¹ While the debate on the background of this formula is itself interesting, it tells us little about the use of the formula by Mark. The phrase, egō eimi, first appears in Mark in 6:50 at the conclusion of the miracle of the walking on water, where Jesus tells the disciples to "take heart, it is I, have no fear." As Bultmann and Lohmeyer have shown there are really two motifs interwoven; one, the stilling of the storm, the other, the walking on water.² The walking on the water is in the form of an Epiphaniegeschichte in which the emphasis is on the appearance of Jesus to his frightened disciples.³ The motif of the walking on the water culminates in the saying of Jesus, egō eimi. In this usage the phrase functions almost in a titular sense and as a revelational formula. The second use of egō eimi is in the eschatological discourse at 13:6 where the deceivers who come in the name of Jesus will say egō eimi and they will lead many astray by using this designation.⁴ In this verse also egō eimi is obviously used as a formula of revelation or identification, and, since it is used as a misappropriation which leads the believer astray, it must sometime in Mark receive its true meaning. Therefore in 14:62 egō eimi is more than a simple affirmation. Such an interpretation would make the uses in 6:50 and 13:6 seem absurd. In these verses it is a revelational

---

¹Norden, Agnostos Theos, pp. 173-200. In a recent survey of the Gnostic literature, George MacRae writes: ". . . we do not find any other instances in the Gnostic sources of the absolute egō eimi to parallel the Marcan and Johannine ones. Instead, there is an extremely common Gnostic parallel which also alludes to the Deutero-Isaian background from which the New Testament egō eimi very probably springs," "The Ego-Proclamation in Gnostic Sources," The Trial of Jesus (Studies in Biblical Theology, Second Series, Vol. XIII; London: S. C. M. Press, 1970, p. 123.

²Bultmann, Synoptic Tradition, p. 216; Lohmeyer, Markus, pp. 131-134.

³Ibid., p. 134.

⁴Pesch, Naherwartungen, pp. 110-111, calls this verse redaction.

formula, the content of which is not determined. Therefore we affirm that in 14:61 Mark uses <u>egō eimi</u> consciously as a revelational formula, the content of which will now be determined by the following verse. It functions in Mark as a "transitional revelation formula" between the question of 14:61b and the answer of 14:62. It is transitional to a Christophany. The Messianic Secret, kept so long throughout the gospel, is about to be revealed by the Christology of 14:62.[1]

The second phrase in the response of Jesus in 14:62 is <u>kai opsesthe</u> which then introduces the saying about the coming Son of Man, in the form of a citation of Ps 110:1 and Dan 7:13. Perrin presents a convincing argument that in the pre-Marcan tradition which combined two independent <u>peshers</u>, one using Ps 110:1 and Dan 7:13 and having its origin in the resurrection while the other uses Zech 12:10ff. and has its origin in the crucifixion.[2] This latter tradition explains, in Perrin's view, the presence of <u>opsesthe</u>, which arises from a word play <u>kopsontai/opsontai</u> on the basis of the Septuagint text of Zechariah.[3] While accepting Perrin's view that early Christian use of the Old Testament was responsible for the formulation of this verse, we feel it necessary to qualify his views in view of the Marcan modifications and use of these traditions. In the concrete he does not mention the Marcan modification of <u>opsontai</u> to <u>opsesthe</u>, and the larger significance of the Marcan use of the verb "to see" in relation to the parousia. In Mark the future (either in tense or meaning) of this verb occurs in the following places:

---

[1] Maurer, "Das Messiasgeheimnis," p. 519.

[2] Perrin, "Mark XIV.62," esp. p. 151; <u>Rediscovering the Teaching of Jesus</u> (New York: Harper and Row, 1967), pp. 173-185.

[3] "Mark XIV.62," p. 153; <u>Rediscovering</u>, pp. 181-183.

13:26   And then they will see (<u>opsontai</u>) the Son of Man coming in clouds with great power and glory.

14:62   And you will see, etc.

16:7   But go, tell his disciples and Peter that he is going before you to Galilee; there you will see him. (<u>opsesthe</u>)

9:1   . . . will not taste death before (until) they see (<u>idōsin</u>) the kingdom of God come with power

13:14   But when you see (<u>idēte</u>) the desolating sacrilege set up where it ought not to be . . .

13:24   When you see (<u>idēte</u>) these things taking place.

In all these instances Mark uses the verb "to see" in connection with some event in the future and an event associated with the parousia, either the coming of the kingdom, or of the Son of Man or of the events surrounding the final crisis which precipitates this coming.[1] The only example which does not immediately fit this pattern is 16:7, but here the reference to Galilee is more than geographical since Galilee represents for Mark the place of the awaited second coming.[2] Therefore the modification of the early exegetical tradition of <u>opsontai</u> to <u>opsesthe</u> is due to Marcan redaction of the earlier tradition and conforms to his normal use of the future of the verb "to see" in reference to the parousia.

At this point it would seem logical to give a full discussion of the conjunction of Dan 7:13 and Ps 110:1 in the response of Jesus. While admitting with Perrin and Lindars that the use of these Old Testament citations in reference to the parousia and exaltation of Jesus is not original with Mark, we will attempt to show in a later chapter that the use Mark makes

---

[1] A. L. Moore, <u>The Parousia in the New Testament</u> (Supplements to Novum Testamentum, Vol. XIII; Leiden: E. J. Brill, 1966), p. 105, notes, "It seems that verbs of <u>seeing</u> are often used in the New Testament in connection with sayings related to the future coming of the Kingdom and of the Son of Man."

[2] Marxsen, <u>Mark</u>, p. 85.

of them in the trial scene shows definite concerns of his theology.[1]

We thus arrive at the second major Marcan redactional activity in the trial scene. He has brought together all the major titles used of Jesus in his gospel in a context which shows he is about to give a definitive meaning to them. The secret so long held throughout the gospel is about to be revealed, and the Son of Man title in 14:62 serves as it does in other parts of the gospel to give content and meaning to the other titles, all of which reappear here.[2] The convergence of titles, therefore, in Mark 14:61-62 is due to Marcan composition and redaction.

The Condemnation

14:63   ho de archiereus diarrēxas tous chitōnas autō legei, ti eti chreian echomen martyrōn

14:64   ēkousate tēs blasphēmias, ti hymin phainetai; hoi de pantes katekrinan auton enochon einai thanatou

In terms of language and style it is difficult to judge whether these verses are due to Mark or come from the traditions available to him. The terminology of the rending of the garments is unusual since throughout the Old Testament, and as in the Matthean parallel to Mark, himatia is generally the object of diarrēxein, and the plural of chitōn is also unusual.[3] The phrase chreian echein is familiar to Mark (2:17; 2:25; 11:3) and the legei in the historical present shows a common Marcan characteristic.[4] The hoi de pantes shows the normal Marcan concern for "universalizing" scenes, and both Schneider and Zerwick

---

[1] Lindars, New Testament Apologetic, pp. 45-51; Perrin, "Mark XIV.62," and infra, Chap. IV.

[2] Perrin, "Creative Use," p. 365.

[3] Arndt-Gingrich, Lexicon, p. 376, list the usage in 14:63 of chitōn in the plural as an unusual usage meaning "clothes in general."

[4] Supra, p. 54, n.2; p. 55, n. 1.

remark that the "indirect formulation" of the concluding section of verse 64 is due to the evangelist.[1] There is also a strong similarity in this verse with the third Passion prediction, Mk 10:33, not only in terms of language (katakrinein, thanatos, emptyein, 14:65), but also in terms of situation--the condemnation followed by the mocking. Therefore while it is difficult to conclude definitively that Mark has composed these verses, simply in terms of language and style it seems that Mark is at work in these verses in a way which brings them into close parallel with the third Passion prediction, which itself is a Marcan composition based on the first prediction.[2]

The charge of blasphemy and the condemnation to death raise special problems in relation to the rest of the narrative. Commentators have noted that there is nothing said explicitly by Jesus which merits this charge and condemnation.[3] It should also be noted that in all the versions of the trial in the New Testament, only Mark and Matthew in close dependence on him record the charge of blasphemy.[4] Beyer has pointed out that one of the sufferings the early Christian communities had to

---

[1] Zerwick, Untersuchungen, p. 30; Schneider, "Gab es," p. 31.

[2] Georg Strecker, "The Passion-and-Resurrection Predictions in Mark's Gospel," Interpretation, XXII (1968), 435-438.

[3] Taylor, Mark, p. 569, notes that "one of the strongest counts against the historical character of the Passion Narrative has been the claim that neither the confession of Messiahship, nor the saying about the destruction of the Temple is blasphemy for which a definite railing against the Divine Name is necessary." For those who seek an understanding of the trial in terms of the historical recollection, this charge continues to pose a constant problem; see, Blinzer, Der Prozess, pp. 151-162, for a survey and an attempt to resolve the problem. Conzelmann, "History and Theology," p. 190, calls the charge an interpretatio Christiana.

[4] Neither Luke (22:71) nor John (18:23-24) record the charge in the trial. However, cf. Jn 10:33, 36 and 19:7 for charge outside of trial.

endure was undergoing the charge of blasphemy, and Haenchen has suggested that the charge arises when Jewish authorities began to consider the messianic claims given to Jesus as blasphemous.[1] Therefore the charge of blasphemy in the trial narrative serves to clarify the Christology of 14:62. It speaks to a Christian community which is called on to undergo the same sufferings as their master when they confess who he is.[2]

The condemnation serves a double purpose, one in the structure of the trial narrative and the other in the context of the whole gospel. In the trial narrative it refers immediately back to the purpose of the Sanhedrin in 14:55 to find witnesses to kill Jesus. Between this verse and the fulfillment of the purpose is the material on the temple saying and the Christological material. The condemnation of 14:64b brings this purpose to its culmination and provides the final specification which makes of the whole scene a trial. In terms of the movement of the whole gospel the mortal opposition to Jesus, begun in 3:6 and which appears at crucial places in the gospel, reaches its apex here. From now on the Passion narrative is simply the playing out of what takes place in this scene. Therefore Marcan literary activity is strong in these two verses. He explicitly mentions the charge of blasphemy to clarify the content of his Christological statement and he adds the condemnation to give to the scene its complete formality of a trial and to bring to a

---

[1] On the community suffering the charge of blasphemy, cf. 1 Cor 4:13; Rev 2:9; 1 Pet 4:4; and Hermann Beyer, "blasphēmia," TDNT, I 623. Haenchen, Weg Jesu, p. 514.

[2] The strongest evidence for this in Mark's gospel is the exhortation in 13:9-11. There like Jesus the disciples will be brought before legal bodies (synedria kai synagōgas, 13:9), they will be questioned (13:11), suffer betrayal (13:12), and be condemned to death (eis thanaton). Pesch notes that, though these verses use traditional motifs of suffering persecution, they are brought to their present place by Mark to speak to the needs of his community, Naherwartungen, pp. 133-135.

culmination a theme which runs throughout his gospel.

The Mocking

14:65   kai ērxato tines emptyein autō, kai perikalyptein autou to prosōpon, kai kolaphizein auton, kai legein autō, prophēteuson, kai hoi hyperētai rapismasin auton elabon.

The mocking appears to be a separate element of tradition introduced by Mark at this point.[1] First of all, its setting is different in Mark and Matthew than in Luke. In Luke it comes after the denial of Peter but before the trial narrative (Lk 22:63-64). Also, in addition to this mocking complex there is another which follows the trial before Pilate and is found in Mark (15:17-20), Matthew (27:28-31), and John (19:2-3), but not in Luke. Therefore, traditions associated with the mocking of Jesus circulated freely in the tradition. A second reason urging the independence of the mocking tradition is its relationship to Isa 50:6. Verbal similarity is found in *emptyein*, *prosōpon*, *rapismasin*. The text is also well suited to the Passion apologetic of the early church since the situation in Isaiah portrays the sufferings of the innocent one before his enemies.[2] We therefore class 14:65 as a piece of traditional material which is associated with the traditions of the suffering of Jesus in the face of unjust accusers and which along with the other Old Testament references in the trial narrative belong to the earliest strata of the narrative.

Conclusion

The thrust of the initial observations of the present chapter was to show that, on the basis of language, style and a

---

[1] Taylor, *Mark*, p. 570; Haenchen, *Weg Jesu*, pp. 514-515; Nineham, *St. Mark*, p. 409.

[2] Other texts which may have influenced this tradition are Isa 53:3-5; Mic 5:1; 1 Kgs 22:24.

recognized Marcan compositional technique (intercalation), the
trial scene is from the same hand as the rest of the gospel. It
is not simply a piece of material which Mark found in the tradition and took over without substantial alteration. The question
then arose as to the extent of Marcan activity within the narrative itself. For the sake of clarity we will suggest a tradition history to the trial narrative, first emphasizing those
elements of the narrative which seem to be pre-Marcan, and then
indicate the areas in which Marcan interest, shown either in the
redaction of traditional material, or in the composition of new
material seems to be strongest.

Our observations reveal that there are three principal
parts of the trial scene which show a strong influence from the
Old Testament: (a) the rising up of the false witnesses in
14:56-57; (b) the silence of Jesus in 14:60-61; and (c) the
mocking in 14:65. The latter of these two allusions comes from
the servant songs of Isaiah, and the first comes from psalms
which portray a situation similar to the plight of the servant
in Isa 53--an innocent man surrounded by unjust accusers.[1] Previous studies of the influence of Isa 53 on the trial narrative
have concentrated on whether the figure of the atoning suffering
servant has influenced the conception of Christ in the trial
scene.[2] This concentration on the figure and function of the
servant has obscured a more basic use of the Old Testament background. Lindars has pointed out that the earliest use of Isa 53

---

[1] Especially in the third (Isa 50:49) and fourth (Isa 52:13-53:12) of the songs is this true. John L. McKenzie, Second Isaiah (The Anchor Bible; Garden City, N.Y.: Doubleday and Co., 1968), p. 133. Christopher R. North, The Second Isaiah (Oxford: Clarendon Press, 1964), p. 238, writes: "The paradox present by the Servant and by Christ in the New Testament is that the man who did not deserve to suffer at all, was the man who suffered most."

[2] Supra, p. 87, n. 1.

was in terms of an apologetic for the Passion, and that the
Christological and soteriological use represents a later stage
of development.[1] Therefore the imagery of Isa 53 provided a
storehouse of sometimes explicit (the <u>paradidonai</u> tradition),
sometimes veiled, allusions to the Old Testament which the early
Christians used in the defense that Jesus was the innocent one
who suffered according to the scriptures.[2] One way in which
this happened was that Jesus was condemned by false accusers,
stood in silence before their accusation and was mocked by them.
We thus suggest that at the pre-Marcan stage the trial narrative
represented a catena of Old Testament texts, brought together
for an apologetic motif. Though Isa 53 may have been the leading text, other texts were freely adduced (Pss 27 and 35) and it
was not the figure of the servant or his role as vicarious suf-
ferer which was normative, but rather the imagery and total setting of Isa 53, the innocent one before unjust accusers. Not
only were such texts ideally suited for an apologetic purpose,
but they also contained in terms of situation and language the
inherent possibility of being cast in a juridical or legal
framework.[3] Thus Mark's use of them in the trial narrative

---

[1] <u>New Testament Apologetic</u>, pp. 77-89.

[2] Dodd, <u>According to the Scriptures</u>, pp. 92-94, gives a complete list of the allusions of this section of Isaiah in the New Testament.

[3] The point here is that the use of legal language in the Old Testament and the situation of the servant on trial provides the basis for the creation of a similar situation in the New. McKenzie, <u>Second Isaiah</u>, p. 131, in commenting on Isa 53:8 says: "This verse suggests that the Servant is the victim of legal in-justice." Commenting on Isa 50:8-9, Christopher North says: "The language of this and the next verse is unmistakably that of the law-court," <u>Second Isaiah</u>, p. 203. The legal language is also strong in Isa 53:8. Examples of this language in the two passages are: Isa 50:8-9, <u>masdîqî</u> (my vindicator); <u>yārîb</u> (who will contend), <u>mišpatî</u> (of my judgment), see, <u>ibid</u>., pp. 203-204; Isa 53:8, <u>mē 'ōser umimmišpat</u>, which North says can be translated either as (a) from imprisonment (custody, arrest) and from judgment (judicial sentence); (b) by reason of an oppres-sive sentence; or, (c) without hindrance and without sentence,

maximizes the possibilities of the texts themselves, and his narrative represents an historicization of Old Testament texts.

When we turn to the narrative itself we find that those verses which give to the narrative its formality as a trial are the very verses which, on the basis of language and style, show the strongest convergence of Marcan characteristics. The assembly of the members of the Sanhedrin requisite for a trial (14:53b), the purpose and plan of the trial (14:55), the listing of charges (14:58), the interrogation (14:60) and the formal condemnation (14:64) show strong Marcan composition.[1] We suggest that in making of what took place a formal trial Mark employs two pre-Marcan traditions, one, the Old Testament allusions mentioned above; the other a historical tradition which dealt with the leading away of Jesus to his condemnation and death, a tradition which lies behind the initial verse of the narrative, 14:53a. The ultimate reason why Mark chooses the form of the trial narrative will be discussed in a subsequent chapter after the main parts of the narrative are considered.

The two major areas of Marcan literary activity in the trial scene are insertion of the temple saying between verses 56 and 59 and the creation of a Christological compendium in 14:61-62. This activity of Mark is partly redactional in the strict sense of the term as working with traditional material and partly compositional in the sense of composing new material. We will show that the temple saying has a tradition history of its own and was originally two sayings which Mark combined into

---

i.e., no one attempted to secure a fair trial for him, ibid., p. 240.

[1] We would suggest that it is for this reason that the trial before the Sanhedrin has created so many problems for historical interpreters. While Mark is anxious to create a narrative which has the formalities of a trial, the technicalities and fine points of Jewish legal procedure are outside his main concerns.

a single saying for a theological reason. The technique of insertion by which Mark calls attention to this saying represents Marcan composition. In the case of the Christological material, Mark is working with titles he receives from the tradition, but, as we have shown, the bringing of them together in this place represents Marcan composition. Also, in the analysis of the use of the Son of Man saying in 14:62 we hope to show that Mark is active in the form and meaning he gives to this saying. Therefore the two major areas of Marcan redaction and composition in the trial narrative are the temple saying and the Christological material, and it is these which make the trial narrative the high point of the Passion narrative.

Marcan activity in the trial narrative can be summarized briefly. He takes over traditions from the early church's exegetical use of the Old Testament and works them into a narrative of the formal trial of Jesus before the Sanhedrin. This narrative then becomes the focus of theological concerns and the culmination of the interest in the fate of Jesus. The two main theological concerns are the preoccupation with the temple which is paramount after ch. 11, and the Christological question of who Jesus is, which is under the veil of secrecy throughout the gospel. The task before us is to show in detail how these concerns come to be united in the narrative and their importance to an understanding of the narrative.

CHAPTER III

THE TEMPLE SAYING OF THE TRIAL NARRATIVE

Introduction

The study of the traditions out of which Mark constructed the trial narrative, as made in the previous chapter, revealed that the temple saying of 14:58 was not part of the original traditions, but was brought to its present place by Mark himself. The primary indication for this was its presence between the Marcan insertion of 14:56 and 59, and the observation that Mark uses this technique to call attention to material which has been put in a definite place for a definite theological reason. Therefore the first major element of Marcan redaction and composition in the trial scene was seen to be the insertion of the saying about the destruction of the temple. At this point further discussion of the meaning of the saying in the narrative and in the gospel as a whole was suspended pending an investigation of the meaning of the saying prior to Mark. Not only has Mark been active in bringing the saying to its present position, but, as will be shown, he is active in the composition of the final form of the saying. Once this has been proven it will be necessary to ask why Mark has created such a saying, one part of which represents a definite anti-temple bias (I will destroy), while the other holds out the expectation of a substitution for this temple (I will build another). In order to see why Mark has created such a saying, it will be necessary to investigate other parts of his gospel in order to see how the statement of the temple saying has influenced his redaction and composition throughout the latter part of the gospel.

Tradition and Redaction of the Temple Saying

The temple saying of 14:58 appears in the following forms and contexts:

The Trial Scene

egō katalysō ton naon touton ton cheiropoiēton kai dia triōn hemerōn allon acheiropoiēton oikodomēsō (Mk 14:58)

houtos ephē dynamai katalysai ton naon tou theou kai dia triōn hēmerōn oikodomēsai (Mt 26:61)

The Crucifixion Narrative

oua ho katalyōn ton naon kai oikodomōn en trisin hēmerais (Mk 15:29)

ho katalyōn ton naon kai en trisin hēmerais oikodomōn, sōson seauton (Mt 27:39)

The Trial of Stephen

. . . they set up false witnesses who said: "This man never ceases to speak words against this holy place and the law, for we have heard him say that this Jesus of Nazareth, houtos katalysei ton topon touton, kai allaxei ta ethnē ha paredōken hēmin Mōyses (Acts 6:14)

The Johannine Account of the Temple Cleansing

apekrithē Iēsous kai eipen autois, lysate ton naon touton kai en trisin hēmerais egerō auton (Jn 2:19)

The presence of this saying in different contexts (temple cleansing, trial of Stephen, trial of Jesus) and in different traditions (Matthew/Mark; Acts; John) confirms the observations by commentators that the saying represents a pre-Marcan tradition.[1] In the case of Mark this is supported by his use of naos for the temple. Mark uses two terms for temple, hieron in 11:11, 15, 16, 27; 12:35; 13:1, 3; and 14:49, and naos in the

---

[1] Bultmann, Synoptic Tradition, p. 120, "In all these examples, it seems that the same tradition has left its mark without making it possible for us to determine which is its original form." Raymond E. Brown, The Gospel According to John (Anchor Bible, Vol. XXIX; Garden City, N.Y.: Doubleday and Co., 1966), p. 120, "The material in John ii 13-22 is not taken from the Synoptic Gospels, but represents an independent tradition running parallel to the Synoptic Tradition." Rudolf Schnackenburg, Das Johannesevangelium, Part I (Herder Theologischer Kommentar zum Neuen Testament; Freiburg: Herder, 1965), p. 365. The synoptics and John are influenced by the same tradition in oral form.

above contexts. The difference does not indicate a difference between the whole temple area and the sanctuary proper, but rather connotes a difference between tradition and redaction since Mark uses hieron in those places which show his strongest redaction.[1]

In form the saying is two part, the first part of which represents a threat of destruction against the temple, while the second part (Acts 6:14, excepted) has reference to the building of a new temple.[2] Though Bultmann despairs of finding the original form of the saying, the fact that it represents a pre-Marcan tradition suggests that such an attempt be made.[3] All previous attempts to suggest a prior form to the saying presuppose that, while two-part, it is, nonetheless, a unified saying.[4] This view is supported by the strong chiastic structure of the saying in its final form.[5] However, the unity is more a

---

[1] G. Schrenk, "hieron," Theological Dictionary of the New Testament, trans. and ed. G. Bromily (Grand Rapids, Mich.: Eerdmans, 1966), III, 235, says that hieron is a generic term for temple, and cites Mt 27:5 to show that naos has a wider extent than sanctuary. Schreiber, Theologie, p. 187, n. 148, asserts that hieron is redactional in Mark.

[2] It is debated whether the lysate of Jn 2:19 should be understood as an imperative or a concessive (if you destroy), see Blass-Debrunner, Grammar, p. 195, par. 378.2. C. H. Dodd, The Interpretation of the Fourth Gospel (Cambridge: University Press, 1958), p. 302, n. 1, favors the concessive and holds that it is a Semitism which suggests that the Johannine form of the saying is earlier than the synoptic form. R. Bultmann, The Gospel of John, trans. G. R. Beasley-Murray (Philadelphia: Westminster Press, 1971), pp. 126ff., holds that the imperative is the ironical imperative found in the prophets (Amos 4:4; Isa 8:9). In this case the "threat" aspect of the saying is clear.

[3] Synoptic Tradition, pp. 120-121; Gospel of John, p. 126.

[4] Ferdinand Hahn, Mission in the New Testament, trans. Frank Clarke (Studies in Biblical Theology, Vol. XLVII; London: S. C. M. Press, 1965), p. 37, n. 1, gives a survey of the opinions.

[5] The chiasm appears in the following form: A, B, c B', A':

A I will destroy   I will build A'

product of the final form of the saying than an index of original unity. The contrast cheiropoiētos/acheiropoiētos is generally admitted to be an addition of the final redactor and not part of the original saying.¹ The contrast between katalyein (destroy) and oikodomein (build), while suggesting an original antithetical parallelism, is attested, outside the present contexts, only in the metaphorical usage of Gal 2:18. These initial observations suggest that there is nothing intrinsic to the saying which demands that it existed as a single two-part saying. Further analysis of the saying in the above contexts indicates close similarity in the first part of the saying. Five of the six occurrences (Acts 6:14, excepted) use naos and all have some variation of the verb (kata)lyein. On the other

B	this temple made with hands		another not made with hands	B'
C		and within three days		

[1] Bultmann, Synoptic Tradition, p. 120, "Mark is secondary in respect of the adjectives, cheiropoiēton, acheiropoiēton." Gaston, No Stone, p. 69, ". . . the words are widely recognized to be additions of the Evangelist." Also, Taylor, Mark, p. 566. These terms are strong evidence that Mark gave the saying its final form in a setting familiar with the literature of diaspora Judaism. The contrast cheiropoiētos/acheiropoiētos is not found in the Old Testament where cheiropoiētos is used in reference to idols (Lev 26:1; Isa 19:1, 31:7) or images of foreign gods (Isa 21:9). In Philo cheiropoiētos is associated with the temple (Spec. Leg. I, 67; Leg. ad Gaius, 290) and with the Jerusalem temple as opposed to the heavenly archetype (Quod Deus sit, 25). C. Spicq notes: "Philon ouvre, en effet, son traité peri hierou par cette déclaration: Dieu a deux sortes de temple, l'un sanctuaire d'en haut et véritable--to men anōtatō kai pros alētheian hieron theou--l'autre bâti de main d'homme--to de cheirokmēton," "Le Philonisme de l'épitre aux Hébreux," RB, LVII (1950), 223. Thus Philo uses cheiropoiētos and cognate terms in the sense of "physical" opposed to "spiritual," a usage which is mirrored in the New Testament (Acts 7:48, 17:24; Eph 2:11; Heb 9:24). See C. F. D. Moule, "Sanctuary and Sacrifice in the Church of the New Testament," JTS, N.S. I (1950), 29-41, esp. 30-33. While not holding that Mark uses the terms in their Philonic/Platonic sense, the Hellenistic background of the terms suggests that Mark is contrasting a present and a future reality. (I am grateful to Prof. Jonathan Smith of the University of Chicago for pointing out the use of the terms in Philo.)

hand, the greatest variation is in the second part of the saying. While Mark and Matthew agree, in Acts the complete reference to Jesus as building the temple is dropped and in its place is sbustituted a new charge about Jesus superseding the law of Moses.[1] In John the ambiguity of the original statement is resolved by the editorial comment that the naos spoken of is the naos of Jesus' body (Jn 2:21). In addition to showing the greatest variation in language, the second part of the saying is that part which is used by the respective authors to interpret the first part in terms of their own theological purpose.[2] Such observations support the view that there are two sayings which are at the basis of the unified saying as found in the above texts.[3]

On the hypothesis that two sayings are at the basis of the present saying, it is clear that there are two lines of tradition which feed into the final form of the saying. The

---

[1] Ernst Haenchen, Die Apostelgeschichte (Kritisch-exegetischer Kommentar über das Neue Testament, 18th ed.; Göttingen: Vandenhoeck and Ruprecht, 1961), p. 224, holds that the saying in Acts is based on Mk 14:58, and that the second half of the saying refers to Jesus' opposition to the Jewish cultic regulations as found in Mark (2:28; 3:2; 7:14; 10:5).

[2] We hope to show this in terms of Mark. In Acts, the subsequent speech of Stephen (7:1-55) develops and justifies Christian opposition to the temple. In John the reference to the resurrection is explicit, in accord with the Johannine theme that "the risen body of Christ will be the center of worship in spirit and truth (4:21ff.), the place of the divine presence (1:14), the spiritual temple whence springs the source of living water (7:37-39)," D. Mollat, L'Evangile de saint Jean (Bible de Jérusalem; Paris: Cerf, 1953), p. 78.

[3] Lohmeyer, Markus, pp. 326-327, gives a reconstruction of the original form of the saying and questions whether the second part belonged to the original form of the saying. Gaston, No Stone, pp. 102-243, suggests that the saying is originally two sayings and traces one part (the anti-temple part) back to a circle of early Christians, represented by Stephen, opposed to the temple, while the second half mirrors an authentic saying of Jesus. Gaston never discusses the importance of the combined saying in Mark.

first part of the saying is in the form of a threat against the temple which Bultmann calls an apocalyptic prediction.[1] In content this threat is similar to the Marcan saying of 13:2 (Mt 24:2; Lk 21:6), <u>ou mē apethe lithos epi lithon hos ou mē katalythē</u>, and the Q saying against Jerusalem (Mt 23:38; Lk 13:34-35).[2] The verb <u>katalyein</u> provides the point of contact between the saying as found in Mk 13:2 and 14:58. Therefore there existed in early Christianity a stream of tradition which attributed to Jesus apocalyptic predictions against the temple and the city.

Observation of the second part of the saying suggests a different line of tradition. Common to the second part is the picture of Jesus as building another <u>naos</u> in place of the one which will be destroyed. In the New Testament <u>naos</u> has different nuances and usages: (a) the physical temple (Mk 14:58, 15:38 <u>et par</u>; Mt 27:5; Jn 2:20), (b) in reference to the body of the individual Christian or the Christian community as a whole (1 Cor 3:16-17; 2 Cor 6:16; Eph 2:21) and (c) the usage in the apocalyptic context of the heavenly eschatological temple (2 Thes 2:4; Rev 11:19, 14:15-17). Independently of the dating of the material in the Apocalpyse of John, we can affirm, on the basis of the Pauline usage, that the communal and eschatological nuances of <u>naos</u> were part of early Christian theology.[3]

---

[1] <u>Synoptic Tradition</u>, pp. 120-121.

[2] The relation between 13:2 and 14:58 is much disputed. Wellhausen calls 13:2 an <u>Abschwächung</u> in relation to 14:58, <u>Marci</u>, p. 99. Bultmann, <u>Synoptic Tradition</u>, pp. 120, 125, 128, holds that 13:2 is more original. G. R. Beasley-Murray, <u>A Commentary on Mark Thirteen</u> (London: Macmillan and Co., 1957), p. 23, holds that the two sayings represent independent traditions as does Taylor, <u>Mark</u>, p. 567. Jan Lambrecht, <u>Die Redaktion des Markus-Apocalypse</u> (Analecta Biblica, Vol. XXVIII; Rome: Biblical Institute Press, 1967), pp. 77-79, and Pesch, <u>Naherwartungen</u>, pp. 89-91, hold the saying is a Marcan composition.

[3] J. Jeremias, <u>Jesus als Weltvollender</u> (Beiträge für die Förderung Christlicher Theologie, Vol. XXXIII; Gütersloh:

Therefore the second part of the saying as found in Mark can maximize the potential meanings of naos and carry with it the overtones of the communal and eschatological temple. It will be the aim of the major part of this chapter to show that it is precisely for this reason that Mark joins the two sayings together. In effect, Mark has created a single saying by joining two traditions, one which affirms opposition to the temple, the other which points to the community as the substitute for the destroyed temple. The redaction-critical question regarding the temple saying can now be posed with some exactitude. Why, in the trial scene did Mark construct a two-part saying, the first part of which puts on the lips of Jesus a threat about the destruction of the temple, while the second part suggests that Jesus is founder of the new eschatological community? We will suggest that from 11:1 forward Mark portrays Jesus in growing opposition to the Jerusalem cult center, and, at the same time, Jesus is pictured as preparing the eschatological community which will function as a substitute for this place.

Before considering the Marcan understanding of the combined saying, it is necessary to consider two principal interpretations which have been given to 14:58. One group interprets the Marcan saying as a reference to the resurrection of Jesus. Evidence for this is found in the dia triōn hēmerōn and the whole saying is understood as a reference to the risen Jesus

---

Verlag C. Bertelsmann, 1930), p. 40, interprets the second half of the saying to mean, "nach der Zerstörung des Tempels wird Jesu Parusie und der Bau des himmlischen Tempels der verklärten Gemeinde erfolgen." See also, Otto Michel, "naos," TDNT, IV, 880-882. The fact that religious groups of the first century used the image of "house" or temple to refer to themselves is attested by both the Qumran literature and the New Testament. See, Bertil Gärtner, The Temple and Community in Qumran and the New Testament (Cambridge: University Press, 1965), and R. J. McKelvey, The New Temple (Oxford: University Press, 1969). Gaston, No Stone, pp. 161-243, also gives an extensive treatment of this theme.

taking the place of the destroyed temple.¹ The difficulty with this view is that in the New Testament oikodomein is never used of the resurrection and also the specification dia triōn hemerōn is not a resurrection formula in Mark. He uses meta treis hēmeras with the verb anistēmi in reference to the resurrection.² The second and dominant mode of interpretation is to understand the saying totally in terms of the religionsgeschichtlich background as an allusion to the expectation that the Messiah would destroy the old temple and build a new one. Therefore Mark is seen as simply taking over a current Jewish expectation and giving a Christian interpretation to it.³ The main difficulty with this view is that it rests more on the authority of figures like Bultmann, Billerbeck, and Jeremias than on the texts they adduce for the view. Bultmann writes:

> Long before the destruction of Herod's temple in A.D. 70 the hope was current that a new and more glorious temple would arise in the Messianic age, and it even suggested on

---

[1] Such a view interprets Mark in light of Jn 2:21. See Nineham, St. Mark, p. 407, and Taylor, Mark, p. 566: "In itself it does not necessarily refer to the resurrection, although this interpretation lies near at hand." More recently, C. F. Evans, Resurrection and the New Testament (Studies in Biblical Theology, Second Series, Vol. XII; London: S. C. M. Press, 1970), pp. 48, 152.

[2] 8:31; 9:31; 10:33. Lohmeyer notes that the "after three days" means the same as "in a short time," Markus, p. 327. The earliest resurrection formulae use the "third day" terminology and the verb egeirein (1 Cor 15:4, see Hans Conzelmann, Der Erste Brief an die Korinther [Kritisch-exegetischer Kommentar über das Neue Testament; 11th ed.; Göttingen: Vandenhoeck and Ruprecht, 1969], pp. 296-302).

[3] Bultmann, Synoptic Tradition, p. 120; Lohmeyer, Markus, p. 327; Jeremias, Weltvollender, pp. 35-44. A complete list of the texts adduced to support this view can be found in H. L. Strack and P. Billerbeck, Kommentar zum Neuen Testament aus Talmud und Midrasch (Munich: C. H. Beck, 1922-1956), I, 1003-1005; Wilhelm Bousset, Die Religion des Judentums in späthellenistischen Zeitalter (3d ed.; Tübingen: J. C. B. Mohr [Paul Siebeck], 1926), pp. 238-240, and Paul Volz, Die Eschatologie der jüdischen Gemeinde in neutestamentlicher Zeitalter (Tübingen: J. C. B. Mohr [Paul Siebeck], 1934), pp. 373-378.

occasion that the "old building" would first have to be done away with.¹

and Jeremias notes:

So unlösich waren tempelerneuung und messianische Parusie in der Volkserwartung verknüpft.²

Thus the view arises that the destruction of the temple, the coming of the Messiah and the building of a new temple formed a pattern in the messianic hope of Judaism and provided a model for Christian re-interpretation of this expectation.

In a recent study Lloyd Gaston has subjected the <u>religionsgeschichtlich</u> evidence to a thorough investigation and found that this "expectation" arises from a conflation of motifs and is not supported by textual evidence.³ The motifs which are conflated are (a) opposition to a defiled temple and the need for its purification, (b) the general messianic expectation, and (c) the hope for a new Jerusalem. The texts most often cited in support of the pattern noted above (destruction, Messiah, new temple) presuppose that the temple is already destroyed and cannot be adduced as evidence that this would be one function of the Messiah. The one text most often cited in support of the view that the Messiah would build a new temple, Enoch 90:28ff., on careful examination, reveals that it is not the Messiah but the "Lord of the sheep" (Yahweh) who will build the new temple.⁴

---

¹<u>Synoptic Tradition</u>, p. 120.   ²<u>Weltvollender</u>, p. 39.

³<u>No Stone</u>, pp. 102-112.

⁴The text of Enoch so often cited in this connection reads: "And I stood up to see till they folded up that old house; and carried off all the pillars, and all the beams and ornaments of the house were at the same time folded up with it, and they carried it off and laid it in a place in the south of the land. And I saw till the Lord of the sheep brought a new house greater and loftier than that first, and set it up in the place of the first which had been folded up: all the pillars were new and larger than those of the first, the old one which He had taken away and the sheep were within it." R. H. Charles, <u>The Apocrypha and Pseudepigrapha of the Old Testament</u>, II, The,

Gaston concludes his investigation with the remarks:

> Our investigation has had negative results. We have found no real parallel to the statement attributed to Jesus in Mk 14:58 in any of the sources. While there is a great deal of opposition to the Jerusalem temple before A.D. 70, only a few questionable passages suggest that it will be the function of the Messiah to destroy it, and it is nowhere indicated that the Messiah will build the future temple.[1]

Independently of Gaston, Eta Linnemann has studied the same material adduced for the supposed expectation that the Messiah would destroy and rebuild the temple and concludes:

> Die Verbindung von Auflösung und Neubau des Tempels als eschatologisches Ereignis ist also hier nicht belegt und hat es als geprägte Vorstellung gar nicht gegeben. Jede Andeutung, dass der Messias oder der Menschensohn der Erbauer des eschatologischen Tempels ist, fehlt.[2]

Therefore, Mark 14:58 cannot be explained as a piece of early Christian messianic expectation which Mark or the pre-Marcan tradition has adapted from contemporary Jewish thought.

While rejecting the religionsgeschichtlich background as an explanation for the Marcan meaning of the temple saying, we will affirm that the type of expectation postulated by proponents of these views—the destruction of the temple and the promise of a new temple—is present in Mark. What we affirm, in contrast to these views is that this expectation is a Marcan creation which arises out of his theological concerns and which is evident in his gospel. It is Mark who joins the destruction of the temple to the hope of the new naos. Mark does this by putting two independent sayings together. In the present

---

Pseudepigrapha (Oxford: Clarendon Press, 1913), p. 258. (Enoch 90:28.)

[1] No Stone, p. 154.

[2] Studien, p. 127. While we agree with Linnemann's denial of this as a background for Mark's statement, we disagree with her conclusion that Mark could not have been referring to the eschatological naos. Linnemann adopts the position that, if there is no contemporary parallel to a Marcan view, Mark could not have held it. Here, as throughout her work, she views Mark only as a collector of pre-existing traditions.

chapter we hope to show the literary evidence in Mark for the influence of these two themes. In a subsequent chapter we hope to show that there is also a good historical reason why Mark creates such an expectation, namely, that he writes for a community which is coming to terms with the destruction of the temple and which looks to the return of Jesus as founder of the new community, which substitutes for the destroyed temple.

The Anti-Temple Theme in Mark

It has already been noted that the temple saying of the trial narrative is found in close connection with the resolution of the Sanhedrin to kill Jesus (14:55). A similar reference is found in four other places in Mark (3:6; 11:18; 12:12; and 14:1b). The last four of these references occur in a context of opposition of Jesus to the Jerusalem cult or temple.[1] These indications will provide initially a structure for the remarks we will make.

Mark 11:1-18: Triumphal Entry, Fig Tree, Temple Cleansing

In his study of the eschatology of Mark, Werner Kelber has shown a definite anti-Jerusalem and anti-temple bias to this section.[2] The acclamation of Jesus takes place outside the

---

[1]Lohmeyer, Galiläa und Jerusalem (Göttingen: Vandenhoeck und Ruprecht, 1936), and R. H. Lightfoot, Locality and Doctrine in the Gospels (New York: Harper Bros., 1938), esp. pp. 111ff., are the precursors of those contemporary redaction critics (e.g., Schreiber and Marxsen) who study the geography of Mark as an entree to his theology. Lohmeyer and Lightfoot also study the anti-Jerusalem motif in Mark which provides the starting point for the present reflections on the anti-temple theme. In Mark there is no real distinction between the city and the temple. When Jesus comes into the city, he is immediately in the temple (11:11, 15, 27). When the temple loses its role, so too does the city. There are no resurrection appearances in Jerusalem and the conclusion of the Gospel (16:1-8) points to Galilee.

[2]Werner Kelber, "Kingdom and Parousia in the Gospel of Mark" (Unpublished Ph.D. dissertation, University of Chicago, 1970), pp. 110-138.

city (11:9-11), and the Marcan addition to the acclamation formula, "Blessed is the kingdom of our father David that is coming" (11:10), points to a substitution of the coming kingdom for the city. Jesus' initial entry into the city is reduced to an eisodos and exodos much like Jesus' entries and exits from temporary locales in the rest of his gospel.[1] The framing of the temple cleansing by the two fig tree references suggests an eschatological visitation on the temple, and the prohibition against carrying "anything" through the temple abrogates the cultic role of the temple.[2] The eschatological "house of prayer for all nations" will replace the temple.[3] In addition to these observations, we might note that the second reference of the plan of the officials to kill Jesus occurs in 11:18, in immediate response to the teaching of vs. 17, but also to the whole action of vss. 15-18. In the beginning of the gospel, after the proclamation of the kingdom and the narratives of Jesus' by-passing of the Jewish cult and ritual in his healings and teachings, a similar reference occurs (3:6), so that Mark has, in effect, made a parallel between the beginning of the ministry in Galilee and the beginning in Jerusalem and has brought the whole

---

[1] Marcan entries: 1:21, 45; 2:1; 3:1; 5:39; 7:17; 7:24; 9:28, 43, 45, 47; 10:15, 23, 24, 25; 11:11; exits: 1:29, 35, 38, 45; 2:13; 5:2; 6:1, 12, 34, 54; 7:31; 8:27; 9:30; 10:17, 46; 11:11; 14;26; 16:8. On the redactional nature of this see Ulrich Luz, "Das Geheimnismotiv und die Markinische Christologie," ZNW, LVI (1965), 14-15, and Kelber, "Kingdom," p. 120.

[2] G. Münderlein, "Die Verfluchung des Feigenbaumes," NTS, X (1963-64), 103, calls the activity "symbolically performed eschatological activity," and says that just as the fig tree was untrue to its nature, so too the temple loses its function. H. W. Bartsch, "Early Christian Eschatology in the Synoptic Gospels," NTS, XI (1964-65), 394, writes: "The demonstration in the temple--I do not call it the cleansing of the temple--also means the end of the cult. . . . The vessels which Jesus forbids them to carry through the temple are cult vessels." Also, Kelber, "Kingdom," pp. 129-130.

[3] Gaston, No Stone, p. 429; Lohmeyer, Markus, p. 237.

ministry under the shadow of the cross.[1] In his study of the anti-temple element of Mark, Kelber did not go beyond 11:26, but it is after 11:26 that we find two more references to the plan to kill Jesus; therefore, we must study the subsequent material.

Structural Considerations

A few remarks about the structure of 11:1-12:44 must serve as an introduction. Previous commentators have suggested that Mark unites here two major blocks of material--the entrance and fig tree incidents, 11:1-12; 20-27, and a series of five controversies: 11:15-17, 27-33; 12:13-17; 12:18-27; 12:28-33; 12:35-37a.[2] Albertz, who first noted this pattern, sees very little Marcan redactional activity in the controversies since they emphasize the authority and power of Jesus and thus stand in tension with the Marcan emphasis on the Messianic Secret.[3] It can, however, be questioned whether the structure and composition of this section is based simply on the juxtaposition of two relatively unredacted blocks of tradition. Between 11:1 and 11:27 there is considerable Marcan redaction shown by the temporal (11:11, 19, 20) and geographical (11:1, 11, 15, 27) designations.[4] Thus it seems that Mark considers 11:1-27 a unit which was to set the stage for the temple discourse delivered on the

---

[1]Lohmeyer, Lord of the Temple, trans. Steward Todd (Edinburgh and London: Oliver and Boyd, 1961), pp. 24-33; Gaston, No Stone, pp. 75-83.

[2]Martin Albertz, Die Synoptischen Streitsgespräche (Berlin: Trowitsch und Sohn, 1921), pp. 16-39, followed by Taylor, Mark, p. 450.

[3]Streitsgespräche, p. 18. However, T. Alec Burkill, Mysterious Revelation (Ithaca, N.Y.: Cornell University Press, 1963), pp. 188-210 ("Strain on the Secret") notes that in this section because of the evangelist's emphasis on the messianic activity of Jesus, the doctrine of the Secret is subjected to great strain.

[4]Schreiber, Theologie, esp. pp. 185-190.

third day of Jesus' activity in Jerusalem (11:28-12:44). The second major aspect of Marcan redaction is the introduction of the parable of the wicked tenants, which destroys the sequence of the controversies.[1]

The parable ends with the second indication of the plan of the authorities to do violence to Jesus. In the following sections the three controversies are patterned after the introduction of specific opponents of Jesus--12:13, the Pharisees; 12:18, the Sadducees; 12:28, the scribes, and the locale is unspecified. Presumably the debates take place in the temple, but in 12:35 there is an explicit mention that Jesus is in the temple when the Son of David question is discussed. The final two sections, the denunciation of the scribes, 12:38-40, and the widow's offering, 12:41-44, are connected by the catchword, chēra.[2] Thus the section from 12:13-44 seems to be a loose Marcan construction by means of sequential appearances of adversaries and catchwords. There are then three major sections in 11:1-12:44: (a) Section One: 11:1-27, the introductory section which sets the tone for the whole section and which is built up around a sequence of careful temporal and geographical references; (b) Section Two: 11:27-12:12, a controversy and a parable neither of which demanded the setting of 11:1ff. as their original locus, but which have been introduced by Mark here and which conclude with the second reference to the opposition to Jesus (12:12); (c) Section Three: 12:13-44, a loose sequence of controversies, given a temple setting by Mark. This structure is confirmed by Pesch's stichometric observations that in

---

[1]Nineham, St. Mark, p. 309; Taylor, Mark, p. 101, "Mark has enlarged the group [of controversies] by inserting the parable of the wicked husbandmen."

[2]Ibid., p. 101, calls it an addition. On Marcan Stichwort composition, see ibid., pp. 409-411.

11:1-26 there are 25 verses, 5 pericopes and 56 lines; in 11:27-12:12 the proportion is 18/2/45 and in 12:13-44, 32/6/84.[1] Therefore, 11:27-12:12 forms the midpiece of the section, and, as we know from other parts of Mark, he is fond of using middle sections to interpret surrounding material, so we can gain some understanding into the whole section by studying the two pericopes of the middle section.[2]

11:27-33: The Authority of Jesus Questioned

The literary history of this pericope is complex. The introduction (11:27) has all the earmarks of Marcan composition--the historical present (*kai erchontai*), *kai* parataxis, localization in Jerusalem and the temple, and the use of *palin*.[3] The designation by name and actual appearance of the constitutive members of the Sanhedrin (*archiereis*, *grammateis*, *presbyteroi*) occurs only here and in the two trial indications of 14:53 and 15:1, so that the whole scene here becomes in effect a "trial" before the Sanhedrin. The debate itself which begins in 11:28 is listed by Albertz as part of the pre-existing complex of Jerusalem controversies.[4] However, it is equally possible that the present debate was a separate piece of tradition put in its present context by Mark. The atmosphere of the controversies in 12:13-17 (taxes to Caesar), 12:18-27 (the debate on the resurrection), 12:28-34 (the great commandment) is notably different. In each of these Jesus gives an answer to some problem

---

[1] Pesch, *Naherwartungen*, p. 65.

[2] Mark's fondness for emphasizing the middle sections is shown primarily by his use of intercalations. See *supra*, pp. 58-63.

[3] *Supra*, p. 55, n. 2 and n. 3; on *palin* see Turner, "Marcan Usage," *JTS*, XXIX (1928), 284-285.

[4] *Supra*, p. 115, n. 2.

posed by his adversaries, but the opponents pose no <u>direct</u> challenge to Jesus or his activity. In each story he emerges as the triumphant teacher of wisdom, as the reactions of the crowds in 12:17 and 12:34 indicate. In 11:27-33 the challenge is directed to his person and activity and the answer is enigmatic. Not only in form is 11:27-33 different from the other debates of this section, but the content also seems out of place. The emphasis on the <u>exousia</u> of Jesus is characteristic of the first sections of the gospel, and the reference to John the Baptist who has so long been out of the picture seems strange here.[1]

Further problems arise in the debate itself. To the question of the Sanhedrin as to the source and nature of his authority, Jesus replies with a counter question which functions both as an answer to and a refutation of the challenge.[2] However, the dialectics of vs. 30 are confusing. When Jesus asks whether the baptism of John was from heaven or from man, he is not giving his opponents optional responses. In positive terms the question of Jesus means: "Just as the Baptist received his <u>exousia</u> from God and not from men, so also have I."[3] The only answer on the part of an adversary who does not want to admit he is bested is the <u>ouk oidamen</u> of vs. 33. There arises, then, a tension between the expected answer of vs. 33 and the deliberations in vss. 31-32. In these verses the opponents interpret the counter question as if there were options presented. Their considerations do not center on the origin of John's baptism, but on the person of John and their own failure to believe in him. The language here evidences Christian concerns in the

---

[1] John A. T. Robinson, "Elijah, John and Jesus: An Essay in Detection," <u>Twelve New Testament Studies</u> (Studies in Biblical Theology, Vol. XXXIV; London: S. C. M. Press, 1962), p. 40.

[2] Bultmann, <u>Synoptic Tradition</u>, p. 20.   [3] <u>Ibid</u>.

emphasis on <u>pistyein</u> and the designation of John as <u>prophētēs</u>.[1]

These literary observations lead to the following conclusions. Mark has written the introduction, making the whole debate refer to the temple cleansing, thus bringing the controversy under the ambit of the anti-temple theme.[2] The debate itself had originally a different setting, most likely associated with the <u>exousia</u> of Jesus which characterized the beginning of Jesus' ministry, and not too far from the Baptist material.[3] Within the debate itself the reference to the baptism of John has been re-interpreted by Mark as a reference to the person and function of John. The following questions then become important. Why is a debate on <u>exousia</u> introduced here? What is the reason for the re-interpretation of the Baptist material here?

The <u>exousia</u> of Jesus is one of Mark's chief theological concerns. After the proclamation of the kingdom of God (1:15), Jesus' initial confrontation with the power of evil is characterized as <u>didaskōn autous hōs exousian echōn</u> (1:22, 27). It is the <u>exousia</u> of Jesus, which, when conferred on the disciples (3:15; 6:7) enables them to do what Jesus has done. The most important use of <u>exousia</u> and the only place other than 11:27ff. where it occurs in a controversy setting is the controversy of 2:6-11. Here, in answer to the murmurings that only God

---

[1]<u>Ibid</u>.

[2]Discussion centers on whether <u>tauta</u> refers to the temple cleansing or to the ministry and teaching of Jesus in general. Taylor, <u>Mark</u>, p. 469, mentions that Wellhausen, Swete, Lagrange, Plummer, and others refer it to the temple cleansing. Of the eight usages of <u>tauta</u> in Mark--2:8; 6:2; 7:23; 10:20; 11:28; 13:4; 13:8; 13:29, all except 13:4 and 13:29 refer clearly to what immediately precedes.

[3]The Johannine order of events (joining of temple cleansing and question of authority at beginning of ministry, near material about John) supports the possibility of such a tradition, see Robinson, "Elijah," p. 40; Lohmeyer, <u>Markus</u>, p. 243.

forgives sins, Jesus manifests his healing power, "in order that you might know that the Son of Man has *exousia* on earth to forgive sin" (2:10). Perrin has discovered that it is only in Mark and in dependence on him that *exousia* is used of the earthly ministry of Jesus, and that it is Mark who makes the earthly ministry of Jesus into a full-scale presentation of the authority of the Son of Man.[1] However, the section 11:1-12:44 is most severely under the Messianic Secret. There is not one Christological title in the section; Jesus is always addressed as *didaskale* or *rabbi*, and Mark is anxious here to portray the mounting blindness of Jesus' opponents. Therefore the lack of any Christological title, and specifically of the Son of Man, is not strange, so that when the opponents fail to recognize the *exousia* of Jesus shown in the temple cleansing, they really fail to see him as the Son of Man exercising his *exousia* on earth. In the second "trial before the Sanhedrin" (14:53-65) this veil of secrecy is lifted. The Christological affirmation of 14:61-62, culminating in the reference to the parousia of the Son of Man, serves to vindicate the anti-temple statement of 14:58. The debate on *exousia* in 11:27-33 serves the same function. It vindicates Jesus' anti-temple activity of 11:1-27, and answers the question of "who" is the one who supplants temple and cult, but the answer is still under the veil of secrecy which in Mark shrouds the ministry of Jesus.

The Marcan additions of vss. 31-32 shift the attention to the person and mission of John. We may now ask how this understanding of the function of John contributes to an understanding of the pericope. When the opponents disbelieve in John in 11:31, they do not see the function Mark has given to John.

---

[1] N. Perrin, "The Son of Man in the Synoptic Tradition," *Biblical Research*, XIII (1968), 20-21.

John marks the end of the Old Testament and the archē of the Gospel (1:1). He is the forerunner and his baptism is in preparation for the messianic age (1:8).[1] Thus John functions as a prophet and a witness to Jesus. When, in 11:31-32, the Sanhedrin refuses to believe in John, they are precluded from recognizing any action of Jesus as part of the new messianic age. Thus, they cannot understand the action in the temple. Also, it should be noted that the text of Malachi 3:1 with which Mark introduces the role of John, speaks of the Lord coming to his temple to purify it (3:1b). It is possible, then, that the allusion to John here takes the reader back to the beginning of the gospel and recalls this verse of Malachi and its ultimate fulfillment in the coming of Jesus to the temple.[2]

We may now summarize the Marcan redactional activity in 11:27-33. Mark begins the middle section of the Jerusalem ministry of Jesus by the introduction of a debate on the exousia of Jesus which was not originally found in the present context. This debate follows immediately upon Jesus' action against the temple, and is in response to it. The opponents in the debate are those who will be the agents of Jesus' death. Thus Mark underscores the fact that the anti-temple activity of Jesus is responsible for the mounting opposition to him. In content the debate makes a Christological statement showing in a veiled

---

[1] Walter Wink, John the Baptist in the Gospel Tradition (Society for New Testament Studies, Monograph Series, Vol. VII; Cambridge: University Press, 1968), p. 4; H. Conzelmann, The Theology of St. Luke, p. 22: "In the pre-Lucan tradition John is understood from the standpoint of the dawn of the new eschatological age. . . . In the tradition John the Baptist stands on the dividng line between the old and the new epoch."

[2] Malachi 3:1 reads: "Behold I send my messenger to prepare the way before me, and the Lord whom you seek will suddenly come to his temple . . ." Since the language of 3:1b is never found in the New Testament, the suggestion made here can never be proven.

manner who Jesus is and by what <u>exousia</u> he performs the actions
of 11:1-27. It is by the <u>exousia</u> which Jesus possesses as Son
of Man that Jesus brings an end to the role of the temple. The
leaders do not recognize this because by their disbelief in John
they cannot understand the role of Jesus. In the discussion of
the following parable we will attempt to show that Mark continues this polemic against the official Jewish leaders who are
rejected because of their disbelief.

12:1-12: The Parable of the Vineyard and the Tenants

Our purpose is not to attempt a reconstruction of the
original extent and setting of the parable, nor to resolve the
question of whether we have a parable or allegory at the basis
of the present text, since the majority of commentators admit
that, in the present context, 12:1-9 is an allegory.[1] Jeremias
writes that in the present context:

> The vineyard is clearly Israel, the tenants are Israel's
> rulers and leaders, the owner of the vineyard is God, the
> messengers are the prophets, the son is Christ, the punish-
> ment of the husbandmen symbolizes the ruin of Israel,
> the "other people" (Matt. 21.43) are the Gentile Church.[2]

Our purpose will be to see how Mark, by the location of the
parable in its present context, by the addition of the citation
from Ps 118:22-23 (12:10-11) and, by the addition of the plan of
the leaders in 12:11, continues the anti-temple theme in vss.

---

[1] J. D. Crossan, "The Parable of the Wicked Husbandmen," <u>JBL</u>, XC (1971), 461, calls it a "strained allegory." J. Jeremias, <u>The Parables of Jesus</u>, trans. S. H. Hooke (6th ed.; New York: Charles Scribner's Sons, 1963), p. 70, "This parable exhibits an allegorical character . . . unique among the par- ables of Jesus." Werner Kümmel, "Das Gleichnis von den bösen Weingärtnern," Aux Sources de la Tradition Chrétienne (Mélanges à Maurice Goguel; Paris: Delachaux et Niestle, 1950), pp. 120- 131, views it as an early Christian product and an allegory on the rejection of Jesus. M.-J. Lagrange, <u>Marc</u>, p. 285, calls it a <u>parabole-allégorie</u>. Taylor, <u>Mark</u>, p. 472, calls it an alle- gory.

[2] Jeremias, <u>Parables</u>, p. 70.

1-10 by giving a specific allegorical interpretation to each of
the details. For him the vineyard and the tower are the temple;
the geōrgoi, the temple officials; the earlier messengers, the
prophets who opposed the cult; and the son, Jesus.[1] In this
case, Lohmeyer's insights are stronger than his evidence. In
the Old Testament, the temple is not called the tower; the
priests are never called geōrgoi, and the vineyard (vine) is
the symbol for the people of Israel or the royal house.[2] We affirm
that the allegory contains an anti-temple motif, but this
is seen not in the details, but in the setting and the Marcan
additions.

The introduction, kai erxato, reveals a standard Marcan
formula, and the autois directs the parable against the adversaries
of the previous debate, the Sanhedrin.[3] As noted, Marcan
editorial activity is also found in the addition of vss. 10-11,
the citation of Ps 118, and in the indication of the plan of the
leaders to seize Jesus. According to some commentators the "beloved
son" (12:6, cf. 1:11; 9:7) is also a Marcan addition which
brings a Christological emphasis to the allegory.[4] The most

---

[1] Ernst Lohmeyer, "Das Gleichnis von den bösen Weingärtnern," Zeitschrift für systematische Theologie, XVIII (1941), 242-259.

[2] The people of Israel: Isa 5:1; 27:2; Jer 12:10; the royal house: Ezek 17:6-8. In fairness to Lohmeyer it should be noted that in Isa 5:1ff. there is a close conjunction of city, temple and people.

[3] On erxato used as a modal verb, see Turner, "Marcan Usage," JTS, XXVIII (1927), 352; Taylor, Mark, p. 48. The referent of autois comes from the setting of the parable within the controversies, see Lohmeyer, Markus, p. 244, "Zum Sanhedrium spricht Jesus," and Walter Grundmann, Das Evangelium nach Markus (Theologischer Handkommentar zum Neuen Testament, Vol. II; Berlin: Evangelische Verlagsanstalt, 1968), p. 238: "Die Einleitung verbindet das Gleichnis mit der Vollmachtsfrage; es ist an die Mitglieder des Synedriums gerichtet und gibt ihnen, sie angreifend, in verhüllter Form eine Antwort auf die Vollmachtsfrage."

[4] On 12:10, Bultmann, Synoptic Tradition, p. 177, "In vss.

common interpretation of the allegory and the additions of vss. 10-11 is that it is an allegory on Israel's rejection of Jesus, and the citation of Ps 118 is used to vindicate Jesus' mission by reference to his resurrection.[1] The apologetic use of this psalm in Acts 4:11, in a clear reference to the resurrection, supports such an interpretation.[2] There are, however, objections to such an interpretation. In the allegory (12:1-9), the final result is not the vindication of the son, but the punishment of the wicked tenants and the transfer of their stewardship to others. The reaction of the opponents in vs. 12, when they perceive that the allegory is directed to them, doesn't make sense if the emphasis is placed on the vindication of Jesus rather than on their rejection. The problem, then, is to see some consistency in the use of Ps 118:22-23, and in the reaction of the Sanhedrin, with the setting and content of the allegory. By the setting Mark directs the allegory against the Sanhedrin, the priestly members of which were custodians of the Jerusalem temple. They are, therefore, like the wicked tenants who exercised their stewardship unfaithfully. We hope to show that the use of Ps 118:22-23 in Mk 12:10f. stresses the replacement of them by Jesus, the cornerstone, and the replacement of the temple by the Christian community.

As Acts 4:11 shows, Ps 118:22-23 was used at a very early stage of the tradition as part of a Passion apologetic. At a much later stage stands the use of the same psalm verses in

---

10f. Mark has inserted yet another polemical quotation," and Lohmeyer, Markus, p. 246. Nineham, St. Mark, p. 312, calls 12:6 a secondary addition and says it relates this section to 1:11. Kümmel, "Gleichnis," p. 131, also views it as secondary.

[1]Ibid., p. 131; Nineham, St. Mark, p. 313; Taylor, Mark, p. 472.

[2]Lindars, New Testament Apologetic, pp. 170, 174.

1 Pet 2:1-10, along with a cluster of "stone" texts (Isa 8:14; 28:16). Lindars has pointed out that, in the context of a baptismal liturgy, by means of a *pesher* type of exegesis the "rejected stone" of Ps 118:22 becomes identified with the person of Christ who is then seen as the cornerstone of the "spiritual house" (1 Pet 2:5) which the Christians are to become.[1] The citation of Ps 118 thus moves from an apologetic to a theological use where Christ is the cornerstone of the Christian community, pictured as the spiritual temple.

We suggest that the Marcan usage of Ps 118:22-23 in 12:10 stands midway between the fully developed community use in 1 Peter and the simple apologetic use of Acts 4:11. In order to show this we must consider Mark's use of other parts of the same psalm. Jeremias has already shown that, at the time of Jesus and in the early Church, the psalm was used in an eschatological messianic sense in reference to the coming of the Messiah.[2] In Mark this usage is mirrored in 11:9 where Ps 118:25-26 is cited, to which Mark adds his own interpretation about the coming kingdom (11:10). The psalm is next cited in 12:10f. in the context of the present allegory. The only other reference to Ps 118 in the synoptic tradition outside of the parallels to the Marcan usage is the Q saying of Lk 13:35, Mt 23:39. Both sayings portray a lament over Jerusalem where Jerusalem acts much like the wicked tenants of Mk 12:1ff. In both Matthew and Luke the house (temple) will be taken away, and Jerusalem will not see Jesus until she says, "blessed is he who comes in the name of the

---

[1] Isa 28:16, "Therefore thus says the Lord God, 'Behold I lay in Zion a stone, a well-tested stone, a precious stone as the cornerstone of a sure foundation.'" Lindars, *New Testament Apologetic*, pp. 175-180.

[2] *Eucharistic Words*, pp. 256-262; *Didache* 10:6 has a parousia use.

Lord." In this context, Ps 118:25-26 does not refer to the entry of Jesus into Jerusalem, but to his future coming. Thus, Ps 118 had two distinct meanings in the pre-Marcan tradition. Verses 22-23 served as a Passion apologetic; vss. 25-26 were used in reference to the coming of Jesus to Jerusalem, either in the context of the narrative of his ministry or at the second coming. Mark adapts these traditions in accord with his purpose. In 11:9, Ps 118:25-26 is cited to bring out the eschatological messianic sense of Jesus' first coming to the temple, and the Marcan addition of 11:10 stresses the substitution of kingdom for temple. The whole bulk of material between 11:9 and 12:10 is then framed by a second reference to Ps 118. Here Mark modifies the earlier apologetic use of vss. 22-23. The emphasis shifts from an apology for the rejected aspect of the stone to its function as cornerstone.[1] In the allegory the last action

---

[1] The exact meaning of eis kephalēn gōnias (Ps 118:22) is very much disputed. Jeremias argues strongly that this phrase and the akrogōniaion of Isa 28:16 means "capstone" or the final stone put on a building, rather than the cornerstone, see, "kephalē gōnias--akrogōniaios," ZNW, XXVIII (1929), 13-20; "Eckstein--Schlusstein," ZNW, XXVI (1937), 154-157; "gōnia," TDNT, I, 791-793. German commentaries have, in general, followed Jeremias on this, see: E. Klostermann, Das Markusevangelium (Handbuch zum Neuen Testament, Vol. III; 4th ed. rev.; Tübingen: J. C. B. Mohr [Paul Siebeck], 1950), p. 123; Julius Schniewind, Das Evangelium nach Markus (Das Neue Testament Deutsch, Vol. I; Göttingen: Vandenhoeck und Ruprecht, 1952), p. 154. Lohmeyer, Markus, p. 247, holds that in the New Testament both cornerstone and capstone are meant. English-speaking commentators have argued that the term means "cornerstone" or a part of the foundation of the building, see: Taylor, Mark, p. 477; Nineham, St. Mark, p. 313. R. J. McKelvey, "Christ the Cornerstone," NTS, VIII (1961-62), 352-359; The New Temple, pp. 194-204, examines Jeremias' arguments and finds that the translation, "capstone," is not as compelling as Jeremias' authority would suggest. The arguments in favor of the translation "cornerstone," are: (a) Even Jeremias admits that in Isa 28:16, akrogōniaion means cornerstone (TDNT, I, 792), (b) at Qumran this stone is understood as a foundation stone, 1 QS 8:7ff., (c) the rabbis interpreted Isa 28:16 as the 'eben $š^e$tiyyah, the stone of foundation (McKelvey, New Temple, p. 202), (d) at times this stone was applied to the figures of Abraham and David who are founding figures, (e) the New Testament meanings outside of Mk 12:10f. et par clearly understand the term as foundation stone. In 1 Pet 2:6-9, three stone texts (Isa 28:16; Ps 118:22;

of the master of the vineyard is to give the vineyard to others
(allois, vs. 9c). After the appended quote from Ps 118, the reaction of the opponents to do violence to Jesus is in response
to this transfer. Since the opponents in the parable are the
Sanhedrin, the opponents of the previous debate, the priestly
members of which are the temple custodians, what triggers their
reaction in 12:12 is their realization that Jesus is to be the
cornerstone of the new temple, and the temple, the allois who
are the nucleus of the new community.

The two parts of the temple saying have thus influenced
Mark in the selection of material, in the structure and in em-
phases placed on different parts, between 11:1 and 12:12. From
11:1 till the end of the debate on exousia, the stress is on the
anti-temple part of the saying and the failure of the leaders to
recognize that Jesus has brought the role of the temple to a
close. Thus the position of the debate and the allegory serve
to reinforce the activity and teaching of Jesus between 11:1 and
11:27. In the allegory of the wicked tenants the anti-temple
motif is present, but the emphasis shifts to the appended psalm
citation where Jesus as the cornerstone of the new temple mirrors the drive of the second part of the saying. The two plans
to harm Jesus come at two high points in the section, at 11:18
and 12:12, where the devaluation of the temple is strong. In
the following section we will indicate that Mark continues the
motifs of the temple saying in ch. 13.

Isa 8:14) are put together. The third text in reference to the
"stone which will make men stumble," suggests a stone at ground
level. Also Eph 2:20b-21a, "Christ Jesus himself being the
akrōgoniaion in whom the whole structure is joined together and
grows into a holy temple in the Lord," understands the term as a
foundation stone.

Chapter 13 and 14:1: Eschatological Discourse,
Plot To Kill Jesus

The final reference to the plan of the officials to kill Jesus comes in 14:1, "they sought how they might take Jesus in secret and kill him." In previous instances this plan has been in reaction to the teaching or the actions of Jesus in opposition to cult or temple. The immediate question is what has prompted the decision of 14:1. If Pesch is correct in viewing ch. 13 as the last addition by Mark to his gospel, then the plan in 14:1 would be in reaction to the complex of material from 11:1 to 12:44.[1] Since our aim is to consider Mark as it stands in the final redaction, we must examine the anti-temple elements of ch. 13, and we will suggest that 14:1 is in reaction both to ch. 13 and to the material of 11:1-12:44.

No chapter of Mark has received as much attention as ch. 13, so detailed investigation of all the technical problems is impossible at this juncture. We will attempt to indicate certain ways in which Mark continues the anti-temple theme in this chapter. While there is much dispute on the internal structure of the chapter, there is growing agreement that 13:1-5a provide the introduction to the discourse.[2] The introductory verses also manifest strong Marcan composition--kai parataxis; the introduction of redactional clauses by a genitive absolute (vss. 1, 3); the use of hieron (vs. 1); the historical present of legei (vs. 1); the emphasis on the private instruction of the disciples (kat' idian, 13:3) and the use of erxato as a modal

---

[1] Pesch, Naherwartungen, pp. 70-73.

[2] Gaston, No Stone, pp. 10-13 (vss. 1-4); Lambrecht, Redaktion, p. 68 (vss. 1-4). These authors see 5a as transitional. The following see 1-5a as the introduction: Lightfoot, The Gospel Message of St. Mark, p. 49; Lohmeyer, Markus, pp. 267-268; Pesch, Naherwartungen, p. 55.

verb.[1] In function the verses look backward (Jesus leaves the city and the temple) and forward (the disciples ask about the future, 13:4) to the discourse itself. The introduction contains a strong anti-temple tendency. When Jesus leaves the temple in 13:1 he never returns to it, and the city of Jerusalem is never mentioned again by name in his gospel.[2] The content of the whole discourse is occasioned by the prediction of the destruction of the temple and the city. The discourse is given by Jesus seated on the Mount of Olives, "opposite the temple" (13:3). In Mark's portrayal of the ministry of Jesus, this mount functions as a substitute for the temple mount. The preparations for the entry into Jerusalem begin here (11:1) as do the preparations for the supper (14:12-16).[3] On this mountain Jesus predicts the final meeting with his disciples in Galilee, completely by-passing Jerusalem.[4] Therefore Mark has prefaced the discourse with an introduction which casts it into a response to the destruction and devaluation of city and

---

[1] On the redaction of the whole introduction, ibid., pp. 93-105; Kelber, "Kingdom," pp. 138-151; on kai parataxis, supra, p. 55, n. 2; the use of the genitive absolute, John C. Doudna, The Greek of the Gospel of Mark (Journal of Biblical Literature, Monograph Series, Vol. XII; Philadelphia: S. B. L., 1961), pp. 57-59; the redactional use of hieron, supra, p. 106, n. 1; the emphasis on didachē, Schweizer, "Anmerkungen," p. 95; the secret teaching, Mk 4:34; 6:31; 7:33; 9:2, 28; on erxato as a modal verb, Turner, "Marcan Usage," JTS, XXVIII (1927), 352-353.

[2] In 14:13 Jerusalem is simply referred to as "the city."

[3] The strong similarity of language between the two incidents suggests that Mark looks on them as parallel accounts, cf. 11:1 apostellei duo tōn mathētōn autou, 14:13, same phrase; 11:2, kai legei autois, 14:13, same; 11:3, kai apēlthon kai heuron, 14:16, kai exēlthon kai ēlthon kai heuron; 11:6, kathōs eipen ho Iēsous, 14:16, kathōs eipen autois. See Lagrange, Marc, p. lxxxv. In Mark's geography Bethany is on the Mount of Olives, 11:1, 11, 12, Schreiber, Theologie, p. 185.

[4] 14:26; C. F. Evans, "I Will Go before You into Galilee," JTS, N.S., V (1954), 3-18.

temple.

In content the discourse consists of an exhortation to care and watchfulness in the face of the deceptions and trials which surround the end-time. In the concrete the major problem facing the disciples seems to be the danger from false messiahs and false prophets who come in the name of Jesus, as is shown by the fact that the major part of the discourse (13:7-20) is framed by parallel references to these deceivers (13:6; 13:21-23).[1] The initial arrival of these deceivers is accompanied by wars and upheaval, but this is not the "end" but the prelude to it (13:7). In the discourse the height of the crisis is reached in 13:14 when the "abominating desolation" stands "where it should not." This will be the signal for the flight of the community and will precipitate the ultimate crisis and occasion the coming of the Son of Man in 13:26-27 which resolves the crisis. Thus the identification of the event referred to in 13:14 provides the key to understanding one of Mark's major purposes in the discourse.

This verse has long been a <u>crux interpretum</u> and will probably remain so for time to come.[2] While the precise identification of the <u>bdelygma tēs erēmōseos</u> remains also problematic, the Danielic background to the phrase and the Matthean alteration of <u>hopou ou dei</u> to <u>en topō hagiō</u> make it certain that the event referred to has something to do with the temple.[3] While it is argued whether the event referred to is the occupation of the temple by the powers of evil, or its destruction, there is

───────────

[1] Pesch, <u>Naherwartungen</u>, pp. 106-118.

[2] <u>Ibid</u>., pp. 139-144.

[3] Mt 24:15 makes the allusion to Daniel explicit by the addition of <u>to rēthen dia Daniēl</u>. In Daniel, 9:27; 11:31; 12:11, the context is the desecration or desacralization of the temple.

no doubt that from this verse on the temple has completely lost its role.[1] The community is now to flee from the temple since it is the seat of evil and opposition. If, then, as Pesch and others suggest, the verse receives its real meaning from the Marcan preface to the discourse, then it is the destruction of the temple which is the sign that the end has come.[2] However, if, as Conzelmann, Pesch, and Kelber have shown, in the discourse Mark is countering a false eschatology which would join the arrival of the parousia to the destruction of the temple, and which is the substance of the teaching of the false messiahs, then Mark has pictured the ultimate devaluation of the temple.[3] The temple is of no importance to his community not only because it is the seat of the powers of evil, but because its destruction is joined to a false eschatology. Therefore in this discourse Mark moves the anti-temple theme from the time of Jesus to the time of his readers. If, as recent studies suggest, the gospel of Mark is written in direct response to the turmoil of A.D. 65-70, and specifically to the destruction of the temple, then the anti-temple theme may reflect the growing estrangement of the Marcan church from Judaism and provide them

---

[1] Pesch, Naherwartungen, p. 142, argues that the reference is to the actual destruction of the temple, while Lohmeyer, Markus, p. 276, is representative of those who deny any political event is alluded to.

[2] Naherwartungen, p. 142; Marxsen, Mark, pp. 180-183, notes that 13:14 must somehow be the answer to the question of 13:2.

[3] Pesch, Naherwartungen, p. 118; Kelber, "Kingdom," pp. 151-159. Hans Conzelmann, "Geschichte und Eschaton nach Mc 13," ZNW, L (1959), 214-215, observes that the discourse is concerned with correcting a false eschatology which joins the fate of the temple and the end of the world. See also T. J. Weeden, "The Heresy that Necessitated Mark's Gospel," ZNW, LIX (1968), 145-158, suggests that an improper understanding of Christology and eschatology is put on the lips of the disciples which precipitates Jesus' discourse of 13:5ff.

with a rationale for understanding its destruction.[1] This rationale is twofold. On the one hand it consists in picturing the ministry of Jesus as in growing opposition to the temple and attributing to Jesus the prediction of its ultimate destruction. Thus the whole movement from 11:1 to 13:5 receives its form and meaning. On the other hand, the temple has lost its significance because in Mark's time it has become the seat of evil powers. However, the community is not to be surprised at this because, according to Mark, Jesus in his action and teaching has shown that this would happen. Therefore, the introduction to the discourse and the occupation of the temple by the "abominating desolation" continue the Marcan anti-temple theme.

In our analysis thus far of the influence of Mark 14:58 we have noted that along with the anti-temple theme, there is the motif of the eschatological community which will replace this temple. There are indications that in ch. 13 Mark looks beyond the destruction of the temple to the formation of the new community.[2] In the discourse of ch. 13 the resolution of the crisis begins with the cosmic phenomena which precede the coming of the Son of Man, which for Mark is the real end-time.[3] At the height of the terror (13:24-25), the faithful will see the Son of Man coming with power and glory. The language in these

---

[1] Pesch, Naherwartungen, pp. 218-223; N. Walter, "Tempelzerstörung und synoptische Apokalypse," ZNW, LVII (1966), 43, date the gospel as post A.D. 70. Also S. G. F. Brandon, The Trial of Jesus of Nazareth (Historic Trials Series; New York: Stein and Day, 1968), argues that Mark is an anti-Jewish Christian apologetic written in Rome after the Jewish wars to disassociate Christians from the Zealot movement.

[2] In separating the destruction from the arrival of the end time, Mark puts the beginning of the final age in the future, Conzelmann, "Geschichte," esp. p. 213.

[3] 13:7, oupō to telos when compared with 13:24 shows that Mark places the beginning of the final period here, Pesch, Naherwartungen, p. 157.

verses is traditional and most commentators view this section as pre-Marcan tradition.[1] There is evidence that in vss. 24-27, Mark has joined two blocks of tradition. There is a tension between the atmosphere created by the use of the Old Testament texts and the role of the Son of Man in vss. 26-27. All the texts, Isa 13:10; 34:4; Ezek 32:7; Joel 2:10, 31, which furnish the images for vss. 24-25 stress the motif of judgment and three of them, Isa 13:10; Joel 2:10, 31, are "day of the Lord" texts.[2] In the New Testament these texts appear also in Rev 6:12-13 and 8:12, but in a context in harmony with their Old Testament background, a context of judgment (cf. Rev 6:16-17). In Mark 13:26-27 the motif of judgment is replaced by the gathering of the elect. Verse 26 begins with the typically Marcan emphasis on "seeing" and then contains the Son of Man saying.[3] Therefore in light of the tension between vss. 24-25 and 26-27, I would suggest that, while the material is traditional, Mark has introduced the coming of the Son of Man with glory as salvation of the elect in the place of a previous judgment saying. With the destruction of the temple (13:2) and its occupation by the power of evil (13:14), the temple has lost its meaning. Salvation awaits the community when the Son of Man comes to gather them into the nucleus of the new community.

We have already noted that along with the anti-temple motif there is the motif of the eschatological community. This does not come forth with the same strength and clarity as the anti-temple motif, but is most evident in the "cornerstone" text

---

[1] Ibid., pp. 157-175; Beasley-Murray, *Commentary*, pp. 87-93; Taylor, *Mark*, pp. 636-644.

[2] Isa 13:9, "Behold, for the day of the Lord comes"; Joel 2:11, "For the day of the Lord is great and terrible."

[3] Cf. 9:1; 14:62; 16:7; *supra*, pp. 93-95.

of 12:10-11 and the gathering of the elect in 13:27. He does not come out with the clarity of a Paul in calling it a <u>naos</u>. The conclusion to the eschatological discourse (13:32-37) suggests a reason for this reserve on the part of Mark. The section begins with a warning to the disciples to watch, for they do not know when the <u>kairos</u> will come. There follows a brief parable in which the servants are given the <u>exousia</u> of the master and again told to watch. In vss. 35 and 37b there is a twofold warning to watch (<u>grēgoreite</u>) into which are inserted the hours of watching.[1] These time designations are the precise time divisions with which Mark divides the material of the Passion narrative.[2] Thus the Passion narrative itself is put into the framework of an eschatological period of watching, a motif which becomes clear at the conclusion of the Gethesemane pericope where the disciples are told, like the servants in 13:37, not to sleep and to watch. The Passion itself is thus a trial of the last days, much like the trials of 13:7ff. Mark thus looks beyond the Passion narrative to the return of the Son of Man. This is the meaning of the second part of 14:58. Jesus will build a new <u>naos</u> in place of the rejected <u>naos</u>. His earthly ministry is the <u>archē</u> of the process; the Passion narrative the last trial prior to its realization, but the realization is still in the future.[3]

---

[1]This is a Marcan insertion technique.

[2]R. H. Lightfoot, <u>Gospel Message of St. Mark</u>, p. 53. The divisions according to three hour intervals are found in:

13:35, <u>opse</u>	14:17, <u>opsias genomenēs</u>
13:35, <u>mesonyktion</u>	14:43-50 (reference is not exact, but arrest is in the middle of the night)
13:35, <u>alektorophōnias</u>	14:72, <u>alektor ephōnēsen</u>
13:35, <u>prōi</u>	15:1, <u>eythys prōi</u>

[3]H. W. Bartsch, "Early Christian Eschatology in the Synoptic Gospels," <u>NTS</u>, XI (1965), 396, and Conzelmann,

The final reference, before the trial narrative, to the plan of the officials to kill Jesus comes in 14:1b. In previous instances this plan has been in reaction to some action or saying of Jesus. The problem in referring it immediately to the eschatological discourse is that, according to Mark, the discourse is private instruction to the disciples (13:3). The closest references of the plan would then be the denunciation of the scribes in 12:38-40, the story of the widow in 12:41-44 and the exit of Jesus from the temple in 13:1-2. Thus, in the context of the final redaction of the gospel, the plan in 14:1 has a double focus. On the level of the flow of the narrative it is in response to the conclusion of the whole section 11:1-12:44 and the complex of anti-temple motifs there. On another level it refers the reader of the gospel to the motifs of the end of the temple and the promise of the new community in 13:5-37. The fact that 14:1 occurs at the beginning of the Passion narrative suggests that Mark portrays the death of Jesus as arising out of his opposition to Jerusalem and the temple, an opposition which culminates in the trial narrative.

Conclusion

In this chapter the aim was to see the implications of the Marcan redactional activity in the trial narrative as this emerged in Chap. II. There it was seen that the presence of what, for Mark, is a true statement on the lips of Jesus is explained by the distinction between tradition and redaction. Mark has taken over an apologetic tradition which used select Old Testament texts to affirm the innocence of Jesus before false and lying accusers. He has modified this tradition of

---

"Geschichte," p. 220, who says that for Mark the period of trial becomes an epoch.

"falseness" to "not in agreement" and inserted a saying of Jesus into this context. Such an observation demanded an analysis of the origin and meaning of the saying.

The saying itself (14:58) as it stands in Mark is twofold, and Mark is the creator of the combined saying. He does this by combining two traditions: one, a tradition which attributed to Jesus a threat or prophetic saying against the temple (13:2), the other, an early Christian theologoumenon of those groups who viewed themselves as the nucleus of the new naos. The combined saying pictures Jesus in opposition to the Jerusalem temple and as founder of the new community. Though previous research has suggested that the origin for such a view is found in the messianic expectation of first century Judaism which joined the coming of the Messiah, the destruction of the temple, and the hope of the new temple, closer analysis of the evidence for this view indicated that such an expectation did not exist. Therefore the presence of such a view of Jesus in Mark is to be explained in terms of his own creative activity. Since we had already noted, on the basis of literary criticism, that Mark is active in the creation of the trial narrative and that he brings to a culmination there themes which run throughout his gospel (opposition to Jesus, the Messianic Secret, the Christological titles) it became necessary to see if the temple saying has influence in other parts of the gospel. Building on the researches of those who have noted an anti-Jerusalem and anti-temple bias to Mark's gospel after ch. 11, we have shown that this bias is influential in certain pericopes thus far not discussed under this rubric.[1] The entrance to Jerusalem becomes

---

[1] Especially the dispute on authority (11:27-33) and the parable of the wicked husbandmen (12:1-12).

a rejection of Jerusalem, the temple and the temple leaders by one who possesses the <u>exousia</u> of the Son of Man and by him who will be the cornerstone of the new community. This community is still in the future and will be realized only with the return of the Son of Man (13:26ff). Its present members are to exist in a state of watching.

Mark writes his gospel not simply to tell a story of Jesus, but to explain the significance of Jesus for readers of his own time. Different authors have postulated reasons why Mark worked an anti-temple theology into his gospel. Pesch holds that Mark wants to disassociate the destruction of the temple from the parousia in opposition to groups who want to join these two events.[2] Whatever the validity of these individual explanations, if, as recent studies suggest, the gospel of Mark was written in direct response to the turmoil of A.D. 65-70, and specifically to the destruction of the temple, then the anti-temple theme may reflect the growing estrangement of the Marcan church from Judaism, and may provide them with a rationale for understanding the destruction of the temple.[3] The definitive end of the Jewish cult center has come. However, all this has happened proleptically in the ministry of Jesus. In his life Jesus is pictured in opposition to the temple, and this opposition caused his trial, his suffering and death. At the same time Jesus is pictured as promising a new temple. The Marcan community is to form the nucleus of this new <u>naos</u>. Their estrangement from Judaism and the sufferings they endured are nothing more than Jesus endured.

---

[1] <u>Naherwartungen</u>, esp. pp. 231-236, "Die Polemik und Apologetik des Evangelisten."

[2] "Kingdom," pp. 151-159.   [3] <u>Supra</u>, p. 132, n. 1.

The treatment of the temple saying in this chapter leaves one major question unanswered. Though Mark has portrayed Jesus as the one who destroys the old temple, he has not said who Jesus is. In effect, this means that the Christological question remains unanswered. As we have seen, the second major area of Marcan composition and redaction in the trial narrative centers on the Christological material of 14:61-62. We have noted all the literary evidence that Mark makes here a definitive Christological statement, but as yet we have not seen what this statement is. Also the relation of the Christological material to the temple saying has not been discussed. Therefore in our study of the theological implications of Mark's composition and redaction in the trial narrative, it is necessary to turn to the Christological material of 14:61-62.

CHAPTER IV

THE CHRISTOLOGY OF THE TRIAL NARRATIVE

Introduction

The literary analysis of the trial narrative completed in Chap. II revealed that there are two major areas where Mark's theological concern is shown by his reworking of traditional material, by his ordering and structuring of material, and by his composition of new material. In this chapter it was seen that the first major area of concern was the insertion of the temple saying of 14:58 into the narrative, and in Chap. III, the theological implications of this insertion were spelled out. The second area of concern, shown in the literary analysis of Chap. II, was the cumulation of Christological titles in 14:61-62. Nowhere else in the gospel are the titles given to Jesus brought into such close interrelation as in these verses. We then observed that Mark has made the trial scene into a compendium of his Christology. However, at that point we made no attempt to explain what this Christology is. Therefore, the major problem of this chapter is to show in detail the meaning of the titles in 14:61-62, their use in the narrative and the relation of the Christological material to the temple saying. Analysis of this saying shows that Mark states what Jesus does. His ministry is portrayed as bringing about the end of the old temple and the anticipation of the new temple, the community. The question still remains as to who Jesus is and when this community will be definitively established. Therefore the problems of Christology and eschatology still remain unsolved. As a necessary prelude to a discussion of these areas, it will be necessary to survey briefly the status of research on the Christology of the trial narrative.

Survey of Research

Previous discussions of the Christology of 14:61-62 have centered on two questions: (a) does the saying there represent an authentic saying of Jesus, and if so, what are its implications for a judgment on the self-understanding of Jesus? and (b) if the saying is not authentic, what stage of the developing Christology of the early church does it represent?[1] On the basis of the survey of research made in Chap. I of the present work, we noted that there was a growing consensus that the trial narrative is secondary to the oldest traditions of the Passion narrative, and that within the narrative the Christological material is a product of the church's theology.[2] More important than the consensus of authors is N. Perrin's observation that there is no pre-Christian Jewish apocalyptic expectation of the Son of Man coming "with the clouds," and that the form of 14:62 found in Mark represents the end-product of early Christian use of the Old Testament.[3] Therefore the first of the two questions posed will not concern us in the present treatment.[4] On the

---

[1] T. Francis Glasson, The Second Advent (3d ed. rev.; London: Epworth Press, 1963); "The Reply to Caiaphas (Mark XIV.62)," NTS, VII (1960-61), 88-93; John A. T. Robinson, Jesus and His Coming (London: S. C. M. Press, 1957); Taylor, Mark, pp. 563-564; Schmid, Mark, pp. 266-268.

[2] Chap. I, esp. pp. 18-25; Wilhelm Bousset, Kyrios Christos, trans. John E. Steely (Nashville: Abingdon Press, 1970), p. 46, is the first to articulate strongly that 14:62 is a product of early Christian theology. The German original of his work was published in 1913.

[3] Perrin, "Mark XIV.62"; Rediscovering, pp. 173-185.

[4] Also it is not directly within the scope of a redaction-critical investigation.

supposition that the Christology of the trial narrative is the Christology of the early church, the questions then arise as to what kind of Christology it represents, and to what stage of the church's theological reflection does it belong. The first of these questions has been the debate on whether a parousia or an exaltation Christology is contained in the answer of Jesus. The proponents of the parousia Christology hold that in the answer of Jesus there is reference to the final vindication of Jesus and his achieving of full authority at the second coming. The proponents of the exaltation Chrsitology hold that in Jesus' answer there is a reference to his status as sitting at the right hand of the Father in virtue of the resurrection. The clearest example of the contrasting positions is the debate between T. Francis Glasson and John A. T. Robinson who argue for the exaltation Christology and Harvey McArthur who argues for the parousia position.[1] In regard to the second question, the stage of the church's theological reflection the Christology represents, the painstaking work of Ferdinand Hahn, The Titles of Jesus in Christology, represents the fullest exposition of the pre-Marcan Christological traditions.[2] Therefore in reviewing the status of research on the Christology of the trial narrative, we will confine our remarks to a study of the parousia/exaltation debate and the work of Hahn. Ultimately we will hold that the previous research is inadequate for our present concerns because the redaction-critical question has not been posed. In effect, the authors discussed have not asked what is the meaning which Mark himself gives to the saying, and how does

---

[1] Supra, p. 140, n. 1, and Harvey K. McArthur, "Mark XIV.62," NTS, IV (1957-58), 156-158.

[2] Hahn, Titles, pp. 11-12, on purpose of work.

this relate to the other Christological statements of his gospel.

The Parousia/Exaltation Debate

The discussion between Glasson, Robinson and McArthur is important not because they offer original contributions to the debate, but because they summarize well the previous discussions and underline the key issues in the debate.[1] Glasson and Robinson who hold that the answer of Jesus in 14:62 refers to his exaltation to heavenly glory through the resurrection and his vindication by it, adduce the following arguments.[2] In Dan 7:13 what is alluded to is the coming of "one like a son of man," to the Ancient of Days to receive authority and a kingdom (7:14), hence the quotation of Daniel in 14:62 points to the conferring of authority on Jesus through his resurrection/ascension. Glasson holds that the alterations in the response in Matthew (ap' arti, 26:64) and Luke (apo to nyn, 22:69) since they stress the continued reign of Christ, support the view that an exaltation Christology is intended by Mark. Glasson further distinguishes the meaning of the two answers to refer not only to the individual resurrection of Jesus, but to the founding of the Christian community through the resurrection.[3]

In his reply to the use of Dan 7:13 by Glasson, McArthur points out that it is always precarious to interpret the New Testament use of Old Testament references simply by the exegesis

___

[1] Glasson, Second Advent, pp. 30-48, 60; Robinson, Jesus, pp. 9-16. For a criticism of their views see N. Perrin, The Kingdom of God in the Teaching of Jesus (London: S. C. M. Press, 1963), pp. 136-145.

[2] Glasson, Second Advent, pp. 54-62; Robinson, Jesus, pp. 48-58.

[3] Glasson, "Mark XIV.62," p. 92.

of the Old Testament text.[1] He also notes that in Mark 13:26, Dan 7:13 is used in a clear reference to the coming of the Son of Man to earth to gather the elect, so that Mark uses Dan 7:13 in this context also in 14:62. Finally he observes that if the reference in 14:62 were to an enthronement or exaltation, the order of the Old Testament texts should be "coming" and then "sitting" rather than the Marcan order. In answer to the argument that Matthew's and Luke's alterations support an exaltation Christology in Mark, McArthur notes that, if this is the case, why didn't they simply take over the Marcan text without the alterations they make in it.

While underlining the key issues--the use of the Old Testament texts (Ps 110:1 and Dan 7:13), the use of the future Son of Man sayings in Mark, and the relation of the resurrection and parousia in Mark, neither view gives a definitive answer to the question. One reason for this is that they interpret the texts in an "either-or" fashion. The answer of Jesus must refer to either the resurrection or the parousia. They also tend to waver back and forth in suggesting an answer either in the setting of the life of Jesus or of the early church. What they do not discuss is Mark's use of the saying and that the ambiguity may be due to a deliberate tension between resurrection and parousia in Mark. In the discussion of the text we will suggest that the answer of Jesus shows a definite concern of Mark's theology, and is not simply a residue of early church tradition.

Ferdinand Hahn

Hahn's work represents a major contribution to an

---

[1]"Mark XIV.62," p. 156. Perrin, Kingdom, p. 143, also notes "that in the Jewish interpretation of Dan 7:13, as soon as the text was interpreted Messianically it was interpreted in terms of a coming on the clouds of heaven."

understanding of how the early church articulated its understanding of the mission and message of Jesus, insofar as this understanding is expressed in the Christological titles. The professed aim of the work is to study the development of Christology prior to Mark's gospel.[1] In the sense that he studies the traditions available to Mark rather than the Marcan use of them, his work is a prelude to redaction-critical studies on Mark. Following the lead of the Religionsgeschichtliche Schule, Hahn seeks to correlate the use of Christological titles with the spread and growth of early Christianity in different geographical and cultural settings.[2] He therefore uses the schematism of Palestinian Jewish, Hellenistic Jewish, and Hellenistic gentile Christianity as the three stages in which Christology developed.

In the case of the major titles, Christos, Kyrios and Son of God, he seeks to show what content the title received at each stage of its use.[3] In Hahn's view the earliest traditions of the life of Jesus never went beyond titles of honor or titles emphasizing his authority as teacher and said nothing about his otherworldly status or his relations to the deity. The major impetus in the development of a Christology comes with the delay of the parousia.[4] Using concepts which are "foreshadowed" in Jewish apocalyptic literature, the early Christians transformed the messianic hope of the earthly reign of the Messiah into an "otherworldly expectation."[5] In the Palestinian community this hope is expressed by the future Son of Man sayings which convey

---

[1] Titles, pp. 11-13.

[2] Ibid., p. 14, n. 6. Hahn acknowledges his debt to Bousset.

[3] Ibid., p. 314, for summary of his views.

[4] Ibid., pp. 129-131.   [5] Ibid., p. 162.

a strong parousia expectation. With the continued delay of the parousia, the emphasis then shifts to the present role of the exalted reigning *Kyrios* which takes place in the milieu of Hellenistic Jewish Christianity. In this environment *Kyrios* becomes the title *par excellence* for Jesus as Son of Man did in the Palestinian community.[1] Only in this community did any exaltation Christology arise. In the Hellenistic gentile communities the titles are used to convey the pre-existent status of Christ, and here Son of God becomes the pre-eminent title.[2] Thus Hahn postulates a linear development in the early church's Christology--parousia expectation, emphasis on the reigning and exalted *Kyrios* to statements about Christ's pre-existence--and finds that certain titles dominate at a particular stage.

In this light, Hahn's view of the Christology of 14:62 emerges. He adduces various arguments to show that the response of Jesus has its setting in the early Palestinian tradition. The surrogate for the divine name "huios tou eulogētou" is primary evidence for this.[3] More important than this is that the citation of Dan 7:13 in the response of Jesus conveys the parousia eschatology of the Palestinian community.[4] The obvious objection to Hahn's view is that the citation of Ps 110:1 with the notation of Jesus sitting at the right hand of the power would seem to connote an exaltation Christology. Hahn answers this by stating that the earliest use of this psalm in the New Testament is in the context of the granting of power to Jesus at the parousia, so that when Jesus is installed in his messianic

---

[1] *Ibid.*, pp. 93-113.   [2] *Ibid.*, p. 304.

[3] See, however, our earlier reservation about this as evidence for a Palestinian setting, *supra*, p. 90, n. 1.

[4] *Titles*, p. 130.

office at the parousia, all power and authority is given him.[1]
Hahn notes that such an eschatological motif used in conjunction
with the sitting at the right hand is found nowhere else in the
New Testament.[2] Therefore he finds it a bit strange that such a
piece of early Palestinian tradition would remain in the Hellenistic gospel of Mark.[3]

The immediate criticism of Hahn is that his view of the
redactional work of Mark is at a minimum. For him Mark would be
reduced to a collector of traditions. Our research, simply from
a literary point of view, has shown that Mark is very consciously working with his material in 14:61-62. Therefore an
answer to the problem of the Christology of the trial scene
simply in terms of the origin of sayings is inadequate. While
Hahn's research is valuable in showing that the contrast between
the parousia and the exaltation of Jesus is at times forced, he
does not show why the parousia expectation gains such prominence
in the trial scene. On a large scale Hahn's schematism is
forced, and he is too anxious to see Christological development
in a linear sense with one title yielding to another in a different environment.[4] Also the keystone of his whole system,
that there is no exaltation Christology at an early stage, is

---

[1] Ibid., pp. 130-133.   [2] Ibid., p. 130.

[3] Ibid., p. 285.

[4] Philipp Vielhauer, "Zur Frage der Christologischen Hoheitstitel," TLZ, XC (1965), 569-588. Vielhauer calls Hahn's schematism einliniges and adduces the following arguments against it (pp. 586-587): (a) his main thesis that the exaltation Christology of the early church develops because of a delay of the parousia is wrong, (b) the "stages" in early Christianity are neither successive nor mutually exclusive, and (c) his attempt to trace the beginning of Christology from the earthly Jesus rather than from the risen Christ is methodologically questionable. See also Horst R. Balz, Methodische Probleme der Neutestamentlichen Christologie (WMANT, Vol. XXV; Neukirchen-Vluyn: Neukirchener Verlag, 1967).

undermined by Perrin's observation that at the basis of 14:62 is a very old Christian exegetical tradition which used Ps 110:1 in a context of exaltation/resurrection.[1] Initial observation of some of Hahn's evidence and the subsequent research in the present chapter will show that the use of the titles was much more fluid than Hahn would allow. For example, in 1 Thes 1:9-10 the community is urged to "wait for the coming from heaven of his son, whom he raised from the dead." Hahn sees this text merely as evidence that Son of God (his son) was used eschatologically in the early church and that the parousia expectation was yielding to an exaltation Christology.[2] However, as Langevin suggests, there is evidence that the "son" of 1 Thes 1:9f. is an allusion to the Son of Man in Dan 7:13.[3] Therefore we have a case where a type of Christology which Hahn assigns to the Palestinian community is found in an Hellenistic environment. In 1 Thes 4:15-17, we find a use of Kyrios who functions much like the Son of Man in the synoptics.[4] He comes down from heaven and is met on the clouds. Therefore, Hahn's conception of the use of the titles is too narrow and exclusive.

In the present chapter our attempt will be to show that Hahn's view of the Christology of the trial scene is inadequate, not simply because he does not ask the redaction-critical question of the trial scene, but also because his view of the history of tradition of the titles is inadequate. We will, like Hahn, discuss the tradition history of the future Son of Man

---

[1] "Mark XIV.62," and Rediscovering, pp. 173-185.

[2] Titles, p. 286.

[3] Paul-Émile Langevin, Jésus Seigneur et L'Eschatologie: Exégèse de Textes Prepauliniens (Studia, Vol. XXI; Paris: Desclée de Brouwer, 1967), pp. 73-85.

[4] Hartmann, Prophecy Interpreted, pp. 181-190.

sayings behind Mark 14:62, but in so doing we will suggest that he has not given sufficient attention to the creativity of Mark in working with these traditions. He has not given sufficient attention to the details and nuances of the imagery surrounding the coming sayings, but has lumped them too generally under the heading apocalyptic. In effect, the main thrust of the present chapter is to show that a treatment of the trial narrative, only from the viewpoint of the history of the traditions contained there, is inadequate.

Philipp Vielhauer

A further treatment of the trial narrative which should be mentioned is that of Vielhauer which represents an approach to the narrative along the lines of redaction criticism.[1] Vielhauer treats the Christology of Mark as structural, i.e., developing in a definite schema throughout the gospel, so that the titles are treated according to their gospel setting. The most important title in Mark is Son of God and the crucial places where it is found are the baptism (1:11), the transfiguration (9:7) and the confession of the centurion (15:39). Vielhauer finds in these places a pattern of adoption and installation (the baptism), proclamation (transfiguration) and acclamation (confession of the centurion). Such a pattern corresponds to the old Egyptian enthronement ritual, so that 14:62 is interpreted as an enthronement Christology. The main problem with Vielhauer's view, in our perspective, is that the trial narrative does not fit into his schema. While admitting its importance because of the cumulation of titles, he does not treat it in his study of Mark's structural Christology. There

---

[1]"Erwägungen zur Christologie des Markusevangeliums," supra, p. 6, n. 2.

is, then, no redaction-critical study which gives due attention to the importance of the Christology of 14:61-62, both in the context of the trial narrative and in the rest of the gospel.

Future Son of Man Sayings and the Christology of the Trial Narrative

Statement of the Question

As a presupposition to posing the redaction-critical question in exact form, certain things must be noted about the trial scene. In Chap. II, we noted that the most important Christological titles or symbols of Mark's gospel--<u>Christos</u>, <u>Huios tou eulogētou</u>, <u>Huios tou anthrōpou</u>, are brought together in the trial scene. Allied to this is the observation first made by Perrin that in the trial scene Mark uses Son of Man to interpret and give content to Son of God.[1] A third observation arises from a consensus among virtually all commentators on the scene that the movement of the trial scene culminates in Jesus' answer <u>egō eimi</u> and that the saying of 14:62 gives content to the affirmation.[2] Therefore, the future Son of Man saying of 14:62 becomes a key to an understanding of the scene.

If 14:62 is the key to the Christology of the trial scene, then it is necessary to examine the relation of the Son of Man saying here to other Son of Man traditions in Mark. Just as was done in the case of the temple saying, the question of Marcan redaction and editorial work on these sayings must be raised. To accomplish this, detailed discussion must be given to the other future Son of Man sayings in 8:38 and 13:26 in order to find if any pattern or structure emerges in the use of

---

[1]"The Creative Use of the Son of Man Traditions by Mark," <u>USQR</u>, XXIII (1968), 360.

[2]Dibelius, <u>Tradition</u>, p. 192; Haenchen, <u>Weg Jesu</u>, p. 511; Grundmann, <u>Markus</u>, p. 300; Taylor, <u>Mark</u>, p. 564.

these sayings. Therefore an attempt must be made to see what traditions were available to Mark, how he modifies these traditions, and how these modifications provide a key to an understanding of the Christology of the trial scene.

Future Son of Man Sayings in Mark: General Comments

Since Bultmann it has been customary to classify in one group those Son of Man sayings which refer to the activity of the Son of Man in the future. They have been called by various names, "coming sayings" (Bultmann, Tödt), parousia sayings (Manson), and apocalyptic sayings (Perrin).[1] They are characterized by a reference to the activity of Jesus in the future, most often in connection with the second coming. They are seen as the group of Son of Man sayings (in contrast to the "suffering" sayings, and those which speak of the Son of Man's activity on earth) which are most influenced by Jewish apocalyptic literature, and the major debate about them has been whether they represent the earliest level of tradition.[2] One effect of this way of looking at the sayings has been to lump together the individual characteristics of the sayings within the group. Yet along with this tendency recent studies have begun to break down the monolithic view of the sayings, by concentrating on the

---

[1] Bultmann, Theology of the New Testament, trans. K. Grobel (Scribner's Studies in Contemporary Theology; New York: Charles Scribner's Sons, 1951), I, 30; Tödt, Son of Man, p. 32; T. W. Manson, The Teaching of Jesus (Cambridge: University Press, 1963), p. 225; Perrin, Rediscovering, p. 164.

[2] Tödt, Son of Man, p. 32, ". . . those strata of the Synoptic tradition which undoubtedly count as the most primary." He is followed by Hahn, Titles, p. 28: "The words concerning the coming Son of Man stand at the beginning of the evolving tradition." They are opposed by Eduard Schweizer, "Der Menschensohn"; Neotestamentica (Stuttgart: Zwingli Verlag, 1963), pp. 58-67, and Vielhauer, "Zur Frage," p. 570.

context and function of the sayings. Käsemann and Edwards have shown that the future Son of Man functions in a context of judgment in the eschatological judgment pronouncements and in the eschatological correlatives.[1] Therefore the first step in a re-examination of these sayings is to investigate the future Son of Man sayings to see if they fit easily into one group.

In the case of the Marcan use of these sayings, authors have seen little Marcan redaction of the sayings since they are thought to be part of the earliest received tradition.[2] In his study of the Son of Man in the synoptic tradition, Perrin, while noting that these sayings form no homogeneous group, did not pursue his research into the Marcan redaction of the Son of Man sayings beyond the study of the suffering and present sayings.[3] In the following sections of this chapter the attempt will be made to show that there was no fixed group of apocalyptic sayings available to Mark, but rather exegetical traditions which used the apocalyptic imagery found in the Marcan sayings, but which did not necessarily use Son of Man. On the other hand, we will attempt to show that there are future references to the Son of Man which did not use the imagery found in Mark. The conclusion of this examination will be that the future Son of Man sayings as found in Mark show considerable Marcan redaction, and in this sense are a Marcan creation.

Future Son of Man Sayings in Mark:
Detailed Argument

The future Son of Man sayings in Mark exist in the

---

[1] Käsemann, New Testament Questions, pp. 66-81, "Sentences of Holy Law." Richard A. Edwards, "The Eschatological Correlative as a Gattung in the New Testament," ZNW, LX (1969), 9-20.

[2] Supra, p. 150, n. 2.

[3] "Son of Man in the Synoptic Tradition," pp. 4-9.

following forms:

8:38   For whoever is ashamed of me and my words in this adulterous and sinful generation, of him will the Son of Man also be ashamed, when he comes in the glory of his Father with the holy angels.

13:26 And then they will see the Son of Man coming in clouds with great power and glory.

14:62 And Jesus said, "I am; and you will see the Son of Man sitting at the right hand of Power and coming with (meta) the clouds of heaven."

The following characteristics emerge from observation of these sayings. The references to the "coming" are present in all three sayings: in 13:26 and 14:62 in the participial form after the future tense of the verb "to see," in 8:38 in the subjunctive (elthē). The clouds are associated with the coming in 13:26 and 14:62, while "glory" is mentioned in 8:38 and 13:26, and "power" is mentioned in 13:26 and 14:62. Two of the sayings have a reference to "seeing" the coming. The saying of 8:38 stands alone in mentioning the "angels" and, in relating the Son of Man to the Father (in the glory of the Father), this saying is unique among all the Son of Man sayings.[1] In the course of the discussion on the Marcan use of the sayings the significance of this imagery will emerge. Here it can simply be noted that it is the imagery--coming, power, glory, clouds of heaven, seeing-- which gives the apocalyptic scenario to the sayings.[2]

In contrast to the Marcan form of the future Son of Man sayings, the future sayings as found in the Q tradition are

---

[1] Maria Horstmann, Studien zur Markinischen Christologie (Neutestamentliche Abhandlungen, N.F., Vol. VI; Münster: Verlag Aschendorf, 1969), pp. 53-54.

[2] By the terminology "apocalyptic imagery" and "apocalyptic scenario," we mean to designate the type of language and images used in those passages of the New Testament which approach the language and images used in what is commonly admitted as apocalyptic on the basis of a study of the Jewish intertestamental literature. See H. H. Rowley, The Relevance of Apocalyptic (3d rev. ed.; London: Lutterworth Press, 1963), esp. pp. 13-166.

noticeably devoid of such imagery. In this tradition the future sayings are found in the following forms:[1]

1. Lk 11:30; Mt 12:40

   For as Jonah became a sign to the men of Nineveh, so too will the Son of Man be a sign to this generation. (Lk)

   For as Jonah was three days and three nights in the belly of the whale, so will the Son of Man be three days and three nights in the heart of the earth. (Mt)

2. Lk 12:8; Mt 10:32

   And I tell you, everyone who acknowledges me before men, the Son of Man also will acknowledge him before the angels of God. (Lk)

   So everyone who acknowledges me before men, also I will acknowledge before my Father who is in heaven. (Mt)

3. Lk 12:40; Mt 24:44

   And you also must be ready, for the Son of Man is coming at an hour you do not expect. (Lk)

   Therefore, you also must be ready, for the Son of Man is coming at an hour you do not expect. (Mt)

4. Lk 17:24; Mt 24:27

   For as the lightning flashes and lights up the sky from one side to the other, so will the Son of Man be in his day. (Lk)

   For as the lightning comes from the east and shines as far as the west, so will be the coming (parousia) of the Son of Man. (Mt)

5. Lk 17:26; Mt 24:37, 39

   As it was in the days of Noah, so will it be in the days of the Son of Man. (Lk)

   As were the days of Noah, so will be the coming (parousia) of the Son of Man. (Mt 24:37)

   And they did not know until the flood came and swept them all away, so will be the coming of the Son of Man. (Mt 24:39)

---

[1] The assignment of a saying to Q is made on the basis of a consensus among authors, Tödt, Son of Man, pp. 47-67; Manson, Teaching of Jesus, p. 215 (following Streeter), and A. J. B. Higgins, Jesus and the Son of Man (Philadelphia: Fortress Press, 1964), p. 119.

The following saying is called a Q saying by Tödt and Manson, but not by Higgins:[1]

> 6. Lk 17:28-30
>
>> Likewise as it was in the days of Lot--they ate, they drank, they bought, they sold, they planted, they built, but on the day when Lot went out from Sodom fire and brimstone rained from heaven and destroyed them all--so will it be on the day when the Son of Man is revealed. (Cf. Mt 24:34ff.)

Tödt has pointed out that two great themes unite these sayings: the threat of judgment and the promise of salvation. He has also noted that they "are not at all dominated by an apocalyptic visionary strain."[2] Perrin, drawing on the research of Käsemann and Edwards and on his own study of the sayings has shown that they form no homogeneous group but have different settings and different functions.[3] What is important for our present purposes is the observation that, beyond alluding to the future coming of the Son of Man, there is little interest in the details of that coming. The future references are connoted with a minimum of description: by the use of estai (Lk 17:24; Mt 24:27; Lk 11:30; Mt 12:40); by the references to the revelation of the "day" of the Son of Man (Lk 17:24, 30); by the use of the term parousia (peculiar to Matthew's version of the Q sayings, Mt 24:27, 37, 39), and by the future of the verb homologein (Lk 12:8). The only use of the verb erchesthai is in the Q saying of Lk 12:40 et par where the present tense is used. Therefore, the Q sayings which refer to the future Son of Man are really called either "coming sayings" or "apocalyptic sayings" in an improper sense.

An examination of the future Son of Man sayings in the material special to both Luke and Matthew yields similar

---

[1]Ibid., p. 119. [2]Son of Man, p. 65.
[3]"Son of Man in the Synoptic Tradition," pp. 4-9.

results. In Lk 17:22 there is a reference to the desire to see the day of the Son of Man. In 21:36 the hearers are exhorted to watch so they can stand before the Son of Man. The only reference to the "coming" of the Son of Man is in the statement of 18:8b, "When the Son of Man comes, will he find faith on the earth?" The material peculiar to Matthew is more complex. Initially we will prescind from Mt 10:23, 19:28 and 25:31 since it is disputed whether these sayings are Matthean or Q.[1] In Mt 13:41 there is reference to the Son of Man "sending out his angels and gathering the elect of his kingdom." Matthew 16:27-28, though showing Matthean redaction, are obviously dependent on Mk 8:38-9:1.[2] Matthew 24:30 is a further development of Mk 13:26 and 24:39b is parallel to Lk 17:28ff. In none of these sayings is there any emphasis on the scenario of the coming which is independent of the Marcan form of the future sayings.

There remain then three sayings which are disputed as to whether they are Q or special Matthew. The attempt here will not be to resolve this dispute, but to show that two of the sayings pose no objection to the present argument, while the third saying has all the earmarks of Matthean redaction. The sayings are:

1. Mt 10:23b

    You will not complete all the cities of Israel until the Son of Man comes.

---

[1] Manson, Teaching, p. 220, and Higgins, Jesus, p. 97, call 10:23, 19:28, and 25:31 Matthean. Tödt, Son of Man, p. 60, calls 10:23 and 19:28, Q, and 25:31 Matthean (p. 73). In assigning 10:23 and 19:28 to Q, Tödt uses criteria of content rather than the normal criteria (presence in Matthew and Luke and absence in Mark) by which sayings are assigned to Q.

[2] Perrin, Rediscovering, p. 16, ". . . the Matthean and Lukan sayings are theologically motivated variations of the Markan."

2. **Mt 19:28**

   Truly I say to you, in the new world when the Son of Man shall sit on his glorious throne, you who have followed me will also sit on the twelve thrones, judging the twelve tribes of Israel.

3. **Mt 25:31**

   When the Son of Man comes in his glory and all the angels with him, then he will sit on his glorious throne.

While the first of these sayings has a reference to the "coming" of the Son of Man, it too lacks the filling out of this coming by the use of apocalyptic imagery. The second saying which is dependent on Enoch (62:26) uses the apocalyptic imagery of the grand assize, but has no reference to a coming.[1] The third saying is a mixture of two motifs: the "sitting" of the Son of Man on his throne of glory and his coming with the angels. In this sense it is best seen as a mixture of the Matthean use of Enoch (cf. Mt 19:28) and the Marcan motif of the coming in glory of the Son of Man.

The survey of the future Son of Man sayings outside of Mark yields the following conclusions. The details which characterize the coming of the Son of Man--in glory, on the clouds of heaven, with power, accompanied by angels--are peculiar to the future Son of Man sayings as they are found in Mark and in the traditions dependent on him. At this point it cannot be determined whether these Marcan sayings are Marcan creations in the strict sense or represent his use of earlier traditions. What the present observations do confirm is that there is no solid block of sayings which can be classified under any single rubric. There are rather different groups of sayings which allude to the future activity of the Son of Man, but derive their

---

[1] For the "throne of glory" see 1 Enoch 45:3; 55:4; 61:8; 62:2, 3, 5; 69:27.

meaning from the context in which they are found. The Q sayings are found in a context of the role of the Son of Man as judge, and the Matthean adaptation of these sayings adopts this function.

The next step in the argument is to examine the apocalyptic imagery found in Mark to see if it exists in other contexts in the New Testament, and then to suggest a way in which it functions in the Marcan future Son of Man sayings. In effect we will say that, while the first part of the argument shows that outside of Mark there are no future Son of Man sayings which emphasize the apocalyptic scenario, there are other texts which contain the apocalyptic imagery, but do not use Son of Man.

Early Christian Apocalyptic

We will begin our observations by examining texts which represent some examples of the earliest Christian descriptive portrayal of the return of Jesus, those from Paul's Thessalonian correspondence.[1] After this we will examine certain texts from the book of Revelation which employ similar imagery.

1 Thes 1:9-10

> For when people speak of us, they tell us what a welcome you gave us, and how you turned from idols to God, to serve a true and living God and to wait for the coming from heaven of his son, whom he raised from the dead--Jesus our deliverer from God's wrath.

The Greek of vs. 10 reads:

> kai anamenein ton huion autou ek tōn ouranōn hon ēgeiren ek tōn nekrōn, Iēsoun ton ryomenon hēmas ek tēs orgēs erchomenēs.

The context of these verses is paraenetic. Paul is encouraging

---

[1] Even if 2 Thes is deutero-Pauline, it is still dated around A.D. 70, see Willi Marxsen, *Introduction to the New Testament*, trans. G. Buswell (Philadelphia: Fortress Press, 1968), p. 44. Feine, Behm and Kümmel, *Introduction*, pp. 188-190, defend the Pauline authenticity of the letter.

his hearers and uses the return of Jesus as a motive for their steadfastness. Both Rigaux and Langevin have noted in vs. 10 a rhythmic style characteristic of pre-Pauline material.[1] The reference to the resurrection uses the pre-Pauline formula, hon ēgeiren. Paul usually expresses eschatological waiting by either nēphein (1 Thes 5:6, 8) or grēgorein (1 Cor 16:13; 1 Thes 5:6; Col 4:2), while anamenein here is a hapax legomenon in the Pauline writings. The formula ek tōn ouranōn (in the plural) is in contrast to the normal Pauline use of the singular (Gal 1:8; 2 Cor 5:2) or ap' ouranou (1 Thes 4:16; 2 Thes 1:7). Thus Paul is using here an early Christian formula of expectation of Jesus who will deliver the believer from the wrath of God.

The Christology of the formula deserves further consideration. In 1 Thes 1:3 the believers are praised for their unwavering expectation of "our Lord Jesus Christ." In 1:10 they are to await the return of "his Son" whom he raised from the dead. There is, therefore, an equation between the kyrios of 1:3 and the son of 1:10. Immediate reflection would suggest that "his son" of 1:10 is a reference to the Son of God since Paul uses "his son" when referring to Son of God in other places.[2] However, the allusion to the son coming "from the heavens" suggests another possibility. The use of Dan 7:13 in both the Marcan future sayings (esp. 13:26 and 14:62) and in Acts 7:55-56 associates the coming of the Son of Man with the heavens. In addition to this verbal contact, the context of 1 Thes 1:10 suggests a parallelism with the early Christian use of Dan 7:13. This text points to a "coming"; the people at

---

[1] Langevin, Jésus Seigneur, p. 49; Béda Rigaux, Saint Paul, Les Épitres aux Thessaloniciens (Etudes Bibliques; Paris: Librarie Lecoffre, 1956), p. 392.

[2] Ibid., p. 393, cf. Gal 1:16; 4:4, 6; Rom 1:39; 5:10.

Thessalonica are to wait for a Jesus who will come (cf. 1 Thes 4:15). The one who comes will be a glorious figure, who will come to save the believers and judge the non-believers, and his coming is an eschatological event.[1] Also it should be noted that Paul never uses the title Son of God in a context of the eschatological return of Jesus. Therefore, there are good grounds for assuming that 1 Thes 1:9-10 is an allusion to Dan 7:13 and that the reference to "his son" is an allusion to the Son of Man of Daniel. The important thing here is that it is not explicitly the use of the title Son of Man which gives the saying its apocalyptic tenor, but the reference to Dan 7:13, and also that Paul equates this son with the kyrios of vs. 3.[2]

Other texts from this same epistle look to a similar eschatological expectation, but do not contain any reference to the "son" but use the title "lord." In 1 Thes 3:13 Paul prays that:

> . . . your hearts may be strengthened and faultlessly pure in the sight of our God and Father, en tē parousia tou kyriou hēmōn Iēsou meta pantōn tōn hagiōn autou.

In the exhortatory part of the same epistle Paul writes to the community:

> For this we declare to you by the word of the Lord, that we who are alive, who are left until the coming of the Lord (tēn parousian tou kyriou) shall not precede those who have fallen asleep. For the Lord himself will descend from heaven (ap' ouranou) with a cry of command, with the archangel's call, and with the sound of the trumpet of God. And the dead in Christ will rise first; then we who are alive, who are left, shall be caught up together with them in the clouds to meet the Lord in the air; and so we shall always be with the Lord. (1 Thes 4:15-17)

---

[1]Langevin, Jesus Seigneur, p. 81.

[2]Perrin has shown a similar phenomenon in the paradidonai tradition where "Son of Man drops out and is replaced by other subjects, Kyrios Iēsous Christos, Gal 1:4, and Son of God, Gal 2:20," see "(para) didonai," p. 212.

This latter text is very interesting for here we have the full apocalyptic scenario where the Lord will come from heaven and the clouds will be the meeting place of the Lord and the believer. Again it is significant here that Son of Man is not the title used in this context but <u>kyrios</u>. In his most recent study of the use of the apocalyptic imagery in the New Testament in general and in Mark 13, Hartmann has shown that Dan 7:13 can have a strong influence on a certain passage even though the reference to the Son of Man is omitted. He writes of the above passage in Paul:

> Thus according to Paul, it is the risen Jesus who is the Son of Man who is brought forward in Dn 7:13. And Paul means that the dead Christians will be brought forward with him.[1]

and

> Thus the detail that the Christians will be caught up to meet the Lord in the clouds evidently goes back to Dn 7:13 which forms the cornerstone of Mc 13:26 <u>par</u>.[2]

A final verse which should be mentioned in the survey of the imagery of apocalyptic expectation is 2 Thes 1:7:

> . . . in the revelation of the Lord Jesus from heaven with the angels of his power.

In the book of Revelation there are three references to Dan 7:13. In 1:7 there is mention of the coming of Jesus Christ (1:5) on the clouds of heaven, but no use of the Son of Man. In 1:13 there is mention of the Son of Man without any reference to his coming on the clouds, and in 14:14 the Son of Man is "sitting" on a cloud, but there is no reference to his coming.

At this point we may summarize our observations as they pertain to uncovering the Marcan redaction of the future Son of Man sayings. The future Son of Man sayings in the Q tradition have a minimum of detail describing the activity of the Son of

---

[1] <u>Prophecy Interpreted</u>, p. 186.   [2] <u>Ibid</u>., p. 190.

Man in the future. On the other hand there is another series of
texts which looks to the return of Jesus and employs descriptive
terms and apocalyptic language which is strongly influenced by
Dan 7:13. The Christological titles in these texts vary from a
reference to "his Son" to kyrios, to Jesus. Therefore there are
two lines of tradition which converge in the Marcan future sayings. On the one hand there is the tradition emphasizing the
return of Jesus as Son of Man who will judge the unbeliever and
save the believer.[1] On the other hand there is the line of
tradition which fills out this return with the use of apocalyptic imagery, but which uses varied Christological titles of
Jesus. In a real sense then kyrios functions for Paul in
exactly the same way as Son of Man in the Marcan future sayings.
Therefore, if the Marcan sayings represent a blending of these
two streams of tradition, Marcan redactional activity is evident
in combining the traditions. It is not affirmed that Mark creates the traditions. He draws on the storehouse of early
Christian exegetical traditions available to him, the main element of which was the use of Dan 7:13 which lies at the basis of
the three Marcan future sayings.

Another thing which should be noted is that the supposed
tension between the use of Ps 110:1 (exaltation) and Dan 7:13
(parousia) in the answer of Jesus in 14:62 is forced. However,
in the texts from 1 Thessalonians, which represent the traditions of a Hellenistic Jewish church, the motif of exaltation
and of the parousia are combined. The people at Thessalonica
are told to wait anxiously for the return of the risen Son or
the exalted kyrios. In this sense then Hahn's schematism for
the use of Christological titles is forced.[2] He cannot simply

---

[1]Tödt, Son of Man, p. 61.

[2]Vielhauer, "Zur Frage," p. 587.

still affirm a linear development of Christology where the parousia expectation yields to an exaltation Christology followed by a Christology of a more philosophical or metaphysical bent. Also it is illegitimate to assign definite titles to each stage. The Christology of 1 Thessalonians shows both that parousia and exaltation Christology existed together and that Son of Man which for Hahn is used at the earliest stage for the parousia Christology is not used, but rather kyrios which for Hahn is a term of exaltation in the Hellenistic environment.

Thus far it has been suggested that Mark does not simply receive the future Son of Man sayings from the tradition but is active in composing the final form of the sayings. The question still remains as to why Mark has done this, and how this activity of his leads to an understanding of the Christology of the trial narrative. In order to answer these questions we must discuss in greater detail the three future Son of Man sayings in Mark.

Mark's Use of Future Son of Man Sayings

Analysis of 8:38 in the Context of 8:27-9:1

The importance of this section to an understanding of the gospel of Mark as a whole has long been recognized.[1] The "Galilean springtime" is over and Jesus turns his face to Jerusalem where he will suffer and die. In a very real sense Mark begins his Christology here. The title, christos, forgotten since the

---

[1] Edward Mally, "The Gospel of Mark," Jerome Biblical Commentary, ed. Raymond Brown, Joseph Fitzmyer, and Roland Murphy (Englewood Cliffs, N.J.: Prentice Hall, 1968), II, 41. Nineham, St. Mark, p. 223, "This passage can only be understood if full weight is given to its position at the opening of a new section of the gospel." Perrin, "Christology of Mark," p. 177.

superscription (1:1), reappears. All the uses of Son of Man, except 2:10 and 2:28, are found after 8:27 and the whole subsequent section is built around the three Passion predictions.[1] In addition to the Christological statements the section is permeated by an emphasis on the instruction of the disciples in the meaning of the death of Jesus.[2]

What has not been noted before is the relation of 8:27-9:1 to the trial scene. There is the same piling up of Christological titles as is found in the trial. The scene begins with Peter's confession in which Jesus accepts the title, Christos (8:29), but commands Peter to silence. This is then followed by the first Passion prediction in the form of a Son of Man saying rooted in the paradidonai tradition (8:31).[3] In the following verses (8:34-38) five scattered sayings on discipleship have been brought together.[4] The scene culminates in the double sayings of 8:38 and 9:1 which combine a threat and a word of consolation.[5] The saying of 8:38 is the first of the Marcan future Son of Man sayings and the first to describe the coming of the Son of Man in apocalyptic imagery. Also, this verse is unique among the Son of Man sayings in relating the Son of Man to the Father.[6] Thus we have the same elements which are present in

---

[1] Ibid., p. 179.

[2] Ibid., and Lightfoot, History and Interpretation, pp. 76-80.

[3] Horstmann, Studien, p. 55, notes that two different Son of Man traditions are joined in the pericope. See also Perrin, "(para)didonai," p. 212.

[4] Ernst Haenchen, "Die Komposition von Mk VIII.28-IX.1 und Par," NovT, VI (1963), 92; Weg Jesu, p. 297.

[5] Haenchen, "Komposition," p. 96, and Günther Bornkamm, "Die Verzögerung der Parusie," In Memoriam Ernst Lohmeyer, ed. W. Schmauch (Stuttgart: Evangelisches Verlagswerk, 1951), pp. 116-119.

[6] Horstmann, Studien, pp. 53-54.

the trial scene--the use of Christos (8:29; 14:61), a relation of Jesus to the Father (8:38; 14:61), the future Son of Man saying (8:38; 14:62), a saying of Jesus which functions as threat to opponents and consolation to the believers (8:38; 9:1; 14:62).[1] The only parallel which is not immediately evident is the absence of a reference to the suffering Son of Man in the trial scene. However, in 8:31 the reference to the suffering Son of Man is in the form of a prediction. In the trial scene this prediction is fulfilled as is evident in the setting, and in the explicit repetition of the three agents of Jesus' suffering (priests, high priests, and scribes, 8:31; 14:53). Therefore, Mark makes here the same sort of basic Christological statement, in relatively the same sequence which he will make in the trial scene.

Since the main focus of the present investigation is on the future Son of Man sayings, we must investigate 8:38 in more detail. Tödt, Käsemann and, most recently, Perrin have subjected this saying to a thorough tradition-historical analysis.[2] Perrin notes that Lk 12:8, "And I tell you, every one who acknowledges me before men, the Son of Man also will acknowledge before the angels of God," represents the earliest form of the saying.[3] In contrast to Tödt who sees an authentic saying of Jesus here, Perrin finds that the saying arises from the early

---

[1] On Mk 14:62 as a judgment against the opponents of Jesus see Klostermann, Markus, p. 156, and Lohmeyer, Markus, p. 329. Taylor says the allusion to Ps 110 is as a symbol of triumph, Mark, p. 569.

[2] Tödt, Son of Man, pp. 40-46, "8:38 is the only Son of Man logion in Mark which with a certain degree of probability can be traced back to Jesus' preaching" (p. 40); Käsemann, "Sentences," p. 77; Perrin, Rediscovering, pp. 185-191. Perrin holds that Mark 8:38 is a reinterpretation of Lk 12:8.

[3] Rediscovering, pp. 187-188.

Church and serves as an "eschatological judgment pronouncement" (Sätze heiligen Rechts).[1] The saying is then expanded by bringing in elements from the apocalyptic Son of Man tradition, evident in 13:26 and 14:62. These would include the reference to the "coming" and to "glory." By doing this Mark maintains the original thrust of the saying which was in the form of a threat to an unbelieving generation, to a generation unwilling to follow him on the way of the cross, but by his reference to the parousia puts the actualization of this threat into the future.

The addition of 9:1, "Truly I say to you, there are some standing here who will not taste death before they see the kingdom of God come with power," is significant for an understanding of this section. The saying has all the earmarks of Marcan redaction. The introduction kai elegen autois is a favorite Marcan introductory phrase.[2] Further Marcan redaction is found in the emphasis on "seeing" the parousia (cf. 13:26; 14:62), the use of power and glory in this connection (8:38; 9:1; 10:37; 13:26) and the similarity in form to 13:30.[3] Thus 9:1 serves as a Marcan conclusion of the section 8:27-9:1 giving the thrust of the whole scene a double focus--judgment and rejection of those who will not follow the suffering Son of Man, consolation and hope to those who do.

The previous analyses of this section thus provide an understanding of the full richness of the pattern Mark

---

[1] Ibid., p. 186.

[2] 2:27; 4:2; 4:21; 4:24; 6:4; 6:10; 7:9; 8:21. Also the historical present is found in the same introductory manner, 1:38; 3:4; 4:13; 4:35; 6:31; 7:18; 10:11; 11:33; 12:16; [14:27,] 30, 32, 34, 36, 37.

[3] On "seeing" the parousia see supra, p. 94; on the relation to 13:30 and other redactional elements see Perrin, "The Composition of Mark ix, 1," NovT, XI (1969), 67-70.

establishes in this section. In the initial verses Mark establishes that to confess Christ involves a willingness to follow in the way of the suffering Son of Man. The coming Son of Man vindicates the suffering Son of Man since it is a judgment on those who refuse to follow this way. The addition of 9:1 which is a source of consolation to those who do follow also brings the arrival of the kingdom into close connection with the arrival of the Son of Man. In this sense Mark re-apocalypticizes the tradition, by expanding the future role of the Son of Man evident in the earlier version of Lk 12:8 into a full blown scenario of the second coming, and by making it the initial moment in the establishment of God's rule on earth.[1] Such an observation is supported by the radical orientation to the future which Mark's gospel takes after 8:27. Prior to 8:27 the kingdom is proclaimed as a present reality manifest in the ministry of Jesus (1:15; 4:11; 4:26; 4:30). After 8:27 the kingdom takes on a future dimension: 9:1, it is coming in power; all the sayings on entering the kingdom come after 8:27 (9:47; 10:23-25). In 11:10 the paean is "blessed in the coming kingdom of God"; in 14:25 the Eucharist is in anticipation of the drinking of wine in the future kingdom, and Joseph of Arithmathea is characterized as waiting for the kingdom (15:43). Also, as has been noted, the future Son of Man sayings are all after 8:27. The resurrection is first mentioned in 8:31 and thereafter seven

---

[1] The third element of the pattern we discuss--suffering, vindication through the coming of the Son of Man, new community--admits of the most variation. It appears in 9:1 as the coming of the kingdom; in 13:27 as the gathering of the elect, and in 14:58 as the new _naos_. What unites these three is the apocalyptic motif of a definitive new stage in human history through the intervention of God. Also the coming of the kingdom in the New Testament has a double focus (a) the establishment of God's rule (kingdom in the active sense), and (b) the effect of God's rule on the faithful who are to share in or be members of this kingdom, see Perrin, _Rediscovering_, pp. 57. 60.

times (9:9, 9:31; 10:27-31; 10:34; 12:18-27; 14:28; 16:6). There are other elements which serve to give the gospel a definite future orientation after 8:27. While in the earlier sections there is no temporal limitation put on the Messianic Secret, in 9:9 the secret is to be kept until the resurrection. The instruction of the disciples which follows each Passion prediction has a definite future orientation, and the request of John and James (10:35-39) has an eschatological orientation in the desire "to sit at your right and your left in your glory." More important perhaps than all these individual observations is that the gospel has in effect a twofold conclusion, in ch. 13 and in the Passion narrative. The discourse of ch. 13 is radically oriented to the future and the Passion narrative concludes with a command to go to Galilee where the disciples will "see" Jesus.

In summary then, the Marcan redaction of 8:38 in the context of 8:27-9:1 shows the following concerns. He has taken over an eschatological judgment pronouncement which used Son of Man and made it into a full-blown apocalyptic scenario. He has done this in definite contexts, the first of which is the gathering together of Christological titles which are important to his gospel, where the titles are understood in interrelation with each other. The suffering Son of Man gives content to Christos and the future Son of Man saying relates the expected Jesus to the suffering Jesus. The second context which he establishes is the pattern of suffering, vindication and judgment, and future coming of the kingdom. In subsequent pages we hope to show that the future Son of Man sayings perform a similar function of giving meaning to other titles and exist in a similar pattern of suffering, vindication, arrival of a new stage of God's activity.

Analysis of 13:26 in the Context of the Apocalyptic Discourse

The second future Son of Man saying in Mark comes at the high point of the eschatological discourse.[1] After the trials associated with the defilement of the temple (13:14), and the arrival of the false christs and false prophets (13:22), the community is given a word of encouragement by the mention of the coming Son of Man. In the use of the Son of Man saying in 13:26, we find the fullest use of the apocalyptic scenario which is connoted not only by the saying itself but by the surrounding verses.[2] Though the section 13:24-27 has most often been thought to be traditional material, there are elements of Marcan redaction which show his theological concerns.[3] The introductory verse, "but in those days, after the tribulation" shows the familiar Marcan technique of a double temporal indication in introductory sentences where the second temporal indication shows a definite Marcan purpose.[4] In this case the coming of the Son of Man will not simply be contemporaneous with the tribulation (in those days) but will follow upon it. Since Mark is anxious to distinguish the false messiahs which come during the tribulation from the Son of Man who comes after it, he has disassociated the parousia from the final tribulation. Here again he has used the Son of Man saying in a radically future sense.

---

[1] Pesch, <u>Naherwartungen</u>, p. 157, "Die vier Versen [13:24-27] bilden das Mittelstück der ganzen Rede."

[2] Tödt, <u>Son of Man</u>, p. 33, says that 13:26 is closest to the sphere of Jewish apocalyptic.

[3] Beasley-Murray, <u>Commentary on Mark Thirteen</u>, pp. 87-93; and Pesch, <u>Naherwartungen</u>, pp. 157-174, show the traditional elements.

[4] 1:32; 35; 10:30; 14:30, 43; 15:42; 16:2, see Hawkins, <u>Horae Synopticae</u>, pp. 139-141, and Pesch, <u>Naherwartungen</u>, p. 157.

The saying itself in 13:26 shows some indications of Marcan redaction. It seems to be dependent on 14:62. While 14:62 in citing Dan 7:13 follows Theodotion in having meta tōn nephelōn, 13:26 has en nephelais which is found in no LXX version.[1] The reference to the "heavens" present both in Daniel and in 14:62 is also omitted and in its place the generalized summary "with much power and glory is substituted." Hartmann has suggested that this is an allusion to Dan 7:14, but even if this is so, Mark is working more freely in 13:26 with traditional material than in 14:62.[2] If we add to this observation the tension already noted between 13:24b-25 which clearly deal with judgment and 13:26-27 which shift the emphasis to the gathering of the elect, then there is good evidence that 13:24-27, though using traditional language, owes its present form to Mark's composition and structure.[3]

It can now be seen what function the Son of Man plays here. As was seen in 8:27-9:1 a definite pattern of suffering, judgment, coming of the Son of Man and establishment of the kingdom emerged. In the Marcan apocalyptic discourse of ch. 13 there is no explicit reference to the suffering of Jesus or the Son of Man. This is explained by the function of the whole discourse which is not to make an explicit Christological statement, but to be an eschatological paraenesis to the believers.[4]

---

[1] Lambrecht, Redaktion, pp. 181-184, discusses the variations in the LXX versions.

[2] Hartmann, Prophecy Interpreted, p. 174.

[3] Supra, pp. 132-133.

[4] Gaston, No Stone, pp. 47-61, stresses the paraenetic nature of the discourse. Lightfoot, The Gospel Message, p. 50, writes: "A remarkable feature of the discourse is that it contains at least as much counsel and warning as apocalyptic revelation."

There are indications, however, that the fate of the believer and Jesus in suffering are brought close together. In 13:9-13 the term *paradidonai* which as Perrin has shown has become a *terminus technicus* for the Passion of Jesus, is used three times in relation to the follower of Jesus (13:9, 11, 12). Like Jesus the Christian will be "handed over" to the Sanhedrin; like Jesus he will be handed over by one of his intimates. The motif of suffering present in 8:31 reappears in ch. 13, but in this case it is the disciple who suffers in place of Jesus. Also the very position of the apocalyptic discourse immediately preceding the Passion narrative makes of it a farewell of Jesus before he begins his own path of suffering.[1]

The motif of judgment arises from the Old Testament texts of 13:24b-25. As was noted earlier these texts employ the imagery of the "day of the Lord" and show that the arrival of the Son of Man will have the same double focus as the day of the Lord--a day of deliverance for those faithful to the Lord and a day of judgment for those unfaithful, a day of wrath as well as a day of salvation.[2] The vindication and salvation of the community comes with the arrival of the Son of Man. As was noted, the future of the verbs of "seeing" in Mark shows a special concern of Mark for the parousia and characterizes it as a manifestation or epiphany.[3] Pesch wants to argue that the subject

---

[1]Lightfoot, The Gospel Message, notes the following contacts with the Passion narrative: the use of the verb "to hand over" (p. 51); the stress on Jesus knowing of the betrayal beforehand (p. 52); the emphasis on "the hour" (p. 52); and the time designations of 13:35 (p. 53).

[2]On the double quality of the "day of the Lord," see Gerhard Von Rad, Old Testament Theology, trans. D. M. G. Stalker (New York: Harper and Row, 1965), II, 119-125, 137, 289, "Jahweh is to come unexpectedly and his day is to bring judgment upon the godless; but for those who fear God, the sun of salvation will shine forth."

[3]Supra, pp. 93-95.

of opsontai in 13:26 are only the unbelievers or deceivers who see the parousia as judgment since this is always the case in the Marcan use of opsontai.[1] However, this view is not supported by 9:1 and 16:7 where it is the faithful ones who will see the parousia. Rather it seems safer to say that the "seeing" emphasizes the revelational quality of the coming of the Son of Man. Whether it is seen as judgment or salvation depends on the disposition of the one seeing, so that both nuances are present in Mk 13:26. The gathering of the elect in 13:27 completes the pattern of suffering, vindication, judgment, and at the same time specifies what the establishment of the kingdom of 9:1 means for the believer of Mark's time. He is given the promise that he will be one of the "elect" the nucleus of the new community which will be initiated only with the coming of the Son of Man.

Therefore, as in 8:38, so too in 13:26 Mark uses a future Son of Man saying with a definite theological purpose. By putting it in the full apocalyptic scenario he is able to make a definite Christological statement that the Jesus who will suffer is the one who will return as Son of Man. He can also make a definite eschatological statement by orienting his community to the return of Jesus, and finally he is able to make an "ecclesiological" statement by saying that the return of Jesus will bring with it the inauguration of the new community.[2]

---

[1] Pesch, Naherwartungen, pp. 167-169.

[2] "Ecclesiological" here is not meant in the technical sense that Mark pictures Jesus as founding an ekklēsia (the word is never used by Mark), but only in reference to Mark's view that Jesus was engaged in forming the nucleus of an eschatological community.

Analysis of 14:62 in the Context of the Trial Narrative

In this section we will attempt to show that the same pattern which existed in the use of the two previous future sayings, that of suffering, vindication and judgment through the parousia, and a reference to a new community, is found in the Christology of 14:62. Secondly, the implications for Mark's theology of the convergence of major Christological titles in the trial scene as well as their interrelation must be studied.

The motif of the suffering of the Son of Man arises here primarily from the context. An essential element of the <u>paradidonai</u> Passion predictions is that Jesus will be handed over to the Jewish officials who are mentioned by name in 8:31 and 10:33. As we have seen the introduction to the trial scene, 14:53, is a Marcan composition which makes the trial scene a fulfillment of these predictions. The mocking in 14:65 is also very close to the third Passion prediction, so much so that Strecker holds it to be a Marcan composition based on the other Passion predictions and on the Passion narrative.[1] Therefore it predicts and anticipates the suffering of the Son of Man in the trial narrative.

The second element in the pattern uncovered was an allusion to the coming of the Son of Man in a context of the vindication of Jesus and judgment on those who do not accept Jesus. In 8:38 the form of the saying as an eschatological judgment pronouncement supports this, while in 13:24-27 the motif arises from the use of the Old Testament texts. Commentators on 14:62 have noted a dramatic irony in the answer of Jesus in 14:62; he who is being judged will pass judgment on his accusers as ruler

---

[1] Strecker, "The Passion-and-Resurrection Predictions," pp. 434-435.

of the world; at the deepest point of his humiliation Jesus is exalted and proclaimed the coming Son of Man.[1] However, in addition to these generalizations there is one specific point which can be underscored as connoting judgment in a strong manner. As was noted earlier, commentators (e.g., Glasson and McArthur) have been too quick to note a tension between the use of Ps 110 and Dan 7:13. It is true that the earliest use of the psalm was in a context of exaltation/resurrection.[2] However, commentators have not given sufficient attention to the use of the whole psalm in the New Testament. Since Hartmann has shown that very often "midrashic meditation" on Old Testament texts without citation of exact words and phrases explains the material in the New Testament which surrounds a single explicit reference, we may attempt to see if further reflection on Ps 110 explains the context of its use in 14:62.[3]

In the Old Testament Ps 110 is a royal psalm, celebrating the enthronement of the king and promising him Yahweh's aid. This enthronement is in terms of a victory (vs. 2) and the king reigns in the midst of his enemies (vs. 3). In the latter half of the psalm (vss. 5-7) the judgment of the Lord on the enemies takes place when the victory is complete.[4] Therefore the imagery of the psalm suggests the enthronement of the king surrounded by his enemies, but vindicated in the face of them and judging them. Such a scene corresponds directly to the trial scene, so that in many respects the trial is a "midrash" on the

---

[1] Conzelmann, "History and Theology," p. 190; Grundmann, Markus, p. 302; Lohmeyer, Markus, p. 329; Nineham, St. Mark, p. 299; Taylor, Mark, p. 569.

[2] Lindars, New Testament Apologetic, p. 32.

[3] Prophecy Interpreted, pp. 145-178, 206-252.

[4] Mowinckel, Psalms in Israel's Worship, I, 54, 63-65.

psalm. Jesus is seen at the right hand of the Father, while simultaneously in the midst of his enemies. His exaltation is at the same time victory over the enemies who are subject to him.

Support for the influence of the total meaning of the psalm on the trial narrative comes from an examination of its use in other places in the New Testament. In 1 Cor 15:24-25, Paul writes:

> Then comes the end, when he delivers the kingdom to God the Father after destroying every rule and every authority and power. For he must reign until he has put all his enemies under his feet. (Cf. Ps 110:1b.)[1]

Conzelmann writes of these verses:

> Gott hat seine basileia für einen bestimmten Zeitraum, von der Auferweckung Christi (die ja seine Erhöhung ist) bis zu dessen Parusie, und zu einem bestimmten Zweck, der Vernichtung der feindlichen Mächte, an Christus delegiert. Dieser gibt die Herrschaft an Gott zurück, "nachdem" er alle Feinde vernichtet hat. Die Vernichtung beginnt mit der Erhöhung; das ist ja der Zweck seiner Inthronisation.[2]

Thus Paul cites Ps 110 in a context wider than the exaltation of Jesus but with reference to the subjection of the enemies, a subjection which will be complete at the parousia (vs. 23). In Romans 8:33-34, Paul writes:

> Who shall bring any charge against God's elect? It is God who justifies; who is to condemn? Is it Christ Jesus who died, yes, who was raised from the dead, who is at the right hand of God, who indeed intercedes for us? (Ps 110:1.)

In the context Paul does not use Ps 110 simply as a proof text for the resurrection of Jesus, but as part of a theolcgoumenon on the justification of the Christian. No one can judge the

---

[1] Paul's Text reads, achri hou thē pantas tous echthrous hypo tous podas autou, while the LXX reads, heōs an thō tous echthrous sou hypopodion tōn podōn sou.

[2] Hans Conzelmann, Der Erste Brief an die Korinther (Kritisch-Exegetischer Kommentar über das Neue Testament [Meyer Kommentar]; 11th ed.; Göttingen: Vandenhoeck und Ruprecht, 1969), pp. 321-322.

Christian because Jesus in his exalted state intercedes for him. The presupposition to the Pauline statement here is that the exalted Jesus has a role in declaring the Christian upright. Therefore Ps 110:1 is cited in a context larger than a proof of the resurrection, and in a context which underlines the role of Jesus in judgment. By considering this usage and the usage in 1 Cor 15:24-25, we see that there is no tension between exaltation, judgment, and parousia. The exaltation of Jesus is the subjection of the enemies to him which will be complete at the parousia. In this light the sequence of 1 Cor 15:24-25 is important. Similarly in Mk 14:62b the addition of Dan 7:13 and the complex of ideas associated with it (judgment, rule, giving of kingdom, cf. 13:26) compliments the meaning of Ps 110:1 in 14:62a and creates a sequence like that of 1 Cor 15:24-25. Thus the scriptural citations become keys to lead the reader to the meaning of the whole psalm, so that the theme of vindication, judgment and victory over enemies is conveyed by the citation, and the pattern of suffering-vindication-judgment, noted in 8:38 and 13:26, is continued.

The final element in the pattern we have discerned is that the arrival of the Son of Man brings with it the inception of a new stage of God's activity in history, in 9:1, the establishment of the kingdom, and in 13:26, the gathering of the elect. In the trial scene the second half of the temple saying which, as we have seen, points to the new community completes the pattern of suffering-vindication-new action of God in history. However, there is a problem with this view. In contrast to the two previous sayings (9:1, 13:26-27) where this new action of God is addressed to disciples and is put directly on the lips of Jesus, the temple saying of 14:58 is not put directly on Jesus' lips, and the Christological affirmation of 14:62 is addressed to opponents, not to disciples. Also in the trial narrative, Jesus makes no definite answer to the question about the temple saying, but merely keeps silent. Though the temple saying is for Mark a true statement of Jesus, Mark does not have Jesus here affirm its truth. The reader is given no assurance that, although Jesus predicts to his enemies his own vindication, the community is immediately involved. In this light, the intercalation of the trial narrative within the story of Peter's denial and its position immediately after the flight of the disciples becomes important. Thanks to the studies of Weeden and Tyson, it can be said that the disciples in Mark assume a "symbolic" role.[1] They represent attitudes of faith present in Mark's community, and their relations with Jesus mirror crises in Mark's time. Since these disciples have left Jesus in the isolation of his Passion there is no direct Trostwort for them to counter the Drohwort of 14:62. The opponents of Jesus will see the return of the Son of Man as judgment. It is not said directly what this means for the disciple. For Mark the inability of the disciples to follow Jesus in the way to the cross means that they will not understand the full implications of the coming of the Son of Man. Also there is no further reference in the Passion narrative to the return of Jesus until after the resurrection and here the message is given to those who actually do follow Jesus on the way to the cross (15:40; 16:1, 7). Thus by joining the Christological material of 14:62 and the temple saying of 14:58 in the trial narrative, Mark

---

[1] T. J. Weeden, "The Heresy that Necessitated Mark's Gospel," and Mark-Traditions in Conflict (Philadelphia: Fortress Press, 1971); Joseph Tyson, "The Blindness of the Disciples," JBL, LXXX (1961), 261-268. See also Alfred Kuby, "Zur Konzeption des Markus-Evangeliums," ZNW, XLIX (1958), 52-64.

continues the pattern of the eschatological expectation of the return of the Son of Man and the founding of a new community, but he does this in a manner which is less clear than in other sections, and in a manner which leaves the future ambiguous for a community which like the disciples denies Jesus at the moment of greatest crisis.

Son of Man and the Other Titles of the Trial Scene

Thus far we have seen how the Christology of 14:62 is related to the other places in Mark's gospel where a future Son of Man saying is also found. Now it is necessary to discuss the relation of the Son of Man title in 14:62 to the other titles of the trial narrative. The question of the high priest reads: "Are you the Christ, the Son of the Blessed?" The answer of Jesus is three part: the affirmation, egō eimi, the citation of Ps 110:1, the reference to the Son of Man sitting at the right hand of power and the citation of Dan 7:13, the Son of Man coming with the clouds of heaven. Neither of the titles of the question appears in the answer, so the answer is not simply an answer, but a new qualification given to the question. The first thing that must be noted is that prior to 14:62 the two titles of the question, Christos and Son of the Blessed (of God) have not been used properly of Jesus. While Christos appears as a designation of Jesus six times in Mark, as has been noted (1:1; 8:29; 9:41; 12:35; 14:61; 15:32), the only places where the use is titular are 1:1; 8:29; 14:62, and 15:32.[1] The usage in the superscription mirrors a Christian usage where Jesus Christ has become a proper name as well as a title. The only

---

[1] Supra, pp. 89-91; 13:21 is not listed since it does not apply to Jesus.

places where Jesus responds when the title Christos is adressed to him are 8:29 and 14:62. At Caesarea Philippi, though Jesus does not reject the title, he enjoins silence and then qualifies its application to him by the saying on the necessity of the suffering of the Son of Man (8:31). In 14:62 Jesus accepts the title openly, but qualifies it in relation to the coming Son of Man. The fact that silence is enjoined in 8:30, while the title is publicly proclaimed and admitted in 14:62 suggests that Mark waits until 14:62 to give the definitive meaning to Jesus as Christos, which appears at the beginning of the gospel. The Christos for Mark is the Jesus who must suffer, but his suffering looks beyond the passion to the parousia at which time Jesus receives the fullness of the messianic office.[1]

We have already noted in Chap. II that huios tou eulogētou is a Marcan surrogate for Son of God.[2] A survey of Son of God in Mark reveals the following pattern.

Usages in which the "Hellenistic" Son of God formula is used:[3]

    3:11   The demons cry out, "You are a Son of God."

    5:7   The evil spirit cries out, "Jesus, Son of the Most high God."

    15:39   The Centurion says, "Truly this was a (the) Son of God."

---

[1] The use of Christos in Mk 15:32 with ho basileus tou Israēl puts a false Christology and eschatology on the lips of the high priests and scribes, infra, pp. 198-201

[2] Supra, p. 90, esp. n. 1.

[3] "Hellenistic" is used to designate the explicit use of huios tou theou. Scholars, in general, hold that the title arose in a Hellenistic Jewish rather than Palestinian Jewish environment under the influence of the theios anēr figures, Hahn, Titles, pp. 222-292; Fuller, Foundations, p. 268; Bultmann, Theology, I, 50.

Usages which are close to Jewish terminology:[1]

    1:11   You are my Son, the beloved (the baptism)

    9:7   This is my Son, the beloved (transfiguration)

    14:61   Are you the Christ, the son of the Blessed?

In general authors who discuss the Son of God in Mark tend to lump all these denominations of Jesus together and discuss the meaning of Son of God in Mark.[2] Betz holds that the combination of the two usages (Hellenistic and Jewish) represents a Marcan combination of the <u>theios anēr</u> title (Son of God) with the title for the eschatological messianic king.[3] Mark has a further purpose in mind in using the two forms of the title. In the case of the first two usages (3:11; 5:7) Jesus counsels silence and does not explicitly accept the title. In the baptism and transfiguration, though the scenes appear public, there is no reference that anyone except Jesus heard the address "my son," and in the case of the transfiguration, silence is again ordered concerning the whole incident. Mark has created, then, a definite pattern to his Son of God Christology. In the public life of Jesus it is on the lips of demons and denotes a Christology which Jesus does not accept. In those places (the Jewish

---

[1] "Jewish" is used to designate the terminology as influenced by the Old Testament. Here the whole people, kings and people with a special commission by God are designated sons of God, Oscar Cullmann, <u>The Christology of the New Testament</u>, trans. Shirley C. Guthrie and Charles Hall (Philadelphia: Westminster Press, 1959), pp. 272-273. The use in Mk 1:11 and 9:7 reflects the influence of Ps 2:7, "You are my son, today I have begotten you," and Isa 42:1, "Behold my servant whom I uphold, my chosen (<u>ho agapētos</u>) in whom my soul delights," Lindars, <u>New Testament Apologetic</u>, pp. 139-152.

[2] Vielhauer, "Erwägungen"; Hans D. Betz, "Jesus as Divine Man," <u>Jesus and the Historian</u>, ed. Thomas Trotter (Philadelphia: Westminster Press, 1968), pp. 114-133.

[3] <u>Ibid.</u>, p. 122.

usages) where the title is accurate, it is not public. Therefore Mark holds the real meaning of the title in suspension until the trial scene. One title is public but inaccurate; the other secret but accurate.

In his analysis of the Marcan use of the earthly Son of Man sayings and the suffering sayings, Perrin has shown that Mark uses Son of Man to counter a false Christology which portrays Jesus as a divine man who did not have to suffer.[1] The work of Weeden suggests that Son of God was a title used of Jesus by proponents of a false Christology.[2] Therefore, just as in the case of <u>Christos</u>, so too does Son of God receive its definitive and correct meaning in the trial scene. Jesus publicly accepts the title Son of the Blessed, but he qualifies it in reference to the future Son of Man. The true meaning of Jesus as Son of God will be known only when he returns in glory as the victorious Son of Man. Therefore, Son of Man serves to give a correct understanding of not only the earthly ministry of Jesus, and his suffering, but also of his status as Son of God.

Conclusion

In order to make a final statement about the Christology of the trial scene, it will be helpful to review some of the conclusions arrived at thus far, in order to see why Mark has brought the titles together in the trial scene and how this

---

[1] Perrin, "Creative Use of Son of Man Traditions by Mark," pp. 385f. Betz holds that Mark accepts the Son of God "divine man" Christology, but re-interprets it in accord with his purpose, "Jesus as Divine Man," p. 122.

[2] Weeden, "The Heresy," pp. 148-154. The use of Son of God by "heretics" in early Christianity is attested by the <u>Didache</u> 16:4, ". . . for as lawlessness increases, they shall hate one another and persecute and betray, and then shall appear the deceiver of the world as a Son of God (<u>hōs huios theou</u>) and shall do signs and wonders."

relates to the Christology of his gospel. Previous research has confirmed the importance of Son of Man to Mark's gospel. His redactional activity is evident in the composition of earthly sayings, and in the structuring of the middle section of his gospel around the suffering sayings. The future sayings were thought to be the area where Marcan literary activity was least evident. We have shown that Mark was active in creating "apocalyptic" Son of Man sayings which do not exist in the tradition prior to Mark or in any other tradition independent of him. The function of these sayings is to emphasize that Jesus comes in solemn glory to judge his opponents and gather in the elect. Mark has worked these sayings into a pattern of suffering, judgment and salvation of the elect. The suffering of Jesus and the meaning of his life will be clear when he returns.

A second major feature of Mark's Christology is that the meaning of Christological titles is held in suspension until the trial scene. Whatever nuances and qualifications are given to the Messianic Secret it is a definite feature of the final structure of Mark's gospel. No Christological title is made publicly and accepted as such by Jesus until the trial scene. Some are made publicly and rejected (Son of God); some are made publicly, accepted, but qualified in their meaning (Christos in 8:29) and silence is enjoined; some are made and accepted (Son in 1:11 and 9:7), but no publicity is connoted. In the trial scene Mark brings together major concerns, the pattern of suffering to vindication begun in 8:27 and the unveiling of the Messianic Secret.[1]

---

[1] De Tillesse, Le Secret Messianique, p. 337, "La question solennelle du grand prêtre et la non moins solennelle réponse de Jésus indiquent que là se trouve, pour Marc, l'aboutissement et le terme de tout son évangile. Tout ce qui avait précédé tendait vers ce moment suprême."

The debate over whether 14:62 connotes an exaltation or parousia reference seems resolved in favor of a parousia expectation, but not in an exclusive sense. For Mark, Jesus is the exalted one who will return. Marcan redaction shows that he has not simply taken over the parousia expectation of earliest Christianity but created his own version of parousia expectation.[1] The Jesus who reigns will return, but his reign has not been definitively established until his return. In 14:62 Mark draws on previous exegetical traditions to make such a statement. The possibilities inherent in these traditions where Ps 110 came to be used for the victorious reign of Jesus and where Dan 7:13 was used for the return of the Son of Man enabled Mark to combine these traditions into a single statement.

The question still remains as to why he took Son of Man as the title *par excellence* for his Christology. Prior to Mark there was no developed Son of Man Christology, but rather various exegetical traditions which used Son of Man. The closest thing to a Son of Man Christology is in Q, but Mark does not seem to know Q, but rather the traditions which Q used.[2] Also Q has no emphasis on the Passion of Jesus, so, even if Mark had known Q, it would have been inadequate for his purposes. The Son of Man Christology as it is found in Mark is then in a real sense a Marcan creation. Why does he create this Christology and why does he use Son of Man?

The discussion of Son of Man as an independent title is misleading. Perrin has shown in contrast to Tödt and the

---

[1] Mark does this in two ways: (a) by combining an exaltation and parousia Christology, and (b) more importantly, by casting his apocalyptic teaching in the form of narrative.

[2] On the Q Christology, see Tödt, Son of Man, pp. 232-283.

prevailing opinions that there was no pre-Christian Jewish apocalyptic figure of the Son of Man which early Christian reflection adopted.[1] In the earliest Christian exegetical traditions what takes place is the use of Dan 7:13 as a reflection on the resurrection of Jesus, in much the same manner that Dan 7:13 was used in the Jewish tradition as a reflection on the translation of Enoch.[2] Thus Son of Man does not enter the Christian tradition as an independent title, but as part of early Christian use of the Old Testament. The fact then that it was used in previous exegetical traditions enabled Mark to modify and adapt these traditions to his own purpose. Its use in traditions associated with the coming of Jesus in judgment (the Q eschatological judgment pronouncements and the eschatological correlatives) enabled Mark to use Son of Man in the fully developed apocalyptic sayings of 8:38; 13:26; and 14:62. Its use in exegetical traditions associated with the resurrection and exaltation of Jesus enabled him to form sayings on the earthly ministry of Jesus as the manifestation of the _exousia_ of the risen Jesus.[3] Finally its use in the _paradidonai_ traditions of the Passion apologetic of the early Church enabled Mark to create sayings about the suffering Son of Man. Thus Mark uses Son of Man precisely because it was not a fixed title but rather a symbol or evocative term to which he could give content in terms of his own purpose.[4]

---

[1] Perrin, "The Son of Man in Ancient Judaism and Primitive Christianity: A Suggestion," _Biblical Research_, XI (1966), 1-12.

[2] _Ibid._, p. 10.

[3] Perrin, "Son of Man in the Synoptic Tradition," pp. 18-23.

[4] In this sense redaction criticism runs counter to the "titular Christology" which has been dominant since Bousset. It is no longer sufficient to simply study either the _religionsgeschichtlich_ background of a title or its use in traditions

By the use of this designation for Jesus, Mark is able to create a consistent Christology and time sequence for his theology. The earthly ministry is an epiphany of the Son of Man. It is also a call to follow Jesus in suffering and death. The future sayings indicate that the real meaning of the earthly ministry and the suffering will be known only in the return of the Son of Man. Mark thus forms a consistent schema for the past of Jesus, the present tribulation of the community and their future hope. This explains the pattern of suffering, parousia and new community which we have noted. Mark is enabled to find one title which applies to Jesus at all phases of his existence, earthly ministry, present status and future activity. No other title of his gospel allowed him to do this, since all these titles receive their proper interpretation only in terms of the corrective Son of Man saying of 14:62.

The long-standing observation that in the synoptic gospels Son of Man is never on the lips of anyone but Jesus confirms this view.[1] Those who wish to hold that Jesus uttered Son of Man sayings invoke this observation in support of their position.[2] There is, however, another explanation. Son of Man is always on the lips of Jesus because it is the only title never associated with false or inaccurate meanings. <u>Christos</u>, Son of God, Son of David, Lord, all were used in ways which had at times to be altered or explained away.[3] This is not true of Son

---

prior to the gospels. The meaning each evangelist gives to a title must be learned from his use of the title.

[1] Mark 2:10 is not clearly on the lips of Jesus and the parenthetical structure there suggests it may be an editorial comment of Mark, Perrin, "Christology of Mark," p. 183.

[2] Cullmann, <u>Christology</u>, p. 137.

[3] We have indicated how Mark re-interprets these titles. <u>Christos</u> was always in danger of being associated with a

of Man, so it becomes the designation par excellence by which Jesus describes his mission in Mark.[1]

Thus far we have noted how the major Christological concerns of Mark come to culmination in the trial narrative. A similar process was noted in the case of the temple sayings where motifs present in the gospel from 11:1 forward reach their high point. The temple saying says that with the destruction of the temple, the new community to be founded by Jesus would take its place. At this point we did not say who Jesus was or when he would found this new community. The Christology of 14:62 answers these questions. The Jesus who will found the new community is the coming Son of Man. He is the same Jesus about whom the gospel is written, who suffered and died, but his work is incomplete. The parousia has not come; it is still awaited. The community will be founded only at the return of Jesus. Therefore Mark has given a radical eschatological dimension to his gospel. He looks beyond the resurrection, the presence of Jesus to his church, and beyond the destruction of the temple, to the coming of Jesus. Until then the community is always in suffering and turmoil and never completely formed. There will

---

political Messiah, Hahn, Titles, pp. 148-158, "The Jewish title of Messiah was as such not tolerable for Jesus and the first Church, but in connection with the Son of Man concept and the thought of suffering it was assimilated later and gradually transformed" (p. 158). Son of God was associated with an incorrect "divine man" Christology and was used by unorthodox groups, supra, p. 180, n. 2. On the necessary modifications made in the Son of David title, Hahn, Titles, pp. 240-265. Kyrios was always in danger of contemination by the term as used in the emperor cult, Bousset, Kyrios Christos, pp. 138-152.

[1]Next to Son of Man, Son of God is the most important designation for Jesus in Mark. When given its proper meaning it becomes in some manuscripts part of the designation of the whole gospel (1:1). Also in 15:39 the centurion can make a proper confession of Jesus as Son of God since the title has been given its proper meaning in 14:62.

always be false prophets, denying disciples and trials to be undergone. Mark writes for such a community, the nucleus of the new naos. Their present situation is the way of suffering, but also the way of expectation.

The orientation to the parousia which is present in the Marcan trial scene is confirmed by the alterations Luke and Matthew make in the scene. Luke completely de-eschatologizes the answer of Jesus. The reference to the seeing is omitted and in place of the double response of Jesus, there is only the citation of Ps 110, "from now on the Son of Man will be sitting at the right hand of the power of God." Luke is interested in the role of Jesus in the period of the Church and the second coming has receded into the background.[1] The Matthean alterations are more subtle. First of all by the addition of dynamai before the temple saying (26:61), he makes an eschatological prediction into a Christological statement focusing on the power of Jesus to perform the act rather than the act to be done. In the answer to the high priest after the affirmative reply of Jesus (26:64), sy eipas, Matthew inserts the adversative, plēn and the temporal designation ap'arti before the reply of Jesus. Thus Matthew retains the reference to the parousia which Luke takes out. Jesus will be vindicated at the parousia and the Sanhedrin itself will be judged. However, the addition of ap'arti (from now on, hereafter) creates a fissure between the Christology and eschatology of the reply of Jesus.[2] Matthew has Jesus affirm the validity of the titles applied to him by the high priest (Christos, and huios tou theou), independent of

---

[1] Conzelmann, Theology of St. Luke, pp. 84-85.

[2] These observations are based on remarks by Tödt, Son of Man, pp. 82-84.

their qualification by the Son of Man saying. The Son of Man saying simply points to the return of Jesus without reinterpreting the titles as it does in Mark. Therefore the Son of Man saying in Matthew no longer has the same function it has in Mark.

At this point certain questions still remain about Marcan literary activity in the trial scene. In the previous two chapters we have attempted to show how the two major areas of Marcan concern in the trial scene, the temple saying, and the Christological material are related to other parts of the gospel and to each other. We have not yet shown how the trial narrative as a whole is related to the Passion narrative and the rest of the gospel. Also as was noted redaction criticism postulates not only a setting in the gospel for a given pericope, but like form criticism has a sociological dimension, in suggesting how a given section of the gospel relates to the community or audience to whom the evangelists addresses his message. This problem will occupy the final chapter.

CHAPTER V

THE TRIAL NARRATIVE IN THE GOSPEL OF MARK

Introduction

In our initial methodological statement we noted that redaction criticism has different aspects. The main aspect was to discover the author's theological purpose through an analysis of his literary activity in any given pericope. The aim of the second chapter was to discover this literary activity and the subsequent two chapters brought out the theological implications of this activity. We noted that Mark makes the trial narrative into a compendium of theological concerns which run throughout the gospel. There are, however, other aspects of the methodology which demand not so much an analytical study of the parts of any given pericope, but rather a statement on the function of the narrative as a whole in the movement of the whole gospel. The first task, therefore, is to study the function of the narrative as a unit in the gospel of Mark. In specific terms, which will become clear in subsequent discussion, this task will demand an analysis of the relation of the trial narrative to the crucifixion narrative (15:20b-41). The second major aspect of redaction criticism not yet treated could be labeled its "sociological dimension." Just as form criticism postulated a setting in the life or worship of the early church for any given pericope, so redaction criticism postulates that the theology of any given pericope and of the gospel as a whole has a setting in the concerns of the community for which the gospel was intended. Therefore the second major concern of the present chapter will be to suggest the function which the trial narrative had for the Marcan community. Finally it was noted that redaction criticism is moving in the direction of applying criteria taken from secular literary criticism to the gospel material. Despite the caution mentioned earlier that this enterprise leads to largely unexplored ground, an attempt will be made to understand the trial narrative precisely as narrative according to the canons of literary criticism.

Trial Narrative and Crucifixion Narrative
(15:20b-41)

The evocative remark of Dibelius that there are two high points in the Passion narrative, the trial narrative and the crucifixion narrative, has already been mentioned.[1] We have already seen how the trial narrative constitutes one high point of the Passion account. Immediate observation of the crucifixion narrative reveals that those two aspects which were dominant in the trial narrative, the temple saying (14:58) and the Christological confession (14:61-62) reappear in two distinct places in the crucifixion narrative--in the mocking of 15:29-32a, and in the account of the death of Jesus and its immediate effects in 15:38-39. Coupled with this similarity in both accounts are observations about the general Marcan mode of composition which suggest that this similarity may be deliberate and show a definite Marcan purpose. Willi Marxsen has shown that there is really a double structure to the gospel of Mark.[2] On one level the gospel moves forward as a vita Jesu. On another level the gospel is composed "backwards" under the shadow of the cross so that Mark has ordered all his material as leading to the

---

[1] Tradition, p. 193; supra, p. 19.

[2] Introduction, pp. 134-135.

crucifixion. If this is so, any given pericope has a double function. On one level it shows the influence of the material which went before it, but on another level it is influenced by what will follow, specifically by the crucifixion narrative. Secondly, as Knox and others have noted, Mark likes to narrate things "proleptically" where the material at a given place prepares the reader for a section which will follow.[1] Therefore the textual similarity and these aspects of Marcan compositional technique urge that a study be made of the relation of the trial narrative and the crucifixion narrative. Initially it will be necessary to study evidence of Marcan literary activity in the crucifixion narrative, and only then can a more detailed statement on the relation of the two narratives be made.

The Crucifixion Narrative

General Literary Considerations

There is a general admission among scholars that the crucifixion narrative shows different levels of composition, so much so that Schreiber has characterized it as "Mosaikartig."[2] Earlier attempts to discover these levels by Weiss, Bultmann, Finegan, Goguel, and Taylor have sought to distinguish the "historical core" from later additions.[3] It is significant that, even by the criterion of historicity, only Taylor

---

[1] John Knox, "A Note on Mark 14, 51-52," The Joy of Study, ed. Sherman E. Johnson (New York: Macmillan, 1951), p. 28, and Herman Waetjen, "The Ending of Mark and the Gospel's Shift in Eschatology," Annual of the Swedish Theological Institute, Vol. VI (Leiden: E. J. Brill, 1965), pp. 114-131.

[2] Theologie, p. 23.

[3] Weiss, 15:15b, 20b-22, 24a, 27, 31-32, 37, 39, 40-41a; Bultmann, 20b-24a, (27), 37; Finegan, 21, 22a, 24a, 26, 37, 40-41; Goguel, 22-24, 26, 34, 37; Taylor, 21-24, 26, 29-30, 34-37, 39. These divisions are listed in Linnemann, Studien, p. 136.

attributes the temple saying by the mockers of 15:29 to the historical core, and only he and Weiss attribute the centurion's confession of 15:39 to this core.[1] However, as Linnemann has pointed out, historicity is not of itself a criterion of literary priority, so that if we want to find where Mark has worked with pre-existing traditions, literary rather than historical criteria must be used.[2] Recently there have been three major attempts by Schreiber, by Schweizer, and by Linnemann to uncover Marcan redaction in the crucifixion account, which can provide a starting point for our detailed study of 15:27-29 and 15:38-39.

Johannes Schreiber

Using the literary criteria of the presence of doublets (15:24-25, 30a-31b; and 30b-32ab, 34-37), and of Marcan grammar and distinctive vocabulary, Schreiber isolates two accounts of the crucifixion.[3] The first and older account which is closest to the historical occurrences is found in 15:20b-22a, and 15:24-27.[4] The second account which is found primarily in 15:25, 26, 29a, 32c, 33, 34, 37-38 is an interpretation of the first using categories of Jewish apocalyptic in which the death of Jesus is portrayed as the death of a _theios anēr_ which is at the same time a judgment on those who caused his death.[5] Mark's redactional activity is found in his joining of the accounts and in the following verses which Schreiber designates as additions of the evangelist: 15:22b, 23, 29b-32b, 34b-36, 39-41.[6] The theology which emerges from an analysis of such Marcan activity

---

[1] Ibid.   [2] Ibid.
[3] _Theologie_, pp. 24-31.   [4] Ibid., p. 32.
[5] Ibid., pp. 35-40.   [6] Ibid., pp. 41-44.

is that Mark imposes on the tradition an Hellenistic Christology of the descent and ascent of a saviour where the crucifixion is the exaltation of the victorious saviour.[1]

Schreiber's analysis is important for our present concerns in that he sees the temple material and Christological titles of 15:29 and 32 as due to the evangelist Mark, as well as the centurion's confession in 15:39. Less satisfying is his isolation of the two previous accounts. The major difficulty with his view is that he places the allusions to Ps 22 in two different accounts.[2] As Lindars has noted this psalm has become "a quarry for pictorial detail in writing the story of the Passion," providing the basis for the death cry of Jesus (15:34, Ps 22:1), the distribution of the clothes of Jesus (15:24, Ps 22:18), the attitude of the onlookers (15:29, Ps 22:7) and their jeers.[3] Therefore to place the allusions to this psalm in different accounts is to miss the fact that at its earliest stage the crucifixion account consisted of the historicization of the verses of this psalm, so that allusions to it belong to the same strand of tradition. Secondly, as we have tried to show in other parts of our work, and as Kelber has shown in direct opposition to Schreiber, Mark's Christology does not focus on the

---

[1] Ibid., pp. 218-243, and "Die Christologie des Markusevangeliums," ZTK, LVIII (1961), 154-183. Schreiber's view of the theology of Mark represents a restatement of Bultmann's position that Mark is "the union of the Hellenistic kerygma about Christ, whose essential content consists of the Christ myth as we learn of it in Paul (esp. Phil 2:6ff.; Rom 3:24) with the tradition of the story of Jesus." Synoptic Tradition, pp. 347-348.

[2] He places 15:24 (Ps 22:18) in account I and 15:29a (Ps 22:7) in account II.

[3] New Testament Apologetic, pp. 90-91; Dibelius, Tradition, pp. 186-187.

exaltation of Jesus but on his parousia as Son of Man.[1] Therefore while agreeing with aspects of Schreiber's literary analysis we cannot accept his conclusions in toto.

Eduard Schweizer

Using the criteria of language and style, Schweizer views the earliest level of the crucifixion narrative as consisting of 15:20b-24a, 26, 27, 29a, 32b, 36a, and 37, so that the material concerned with the temple in 29b and 38, and the Christological material in 31 and 39 are both secondary to the oldest account.[2] In the case of 15:38-39 Schweizer makes no detailed attempt to suggest Marcan activity in these verses, but he does suggest an interesting development to the tradition of 15:29b-32a. The first thing he notes about these verses is that they appear to be an insertion between 15:27, "And with him they crucified two robbers, one on his right and one on his left," and 15:32b, "Those who were crucified with him also reviled him" since the latter verse is the logical continuation of the former.[3] He then suggests that the original reference to the mocking consisted of the short indication of 15:27a, "those passing by blasphemed him," which he notes, "completely contradicts the Markan tendency to accuse only the authorities and excuse the general public."[4] At a later stage the Old Testament reference in 15:29a would have been added as well as the temple saying. He then suggests that vss. 31-32a with the mention of the usual

---

[1] Supra, Chap. IV; Kelber, "Kingdom and Parousia," p. 3, calls his work a refutation of Schreiber.

[2] Linnemann, Studien, p. 136.

[3] Mark, p. 349. The technique of interrupting the flow of the narrative is similar to the recognized Marcan technique of intercalation.

[4] Ibid.

opponents of Jesus in Mark, the high priests and scribes, represents another version of the same story which Mark has inserted at this point. In our opinion Schweizer has correctly uncovered the fact that vss. 29-32a interrupt the flow of the narrative and represent a Marcan concern. The main modification we will suggest is that the temple saying of 15:29b is also due to Marcan redaction.

Eta Linnemann

While accepting Schreiber's argument that the presence of doublets indicates levels of tradition in the crucifixion narrative, Linnemann does not follow his division into accounts, but suggests a tradition history of her own.[1] Her basic argument against any unified account as a basis for the Marcan narrative is that in the present narrative the only connection between the various incidents comes from their close connection by means of temporal indications. When divorced from the indications of the different hours they have no other mutual relationship than their general relationship to the crucifixion, so that the order and sequence is totally due to Mark.[2] She then proceeds to a verse by verse analysis which seeks to show the "free floating" quality of the material prior to its incorporation in the Marcan account. She postulates that at the basis of the Marcan account was a simple account consisting of the following verses: 15:22a, 24a, 25a, 33, 34a, 37, 38, and that the splitting of the temple veil in 15:38 constituted the high point of the account.[3] She finds the activity of Mark present in the following areas: (a) he joins together the isolated episodes, (b) he forms 15:26,

---

[1] Studien, pp. 137, 146-158. [2] Ibid., p. 146.
[3] Ibid., pp. 157-158.

the inscription, in relation to 15:2, the trial before Pilate; he forms 15:29b-30 as a <u>redaktionelle Verknüpfung</u> to 14:58 and 15:31a-32ab in relation to 14:61 and he forms 15:32c in relation to 15:27, (c) he adds 15:39 to the account.[1] Linnemann is not sure whether 15:40 (the mention of women) is formed by Mark but its location in the narrative goes back to Mark.

The work of the three above authors has been surveyed not as a prelude to a full-scale discussion of tradition and redaction in the crucifixion narrative, but as authoritative support for our analysis of 15:29-32a and 15:38-39. Starting with different presuppositions and using different methodologies, all the above authors see the temple saying of 15:29 and the Christological titles of 15:32a and 15:39, as due to Mark either in their composition or in their present location. Significant for our present purpose is that it is precisely these parts of the crucifixion narrative which provide the point of contact with the trial narrative. Therefore we must examine the above redactional verses in more detail.

<u>15:29-32a</u>

In these verses the first group which mocks Jesus repeats the saying of the trial scene in abbreviated form, "Aha, you who would destroy the temple and build it in three days, save yourself and come down from the cross." As we noted in our initial study of the saying, it represents a saying created by Mark out of pre-existing traditions in which the ministry and work of Jesus is portrayed in opposition to and spelling the death of the old temple cult, while at the same time preparing the new eschatological community. In the trial narrative Jesus' opposition to the temple is one of the factors which precipitates the

---

[1]<u>Ibid</u>., p. 158. Grundmann, <u>Markus</u>, p. 312, and Haenchen, <u>Weg Jesu</u>, p. 535, also note the redactional nature of 15:29b-30 and 15:31a-32b in relation to 14:58 and 14:61-62 respectively.

final decision to put him to death. The question then arises as to why Mark reproduces this saying in the crucifixion narrative. An immediate response is that by so doing he relates the final decision to execute Jesus for his opposition to the temple to its carrying out in the crucifixion. There are, however, further reasons why the saying has been added here--before the actual death of Jesus. Both Taylor and Lohmeyer have remarked that the intention of the mockers in 15:29-30 (come down from the cross) is that Jesus perform an eschatological miracle which would save himself and enable them to believe.[1] Though translators and grammarians have understood ho katalyōn as a substitute for a conative tense in the sense "you who would destroy the temple," it is equally good grammar to understand it in its literal sense as "you who are destroying."[2] If the phrase is taken in this sense then there is an intended irony in the mocking. The mockers in effect say, "if you are now destroying the temple, come down from the cross." The question then arises as to why Mark put such a phrase on their lips. We have already noted that one of the purposes Mark had in the redaction of ch. 13 was to disassociate the destruction of the temple from the parousia.[3] The trials and turmoils surrounding the destruction

---

[1] Taylor, Mark, p. 591; Lohmeyer, Markus, p. 344.

[2] Blass-Debrunner, Grammar, No. 339, 3, call the usage "conative." However, this is in contrast to the general principles that participles gain their temporal function in relation to the main verb, in this case sōson (present tense), Grammar, No. 339. G. B. Winer, Grammar of New Testament Greek, trans. W. F. Moulton (Edinburgh: T. and T. Clark, 1882), p. 444, says that the participle here is a substitute for a noun which would support our interpretation of the phrase. Also it should be noted that in the New Testament participles are used very frequently in a conditional sense, James Hope Moulton, A Grammar of New Testament Greek (Edinburgh: T. and T. Clark, 1908), I, 230-231, cf. 1 Cor 11:29.

[3] Pesch, Naherwartungen, p. 118; Conzelmann, "Geschichte und Eschaton," pp. 214-215; supra, pp. 130-132.

of the temple were the prelude, not the end itself (13:7). It was also noted that the time indications at the end of ch. 13 which link it to the Passion narrative, make of the period of destruction an eschatological period of waiting before the death and second coming of Jesus.

With these observations in mind we can arrive at an understanding of the function of the temple saying in 15:29. Mark in effect puts an incorrect eschatology on the lips of the mockers and an incorrect understanding of Jesus' Passion. The incorrect eschatology would join the coming of Jesus as saviour with the destruction of the temple which is now taking place. The incorrect understanding of the Passion would obviate the necessity of Jesus to complete the way of the cross before his vindication. Therefore Mark introduces the temple saying again at this exact point before the death of Jesus as a foil for an eschatology and Christology which he rejects throughout his gospel. In regard to the Passion of Jesus Mark wants to affirm two things, its necessity and the necessity of the Christian disciple to follow Jesus on this way; and the fact that the Passion is a prelude to the parousia. By having the challenge of the mockers not accepted by Jesus, Mark again affirms the necessity of the way of suffering as a prelude to the eschaton.

The second mocking by the high priests and scribes which Mark has also inserted at this point also serves as foil for an incorrect understanding of Jesus, and elements in the taunt confirm this. First of all the precise title given to Jesus by the priests must be examined. They mock him as "king of Israel," a title which in the synoptic tradition appears only here and in the Matthean parallel (27:42). This title stands in tension with the other kingly title given to Jesus in the Passion narrative, "king of the Jews," which appears in the trial before

Pilate (15:2; 15:12), the first mocking by the soldiers (15:18) and in the inscription on the cross (15:26). This latter title in terms of tradition history is the older title since it appears in different traditions (the synoptics and John 19:19, 21) and also is close to what historians tell us would have been the proper titulus used by the Roman executioners of Jesus.[1] However, the relationship between "king of Israel" and "king of the Jews" still remains unsolved. Caution must be exercised in simply equating the titles as, for example, Cullmann does when he treats them as synonyms.[2] The second main way of viewing them has been to follow the lead of Kuhn and Gutbrod and see them as examples of the terminological distinction in vogue since Maccabean times where Ioudaioi is used when pagans speak of the people of Israel and Israēl is used by the Jews as a self designation.[3] In this case then the taunt of the high priests would consist simply of a taunt to Jesus to adopt the political idea of messiahship and save Israel.[4]

There is however another sense in which "king of Israel" is used and which can contribute to an understanding of the taunt here. Starting with the observation that Israēl is a religious term for the sacral people, we can observe that it is also an eschatological term. Along with the expectation of the coming of the kingdom of God and the Messiah was the expectation that at this time the true Israel would be established.[5] In the

---

[1] Winter, Trial of Jesus, pp. 108-109; Burkill, "Trial of Jesus," p. 16; Brandon, Trial of Jesus, p. 104.

[2] Christology, p. 221.

[3] Karl Georg Kuhn and Walter Gutbrod, "Israēl," TDNT, III, 359-375.

[4] Cullmann, Christology, p. 221; Taylor, Mark, p. 579.

[5] Perrin, Kingdom, pp. 170, 179; Rudolf Schnackenburg, God's Rule and Kingdom, trans. John Murray (New York: Herder

New Testament this part of the general messianic expectation is mirrored primarily in the Q saying of Mt 19:28, in the saying put on the lips of the disciples by Luke in Acts 1:6, "Lord, will you at this time restore the kingdom to Israel?" and in the church's understanding of itself as the new Israel in Gal 6:16.[1] Therefore the title given to Jesus by the high priests in 15:32 is primarily religious, not political, and in its religious sense addresses Jesus as the king of the eschatological Israel. In this case then Mark is again putting a false eschatology on the lips of Jesus' opponents. They say in effect that the eschatological people should be established by Jesus in some miraculous fashion without his undergoing death on the cross.

The anticipated response of the high priests confirms the eschatological dimension of the taunts. They say that if Jesus comes down from the cross they will "see" and believe. It has already been noted that "seeing" in Mark is primarily associated with the "seeing" of Jesus at the parousia (13:26; 14:62). By

---

and Herder, 1968), pp. 41-54. For examples of Israel used in the "eschatological" sense see, As Mos 10:7-10; Jub 1:15-19, 23-24, 29; Ps Sol 10:17; Test Sim 7:2; Test Levi ch. 18; Test Jud 22:2-3; Test Dan 5:12-13; Test Napth 8:1-3. In this context Test Dan 6:6 is often cited. However the translation as given by Charles (Pseudepigrapha, p. 335), "And it shall be the time of lawlessness of Israel that the Lord will not depart from them, but will transform them into a nation that doeth his will, for none of the angels will be equal to him," is not supported by the new edition of the Testaments by de Jonge. The Greek text as he reconstructs it does not have the "not" in the phrase "the Lord will not depart from them," and in place of "will transform" de Jonge reads meteleusetai, "he will seek out." See M. de Jonge, Testamenta XII Patriarcharum (Leiden: E. J. Brill, 1964), and Marc Philonenko, Les interpolations chrétiennes des Testaments des Douze Patriarches et les manuscrits de Qoumrâm (Cahiers de la Revue d'histoire et de philosophies religieuses, Vol. XXXV; Paris: Presses Universitaires de France, 1960), esp. p. 45.

[1] On Mt 19:28, "judging the twelve tribes of Israel," Tödt, Son of Man, p. 63. On the other texts, Gutbrod, "Israēl," pp. 386-387.

putting such a request on the lips of the high priests at this
point, Mark in effect makes them desire a "seeing" which will be
an illegitimate substitute for the parousia. He also by using
the verb here prepares the way for the proper "seeing" by the
centurion which comes only after the death of Jesus. Therefore
both the taunts of the passersby and of the high priests and
scribes are introduced by Mark at this point as foils for an
eschatology and Christology which he has consistently rejected.
By putting their request immediately before the death of Jesus,
he affirms the necessity of the way of the cross for Jesus and
his followers. By putting false eschatological hopes on their
lips he shows that he at the same time looks beyond the cross to
the parousia for the proper eschatological understanding. By
mentioning both the temple saying and Christological titles, he
prepares for the final statement on the temple saying and
Christological titles in 15:38-39.

15:38-39

After the death of Jesus in 15:37, Mark recounts two
events, the splitting of the veil of the temple (vs. 38) and the
confession of the centurion (vs. 39). The first of these events
is described by Taylor as a "legendary addition doctrinal in
origin."[1] What is intended by the mention of the splitting of
the veil and the interpretation of the splitting is widely disputed. One major group interprets the veil as the veil which
covered the entrance to the Holy of Holies, and sees in the
splitting of the veil a sign that through the death of Jesus,
all men and not simply Jews are given access to God.[2] A second

---

[1] Taylor, *Mark*, p. 596.

[2] Taylor, *ibid.*, lists the following as favoring this
view: Weiss, Swete, Billerbeck, Rawlinson. Linnemann,

group of commentators holds that the splitting refers to the veil hung in front of the whole sanctuary, and that its splitting is a symbolic reference to the destruction of the temple.[1] Billerbeck, who has studied the use of language in the verse and its Old Testament and Intertestamental antecedents, finds that the evidence is inconclusive and that the meaning of the verse must be decided on theological rather than linguistic or historical grounds.[2]

There is, however, one element of the language of the verse which has not been sufficiently considered. While previous discussion has centered on the meaning of katapetasma, insufficient attention has been given to the fact that the veil is called the veil of the naos.[3] In the Septuagint the Holy of Holies is not called a naos, and when Josephus describes this part of the temple he calls it to endotatō meros (the innermost part).[4] More significant is the fact that in the epistle to the Hebrews the Holy of Holies is never referred to as a naos. In

---

Studien, pp. 158-163, favors this view but says that the real meaning of the sign of the splitting is now that the majesty of God appears to all men paradoxically in the death of Jesus.

[1] Lohmeyer, Markus, p. 347; Klostermann, Markus, p. 186; Schweizer, Mark, p. 353, signifies the end of the temple cult; Lightfoot, History and Interpretation, p. 86.

[2] Kommentar, I, 1045.

[3] On the various meanings of katapetasma, Billerbeck, Kommentar, I, 1043-1045.

[4] In 1 Kgs 6:16 (LXX III Kingdoms 6:16) in section on the building of Solomon's temple the area is described as to dabir eis ton hagion tōn hagiōn (cf. 6:16, 19, 21, 23, 31); the area in front of this is called naos (16:7). In 26:33ff. the place is called hagion tōn hagiōn, and in Ez 41:3, tēn aulēn, tēn esōteran. Jewish War 5.5,5 # 219 (hereafter abbreviated JW). Citations from Josephus are taken from: Josephus, translation and notes by Henry St. John Thackeray (Loeb Classical Library; New York: G. P. Putnam's Sons, 1927), 8 vols. Vols. II-III comprise the Jewish War.

Heb 6:19, the author writes of that hope which enters into the inner shrine which is behind the curtain (<u>eis to esōteron tou katapetasmatos</u>). In 9:3, he notes that behind the second curtain stood a tent (<u>skēnē</u>) which is called the Holy of Holies, and in 10:19 he gives a symbolic interpretation to the death of Jesus as entrance into the Holy of Holies. Though the <u>RSV</u> translates the initial part of vs. 19 as "we have confidence to enter the sanctuary" the word <u>naos</u> is not used but rather <u>tēn eisodon tōn hagiōn</u>. Therefore there is little evidence that by the splitting of the veil of the <u>naos</u> the Holy of Holies could be intended.

The terminological indication that the whole temple rather than the innermost sanctuary is intended in Mark 15:38 is also supported by the sequence of temple material in Mark. We have already noted that from 11:1 on Mark develops an anti-temple theme in which Jesus is pictured in opposition to the Jerusalem temple, predicting its destruction and being condemned to death because of this prediction. In this light 15:38, whatever its original significance in the pre-Marcan tradition, is used by Mark to bring this theme to culmination. At the precise moment that Jesus dies the temple loses its significance. What has been destroyed in anticipation in the ministry of Jesus, is now destroyed in fact.[1]

The second thing which happens at the death of Jesus is the confession of the centurion. Commentators have speculated that Mark added this verse here to designate the response of the pagan world to the death of Jesus. For the Jews it meant the end of the significance of the temple, for pagans the opening of

---

[1] Conzelmann, "History and Theology," p. 186.

the way to God through Jesus' death.[1] There are, however, deeper dimensions to the centurion's confession which must be examined. First of all it should be noted that there is an awkwardness in the description that the centurion sees that "crying out in such a way, he breathed his last" (15:39b).[2] Logically in place of the verb idōn which begins the verse there should be some reference to the centurion's hearing the cry of Jesus, since it is not mentioned what he saw.[3] Recalling that the forms of the verb "to see" in Mark are used in primary reference to the "seeing" of Jesus at the parousia, we would suggest that Mark introduces the verb idōn at this point precisely to make of the centurion's confession a symbolic presentation of the parousia confession.

In this light the title of Jesus used by the centurion, Son of God, receives its definitive meaning. We have noted that throughout the gospel this title is corrected by Son of Man. In the earthly ministry of Jesus, the manifestation of Jesus' power is not simply that of an Hellenistic theios anēr figure called a Son of God, but the manifestation of the exousia of the Son of Man who must suffer and die. In the trial scene we noted that Son of God is qualified by reference to the future coming Son of Man. It is only when Jesus is fully recognized as the one who suffered and died and will come again, that he can be called Son of God in the proper sense. In this sense Mark can designate his whole gospel the gospel of Jesus, the Messiah,

---

[1] Lightfoot, History and Interpretation, p. 86; Nineham, St. Mark, p. 430; Lohmeyer, Markus, p. 347.

[2] Schreiber, Theologie, p. 44, notes this tension.

[3] Schreiber (ibid., p. 46) makes the suggestion that what the centurion saw was how quickly Jesus died, but this interpretation is not borne out by the text.

the Son of God (1:1). We would suggest that Mark has introduced the centurion's confession at this point precisely for the symbolic presentation of such a proper confession.

Such a view is supported by the addition in 15:40 of the presence of the women who had "followed" Jesus and ministered to him in Galilee (vs. 41). The mention of the women at this point performs a double function. On the one hand it leads the reader to the instructions to the disciples in 16:7, "But go, tell his disciples and Peter that he is going before you to Galilee; there you will see him" (opsesthe). On the other hand the mention of the women ministering to Jesus in Galilee recalls 14:28 where Jesus says that after the resurrection he will go before the disciples into Galilee, which in Mark is a substitute for Jerusalem and also the place of the final revelation of Jesus as Son of Man.[1] Therefore the introduction of the women at this point immediately after the death of Jesus serves to point the reader beyond the cross to the parousia, and to recall that the whole Passion itself is a prelude to the parousia.

In summary, then, we can see how in those verses which show particular Marcan concern he has made the crucifixion narrative into the second high point of the Passion narrative. By introducing the temple material and the Christological confession both before and after the death of Jesus, Mark is enabled to make his final statement on the significance of these elements of his gospel. In 15:27-29 he portrays the false eschatology and false Christology which would deny the necessity of the death of Jesus. In 15:38-39 he portrays the significance of the death of Jesus. The temple has lost its meaning, and the present time is the time for proper confession. Son of God has

---

[1] Lohmeyer, Markus, p. 356; Nineham, St. Mark, p. 440.

become a title which for Mark can properly be used of Jesus, but only with the qualifications and meaning he has given to it. It can be used only of the Jesus who had to suffer and die and will come again. It is therefore oriented to the parousia. Mark's eschatology is, therefore, twofold. In one sense the death of Jesus is "the end," but it is also the beginning. It is the end of the temple and its significance, but it is a prelude to the real end which is the revelation of the Son of Man. Those who are to follow Jesus exist in such a period, a period of confession of Jesus in the face of the cross and the destruction of the temple.

Trial Narrative and Crucifixion Narrative

Earlier we recalled Knox's observation that Mark narrates things proleptically and Marxsen's remarks on the double direction in Mark.[1] There are numerous instances in Mark where he prepares the reader for what follows. The summary of 1:14-15 sets the tone for the meaning of the whole first part of the gospel--the preaching of the kingdom of God in Galilee.[2] The indications of the plans to kill Jesus (3:6; 11:18; 12:12; 14:1) prepare for the cross. The motif of prediction exemplified in the Passion predictions (8:31; 9:31; 10:33) and in 14:27 is an instance of this tendency. The discourse of ch. 13 ends with the time designations proper to the Passion narrative.[3] These examples stress one facet of Marcan composition--his penchant

---

[1] Supra, p. 190, n. 2, and p. 191, n. 1.

[2] Leander E. Keck, "The Introduction to Mark's Gospel," NTS, XII (1965-66), 352-370.

[3] To these examples might be added the presence of the young man in 14:51 and 16:5, see Waetjen, "The Ending of Mark," passim.

for preparing the reader for what follows. However, an analysis of certain parts of Mark which reveal in a special way his compositional techniques will show that in addition to anticipating what will follow Mark uses the same section to recapitulate and anticipate at the same time. Therefore, we will select for analysis the Sammelberichte of 1:14-15; 3:7-12; and 6:30-33.[1]

The initial Sammelbericht of 1:14-15 serves both as a conclusion to what has happened previously and an introduction to what follows. Jesus is said to begin his ministry after the "handing over" of John who has dominated the presentation from 1:2-9, and Jesus goes into Galilee which will be the center of his ministry in the following chapters. Thus not only is the period of Jesus and of John clearly distinguished, but the location and content of Jesus' initial activity is specified. The function of the second Sammelbericht we will treat can best be illustrated graphically.

Recapitulates	Summary Statement	Anticipates
1:35 Jesus alone with disciples	3:7 Jesus withdraws with disciples	3:13 Private choice of disciples
2:23 Jesus and disciples in cornfield		4:10 Jesus alone with disciples
		4:34 Private instruction to disciples
		6:1 Only disciples come with him

---

[1] Taylor, Mark, p. 85, calls Mk 1:14-15 and 3:7-12 the two most important Sammelberichte. The Christology of these sections has been studied by Vernon K. Robbins, "The Christology of Mark" (unpublished Ph.D. dissertation, University of Chicago, 1969), and K. Kertelge, Die Wunder Jesu im Markusevangelium. Eine redaktionsgeschichtliche Untersuchung (Studien zum Alten und Neuen Testament, Vol. XXIII; Munich: Kösel Verlag, 1970).

Recapitulates	Summary Statement	Anticipates
1:32 Whole city is gathered	3:8-9 Crowds press on Jesus (by the sea)	3:20 Crowd gathers at home
2:1 Crowds gather at door		4:1 Large crowd gathers at sea
2:13 All the crowd gathers by the sea		5:21 Large crowd gathers at sea
		5:24 Large crowd gathers
1:31; 1:41-44; 2:1-12; 3:1-6, healing miracles	3:10 He heals many	5:1-43 Healing of woman with issue of blood and Jairus' daughter
		6:5 He heals some
1:34 He casts out demons	3:11 He confronts demons	5:1-13 Demoniac of Gerasa
1:34, 44 Silence commanded	3:12 Commands to silence	5:43 Command to silence

Thus each element of the summary report at one and the same time summarizes what has gone before in the gospel and at the same time prepares the reader for what follows. The summary report of 6:30-33 on the return of the disciples recalls the sending out of the disciples in 6:7-13 and at the same time supplies "what is presupposed for the following story of the feeding of the five thousand," the crowds of people and the location in the desert place.[1] Such examples confirm that we are in the area of a definite Marcan compositional technique.

With this technique in mind we can now see the function of the trial narrative, from the viewpoint of structure, in the gospel of Mark. As was noted in our study of the content of the

---

[1] Bultmann, Synoptic Tradition, p. 340.

narrative, major themes of Mark's gospel, the anti-temple theme and his Christological concerns, culminate in this narrative. At the same time we saw that these two elements appear in the crucifixion narrative. Therefore, in terms of the structure of the gospel, the trial narrative, like the summary statements, recapitulates and at the same time anticipates what will follow.[1] In addition to this structural function the content of the trial narrative throws light on an understanding of the crucifixion narrative. In the trial narrative Mark shows that the anti-temple activity of Jesus crystallizes the mortal opposition to him, an opposition which is played out in the crucifixion. He portrays Jesus as the destroyer of the old temple and as the founder of the new community. In the crucifixion narrative the temple is symbolically destroyed in the death of Jesus, and the women of 15:40 point to their message of 16:7 to the disciples to be the nucleus of the eschatological community. In the trial narrative he has used Son of Man to give a proper meaning to Son of God, so that in the crucifixion narrative the title can be used in a proper sense by the centurion. Therefore, analysis of Marcan redaction and composition in both the trial and crucifixion narratives in light of his literary activity in the rest of the gospel reveals that he has made of the trial narrative an "anticipatory commentary" on the crucifixion narrative.

The Trial Narrative and the Marcan Community

Redaction criticism, as was noted, has a "sociological" aspect. Once a statement has been made about the meaning of a

---

[1] This is also an argument in support of the fact that Marcan compositional activity is present in the trial narrative. It performs the same function as the Sammelberichte.

certain pericope in the context of the gospel narrative, as well
as about the religious meaning it conveys, the question can be
raised about the audience for whom this meaning was intended or
had relevance. Thus redaction criticism raises anew questions
about the destination and purpose of a given gospel. Marxsen
raised this question in his initial work by suggesting that Mark
was written for people fleeing from Jerusalem and the turmoil of
the Jewish War of 66-70.[1] Pesch continued this trend by suggesting that the gospel is post A.D. 70, written against people
who wrongly associated the destruction of the temple with the
imminent parousia.[2] Weeden has suggested that Mark was written
to counteract proponents of an incorrect theios anēr Christology
in the Marcan community.[3] Whatever the intrinsic merits of
these individual suggestions, their work indicates that internal
criticism of the Marcan gospel is an entree to the external
situation in which the gospel was composed.

In the case of the trial narrative the question of the
community for which the gospel was intended can be approached in
two ways. First of all the content of the theology there ex-
pounded could serve as an index of the community needs for which
this theology would be a response. Here the question would be
asked as to what community would respond to a theology which
pictures the earthly ministry of Jesus as an epiphany of the
coming Son of Man who, in his earthly ministry, was put to death
for his opposition to the Jewish temple, but who will be vindicated when he returns as glorious Son of Man to found the new

---

[1] Mark, pp. 171, 184.

[2] Naherwartungen, pp. 117, 118.

[3] "The Heresy that Necessitated Mark's Gospel," passim, esp. pp. 154-157.

community. There is, also, a second way of gaining access to
knowledge of the Marcan community through the trial narrative.
Here the question would not be asked about the content of the
trial narrative but about its form <u>precisely as trial</u>. The
question to be raised would be: why did Mark choose to cast so
much of his theology in the narrative of a trial before Jewish
officials? In seeking knowledge of the Marcan community we will
first discuss the <u>form</u> of the narrative and then return to
questions of content.

The most common explanation of those who do not hold that
the trial narrative is present for primarily historical reasons
is that Mark has composed it in imitation of the Roman trial
(15:1-5) for apologetic reasons and to involve the Jews in the
death of Jesus.[1] There are, however, possibilities evident from
Mark's gospel which suggest another reason. It will be our argument that one of these possibilities is that Mark's community
had undergone trials before Jewish officials, and that one of
Mark's purposes in picturing Jesus as being tried is to encourage his community in their trials and to give them a
theology for understanding their situation. It will be necessary, then, to examine some of the sections of Mark which point
directly to the sufferings undergone by his community.

There is ample indication that one of the major concerns
of Mark is to stress the necessity for the disciple to follow
Jesus in suffering. Our earlier analysis of the intercalations
shows that Mark uses this device to relate the fate of Jesus to
the disciples.[2] The three Passion predictions are articulated

---

[1] Georg Braumann, "Markus, 15,2-5 und Markus 14,55-64,"
pp. 273-278; Brandon, <u>The Trial of Jesus</u>, esp. pp. 105-106.

[2] <u>Supra</u>, pp. 58-63.

in a context where Jesus is on his hodos to Jerusalem and his death.¹ In this context teaching on the cost of discipleship is brought by Mark to this section of his gospel (8:34-38).² In addition to these more general observations on the necessity of suffering, there is a section of the discourse of ch. 13 which mentions explicitly the sufferings to be undergone by the community.³ An analysis of this will help us to understand why Mark places emphasis on the trial of Jesus.

Mark 13:9-13

Despite Beasley-Murray's contention that these verses represent authentic sayings of Jesus, there is evidence that they are rather a combination of early church tradition and Marcan redaction.⁴ One of the things which holds the section together is the threefold reference to the handing over (paradidonai) of the disciples (13:9, 11, 12). Perrin has shown that the earliest use of this term was in the early church's reflection on the Passion of Jesus.⁵ Once this tradition was established the further step was to apply it to disciples who suffer the same fate of Jesus, which happened in the case of John (Mk 1:14) and is here applied to all followers of Jesus. Also the verses mirror the terminology of the early church with emphasis on the kerygma and the eschatological "hour."⁶ There are also elements of Marcan redaction in the verses. The loose joining

---

¹8:28; 9:33; 10:32; cf. also 8:3 and 10:52, and Wilhelm Michaelis, "hodos," TDNT, V, 67, 69-78.

²Perrin, What Is Redaction Criticism? pp. 44-45.

³Mk 13:9-13.

⁴A Commentary on Mark Thirteen, pp. 40-52.

⁵"(para)didonai," pp. 208-209.

⁶Lohmeyer, Markus, pp. 270-273.

of material by <u>kai</u> parataxis is a recognized Marcan characteristic. Pesch has shown that the second half of vs. 9, <u>eis martyrion autois</u>, betrays the familiar Marcan technique of addition of a qualifying phrase after <u>heneken emou</u>.[1] The statement in vs. 10 which represents a further explicitation of <u>martyrion</u> interrupts the two statements in vss. 9 and 11 about standing trial and also represents the particular Marcan interest in <u>euaggelion</u>, so that Marxsen ascribes it to Mark the evangelist.[2] Also, Hartmann notes that 13:9-13 is the part of the discourse least associated with Old Testament references, so that it seems that Mark is here bringing different traditions to the discourse.[3] The final indication of Mark's redaction in these verses is that he locates them between the beginning of the trials which are associated with the false prophets and the outbreak of the war (13:6-8) and those which are associated with the height of the crisis, the desecration of the temple and the flight from Jerusalem (13:14-19).

In 13:9-13 Mark lists the different persecutions and trials the community will have to undergo: handing over to Jewish officials (13:9a), scourgings (13:9b), appearances before gentile rulers (13:9), betrayal by loved ones (13:12), hatred by outsiders (13:13). The question arises as to whether Mark has in mind actual persecutions which his church has undergone in the turmoil of A.D. 66-70 or is he giving general teaching on persecution? Our answer to this question will proceed in a twofold manner. First of all, we will analyze the way in which

---

[1] 8:35, <u>kai tou euaggeliou</u>; 10:29, <u>kai heneken tou euaggeliou</u>, Pesch, <u>Naherwartungen</u>, pp. 115-116.

[2] Marxsen, <u>Mark</u>, pp. 174-176.

[3] <u>Prophecy Interpreted</u>, pp. 167-168.

Matthew and Luke alter the Marcan material in order to show that they do not reflect the immediacy of the persecution in Mark. Secondly we will suggest a situation to which the immediacy of the persecution in Mark corresponds.[1]

The first major change we note in the Matthean treatment of this material is that Matthew disassociates these verses from the context of the eschatological discourse (Mt 24:9-10) and relocates them in the missionary instruction of ch. 10.[2] The immediacy of persecution is not present in Matthew. When rewriting Mk 13:9, "they will hand you over to synagogues," Matthew adds to synagōgais the crucial qualifying phrase, autōn (10:17b). In Matthew the synagogues are already "their synagogues," so that Matthew pictures a situation in which church and synagogue are already separate.[3] In Mt 10:18 Matthew omits the reference to Mk 13:9 where the giving of witness is connected with the proclamation of the gospel. As Hare has noted, in Mark the persecution provides the occasion for witnessing, while in Matthew it is the result of witnessing.[4] Finally, Matthew makes a crucial alteration in the final verse of the section. Where Mark in 13:13b concludes with the exhortation, "But he who endures to the end will be saved," Matthew, though returning to the Marcan order at this point, adds the saying (24:14), "And this gospel of the kingdom will be preached throughout the whole

---

[1] Gaston, No Stone, p. 23, concludes his study of the sayings: "The church which transmitted these sayings has known persecution."

[2] Douglas R. A. Hare, The Theme of Jewish Persecution of Christians in the Gospel According to St. Matthew (Society for New Testament Studies, Monograph Series, Vol. VI; Cambridge: University Press, 1967), p. 99; Marxsen, Mark, pp. 200-201.

[3] Hare, "Theme," p. 105.

[4] Ibid., p. 100.

world, as a testimony to all nations; and then the end will come." Thus Matthew has separated the persecutions from their eschatological context and, in so doing, envisions a period when the church will undergo many persecutions so that it needs instructions on them. They are no longer the pangs of the last day. The last day will come only when the gospel is preached to the whole world. Persecution is a fact of Christian existence rather than an imminent crisis for Matthew.

The Lucan additions move farther away from the immediacy of the Marcan concerns and point to a period of the church. First of all he alters <u>heneken emou eis martyrion autois</u> of Mk 13:9 to <u>heneken tou onomatos mou; apobēsetai hymin eis martyrion</u> (21:12c-13). The <u>RSV</u> translates Lk 21:13 as "This will be a time for you to bear testimony," but this destroys the literal sense of <u>apobēsetai</u>, "it will lead" to testifying.[1] More explicitly than Matthew, Luke has made the Marcan statement on the relation of persecution and witnessing into a general teaching on the meaning of persecution. The second major Lucan addition is that he adds sayings to the Marcan statements which soften the harshness of the threat of persecution. To Mk 13:11 where it is simply said that the Holy Spirit will be given to the disciples, Luke in 21:15 adds that the disciples will be endowed with a wisdom which "none of your adversaries will be able to withstand or contradict." To the statement of Mk 13:13 that "you will be hated by all men," Luke (21:18) adds the Q saying, "But not a hair of your head will perish." Luke has thus changed the Marcan exhortation to fearless witnessing into a theology of martyrdom. Luke writes for a church which experiences persecution, but it has become a standard event in his

---

[1] Arndt-Gingrich, <u>Lexicon</u>, p. 88.

church and he is constructing a catechesis on the meaning and value of persecution. Persecution is less a recent onslaught against the church than a way of life.[1]

Thus, both the Matthean and Lucan alterations of the Marcan material move away from the immediacy of persecution which we find in the Marcan account. The question then arises as to what persecution Mark may have in mind. Brandon is illustrative of those who hold that 13:9-13 dates from the persecution under Nero.[2] This theory suffers under two principle objections. If the persecution of Christians took place in the city of Rome, the allusion to the handing over to Jewish synagogues would make no sense since there is no evidence that Christians were tried by Jews during the Neronic persecution. If the persecution is thought to extend beyond the city of Rome to areas where Jewish synagogues had power, the problem arises that there is little evidence that the persecution under Nero signalled any outbreak against Christians throughout the empire. As Robert Grant has written: "Nero set a precedent for dealing with Christians in the city of Rome, not outside it."[3] The later persecutions under Domitian are not only not certain, but, if they did occur, they occurred toward the end of his reign (A.D. 81-96), so they could not influence this part of Mark's gospel.[4] Therefore the exact persecutions and trials which lie behind Mark 13 can never

---

[1] Conzelmann, Theology of St. Luke, pp. 209-213.

[2] S. G. F. Brandon, Jesus and the Zealots (New York: Charles Scribner's Sons, 1967), p. 240; Taylor, Mark, p. 641.

[3] Robert M. Grant, Augustus to Constantine (New York: Harper and Row, 1970), p. 79; Eduard Meyer, Ursprung und Anfänge des Christentums (Stuttgart: J. G. Gotta'sche Buchhandlung, 1923), III, 510-511.

[4] Grant, Augustus, pp. 79-80, is doubtful of the existence of a persecution under Domitian.

be specified. The methodological problem here is that the only entree to the historical situation which underlies the gospel of Mark is the gospel itself, so that the situation addressed by the gospel must remain always a postulate. In the following pages we will suggest that there are elements in the tumultuous history of the years A.D. 66-70 which may provide a backdrop for the realism of Mk 13:9-13. What is certain is that Mark has in view real persecutions suffered by the community and that he constructs a theology to help his community meet this situation. What remains conjecture is the precise historical situation which touched off the persecutions.

Outside of the gospels the only available source for a picture of the turmoil in the years 66-70 is the account left by Josephus. There are problems, however, in the use of Josephus for this period. On the one hand his work is highly tendentious and he exhibits a definite anti-Zealot bias.[1] On the other, there is no <u>direct</u> contact between Josephus and the gospel narrative either in events described or persons mentioned, so to claim that they are talking about the same event always remains a matter of conjecture. What we will attempt to suggest is that there is in Josephus evidence of a situation which would explain both the fact that Christians might have been persecuted in Palestine in the years A.D. 66-70, and that the charges against them as mirrored in Mark would also fit in with the intellectual climate of this period.

One of the aspects of this period mentioned by Josephus is that, immediately prior to the war with Rome, there was a series of pogroms and violent acts against Jews throughout the

---

[1] On Josephus' purpose and plan in writing see, <u>JW</u>, 1,1-12 # 1-30, esp. 1.4 # 9-12, on his anti-Zealot bias see also 7.7,1 # 259-274.

area of Syria and Palestine.[1] Allied to this was constantly recurring civil strife in Jerusalem itself.[2] It is quite possible that Christians in Judaea would have been caught up in these struggles. More than these general features there are three aspects of Josephus' account which bear directly on our present concerns: (a) his notation that the Zealots held trials when they took over Jerusalem, (b) his testimony that preoccupation with the temple and its fate was very much in the air in the latter years of the war, and (c) the mention of messianic pretenders associated with the war against Rome.

Josephus mentions the Zealot trials in Jewish Wars and gives one instance of a man who was innocently condemned by one of the Zealot courts.[3] Since the Zealots had also pre-empted the appointment of high priests, hence the head of the Sanhedrin, it is logical to assume that at times the whole legal machinery was in the hands of whatever Zealot faction was then in power.[4] It is quite possible that Jerusalem Christians could have suffered under the excesses of Zealot summary trials and had to stand trial before Jewish courts. The reference to handing over to gentile authorities (Mk 13:9) is not only paralleled by Paul's fate as recorded in Acts, but also by an event which Josephus records as taking place seven years before the war during the rule of Albinus (62-64).[5] Josephus recounts the fate

---

[1] JW, 2.13,6-7 # 264-270; 2.18,1-2 # 457-465; 2.18,5 # 477; 2.18,7-9 # 487ff.

[2] JW, most of book IV, especially 4.3,2 # 130.

[3] JW, 4.5,4 # 335-344.

[4] JW, 4.3,6 # 147-150; Brandon, Jesus and the Zealots, p. 140; Martin Hengel, Die Zeloten (Arbeiten zur Geschichte des spätjudentums und Urchristentums, Vol. I; Leiden: E. J. Brill, 1961), pp. 224-225.

[5] On Paul see Acts 18:12ff.; ch. 22ff.

of an enigmatic figure named Jesus, son of Ananias who appeared in Jerusalem proclaiming the following:[1]

    A voice from the east, a voice from the west

    A voice from the four winds

    A voice against Jerusalem, and the sanctuary (naos)

    A voice against the bridegroom and the bride

    A voice against all the people.

Josephus mentions that this Jesus was turned over to Albinus who had him scourged and let him go. He then continued his refrain until he was killed in the early phase of the siege. The important thing about the story of Jesus is that it indicates that in Jerusalem there was prophetic activity against the temple, and that this activity was summarily suspect in the eyes of Jewish officials.

    Josephus also notes that the temple played a significant role in the ideology of the Jewish war against Rome.[2] Warring Zealot factions fought for control of the temple. The ultimate fate of the temple was very much associated with the outcome of the war. In his opposition to the Zealots, Josephus records an ancient oracle (palaios logos) to the effect that the city would be taken and the temple burnt to the ground when the city was afflicted with sedition.[3] He records a series of ominous portents surrounding the temple which occurred during the siege of the city, and notes that the taking of the city would be associated in an enigmatic way with an event in the temple.[4] Thus Josephus is a witness that in Palestinian Judaism in the years

---

[1] JW, 6.5,3 # 300-304.

[2] Hengel, Die Zeloten, pp. 289-293.

[3] JW, 4.6,2 # 388.

[4] JW, 6.5,3 # 289-309, 311; Hengel, Zeloten, pp. 246-247.

A.D. 66-70 there was a renewed interest in the meaning of the temple and its relation to the fate of the nation. In this context Jewish Christian opposition to the temple could be conceived by groups in control as tantamount to sedition, and bring on them the trials and persecutions similar to those mentioned in Mk 13:9-13.

Finally at the time of the war there was an upsurge of messianic expectation.[1] Josephus says that the leading thing which spurred the resistance to Rome (to de eparan autous malista pros ton polemon) was an "ambiguous oracle" (chrēsmos amphibolos) that one from their (the Jews') country would be ruler of the world.[2] During this period various messianic figures arose. Josephus mentions Menahem, son of Judas who came hoia dē basileus to Jerusalem, occupied the temple and became eventually a tyrant.[3] Another messianic figure was Simon bar Giora who was admitted to the city by the Idumean allies of John of Gischala who had occupied the temple and was acting in a tyrannical manner.[4] Simon was hailed by the people as a saviour (sōtēr hypo tou dēmou), and one of his first acts was to try to regain control of the temple.[5] Hengel speculates that the coins issued in the fourth year of the war on which was inscribed "for the salvation of Zion," stem from the rule of Simon in Jerusalem and confirm that he appropriated a messianic role to himself.[6] Further support for the fact that the nationalistic movements of

---

[1] Billerbeck, Kommentar, IV, 996-1015; August Strobel, Kerygma und Apokalyptik (Göttingen: Vandenhoeck und Ruprecht, 1967), pp. 104-106. Kelber, "Kingdom and Parousia," pp. 186-188.

[2] JW, 6.5,4 # 312-313.

[3] JW, 2.17,8 # 434; Hengel, Zeloten, pp. 299-302.

[4] JW, 4.9,11 # 566-576; Hengel, Zeloten, pp. 303-304.

[5] JW, 4.9,11-12 # 575-578.   [6] Zeloten, p. 303.

that time involved the upsurge in messianic figures comes from
the later Roman suppression of descendants of the Davidic line,
as well as from the career of Bar Kochba.[1] The important point
for our present concern about the presence of these messianic
figures and the factions and divisions they caused is that they
help us not only to understand the Marcan warning against false
messiahs and false prophets (13:6, 22), but their presence suggests that any Christians who made messianic claims for Jesus
and who looked for his speedy return would be caught up in the
maelstrom of civil strife in Jerusalem.

Therefore, there is a parallelism between the events Mark
warns his community about in ch. 13 and the picture of the last
years of Jerusalem as recorded by Josephus. What Mark says is
in store for his community especially in 13:9-13--trials before
Jewish courts, being handed over to gentiles, scourging, factionalism and betrayals--are all events which Josephus pictures
the inhabitants of Jerusalem as having suffered. This is not to
affirm as Brandon does that Jerusalem Christians were involved
in the Zealot movement, but that they could not have avoided the
consequences of the times in which they lived.[2] Even if these
individual events are not the events reflected in Mark 13, the
whole context of the discourse as a response to a question about
the relation of the temple to the end time, parallels similar
speculations in contemporary Judaism.

The redactional verse, 13:10, "And the gospel must first
be preached to all nations," is added evidence that Mark envisages a situation of real persecution and real trial. The

---

[1] Ibid., pp. 304-307.

[2] Brandon, *Jesus and the Zealots*, ch. IV, "Jewish Christians and the Zealot Ideal," pp. 146-220.

context of 13:9-13 is, as Gaston notes, eschatological paraenesis.[1] Mark exhorts his readers to be witnesses in the face of persecution and the function of this witness is that the gospel be proclaimed to all nations (13:10). What is the gospel which is to be proclaimed? In his penetrating analysis of the Markan understanding of euaggelion Marxsen has shown that gospel is less a matter of content than a way of re-presenting Jesus to the time of the reader. The gospel "makes contemporary the one who has come and the one who will come."[2] This means that the Christian of Mark's time, when suffering the same things which Jesus suffered, is making Jesus present to his world and the gospel is, in effect, proclaimed. In this light we can suggest why Mark wrote a full blown narrative of the trial of Jesus before Jewish officials. The form, trial, comes from a desire to portray Jesus standing trial as his followers had done. Its function is to give them the paradigm of the good confession in the face of trial. To them as to Jesus the response they must make at that time will be given (13:11; 14:61). The intercalation of the trial narrative within the denial of Peter supports this view of the function of the trial narrative. In a recent study of the denial of Peter, Max Wilcox suggests that "The story is not primarily about Peter, but about a time of testing and trial," so that the intercalation of the trial narrative within the story of Peter's denial is another way to exhort the Christians of Mark's time not to fail in the hour of trial as Peter did.[3] Therefore we suggest that Mark composes a trial of

---

[1] No Stone, pp. 41-60; Lightfoot, Gospel Message, p. 50, "A remarkable feature of the discourse is that it contains at least as much counsel and warning as apocalyptic revelation."

[2] Marxsen, Mark, p. 148.

[3] Max Wilcox, "The Denial Sequence in Mark xiv.26-31, 66-72," NTS, XVII (1970-71), 435.

Jesus precisely as trial to meet the experiences and demands of the community for which he is writing, a community caught up in the civil strife and trials in the years during and immediately following the Jewish War.

Not only is the form and function of the trial narrative explained by postulating a setting in the life of a community which has recently experienced the horrors of the Jewish War, but the theology of the trial narrative fits in with such a setting. We have noted that the two principal parts of the trial narrative are a saying concerned with opposition to the temple and the Christological or messianic confession of Jesus. These certainly fit in with what we saw were two factors very much alive in Jerusalem in the latter years of the war. We have seen that Mark constantly portrays Jesus in opposition to the temple while at the same time his death spells the downfall of the significance of the temple (15:39), while in his ministry Jesus prepares his community to be the nucleus of the new temple which will be established at his return. In a situation where the Christian church experienced the destruction of the temple such a theology would have great meaning. The Jewish Christians are not to view the events of A.D. 70 as a horror, but as the culmination of a process which began in the ministry of Jesus. The anti-temple material thus becomes a way for Jewish Christians to come to terms with the destruction of the cult center and to view the community as its replacement. Also, the pattern we noted in the use of the Son of Man sayings--suffering, vindication through the return of the Son of Man, new community--fits in with the situation of a Church where members are suffering and looking for hope in their suffering. They are to look to the return of Jesus for their vindication and not to see in the destruction of the temple the end.

Therefore we suggest that a redaction-critical analysis of the trial narrative and its form and function in Mark suggests that Mark was destined for a Jewish Christian community who had recently experienced the horrors of the Jewish war, including the destruction of the temple. The community was brought to trial and would continue to be for their proclamation that Jesus was the only messiah, that he would return as Son of Man to vindicate his elect, and that they were the new temple replacing the destroyed sanctuary which had lost its relevance when its officials rejected Jesus. Thus Mark gives his readers not only an apology to their critics, but also a way of coming to terms in their own minds with the destruction of so much of their Jewish heritage in the war.

The Trial Narrative as Narrative

In the previous section we noted certain reasons why Mark cast 14:53-65 in the form of a _trial_ narrative. Here we will direct our attention to the _narrative_ aspect of the trial narrative. At this point contact is made between secular literary criticism and redaction criticism. Also, at this point because of the uncharted nature of the area we are entering, our discussion is more in the line of suggestions than of definite conclusions. A surprising fact is that secular literary critics and biblical literary critics, though devoting the major portions of their lives to analyses of texts, have so rarely entered into dialogue. Northrop Frye has criticized biblical literary critics for viewing the bible "as a scrapbook of corruptions, glosses, redactions, insertions, conflations, misplacings and misunderstandings."[1] Yet, his suggestion that all parts of the bible be interpreted in light of a typological scheme which goes from Genesis to the Book of Revelation, would hardly meet with acceptance from biblical critics. However, Frye's charge is often justified in light of the dominant methodology of New Testament studies after K. L. Schmidt and the form critics who viewed the evangelists primarily as collectors of pre-existing small units, and who devoted most of their efforts to discovering the form and function of these units. Allied to this problem is that the gospels have been seen as a form of "oral literature" or folk literature, unsophisticated in their composition and execution. This has hindered scholars from applying criteria taken from more consciously articulated literary works such as the novel and the drama to gospel material. Another problem arises when the gospels are viewed either as kerygma or confessional documents. Modern literary critics have stressed the need for "objective criticism," letting the work speak for itself, and the need to avoid the "intentional fallacy," of interpreting the work purely in terms of the author's intention.[2] The theological interpretation of the gospels would seem to conflict with this view.

There are, however, presently both within the realm of secular literary criticism and biblical studies movements which suggest answers to the above problems, and provide directions for a rapprochement between the disciplines. Redaction criticism which concentrates on the final product rather than its pre-history and seeks to find the meaning of a gospel by

---

[1] Northrop Frye, Anatomy of Criticism (Princeton, N.J.: University of Princeton Press, 1957), p. 315.

[2] William K. Wimsatt, The Verbal Icon (New York: Noonday Press, 1954), pp. 3-18.

internal analysis counters the objection that the gospels are a simple collection of "glosses, redactions, misplacings and misunderstandings." The gospels represent consciously articulated literary products which are more than a sum of their parts. Among literary critics there is a growing disenchantment with purely "objective criticism." Wayne Booth's Rhetoric of Fiction, as the title suggests, represents a break with the schools of criticism which would preclude any statement about the author's judgment or intent from an evaluation of a work. He notes:

> In short the author's judgment is always present, always evident to anyone who knows how to look for it. . . . As we begin to deal with this question, we must never forget that, though the author can to some extent choose his disguises, he can never choose to disappear.[1]

Support for the relevance of redaction criticism to secular literary criticism comes also from the statement of Wellek and Warren that:

> The creative process should cover the entire sequence from the subconscious origins of a literary work to those last revisions which, with some writers, are the most genuinely creative part of the whole.[2]

These observations suggesting that there is a point of contact between secular literary criticism and redaction criticism of the gospels, do not tell us in the concrete what the point of contact is. The problem is to find a category under which the insights of literary criticism can be applied to the gospels. This problem is especially acute because the gospels and even the individual gospels seem to represent sui generis products which are not repeated in subsequent literature. The

---

[1] Wayne Booth, The Rhetoric of Fiction (Phoenix Books; Chicago: University of Chicago Press, 1967), p. 20.

[2] R. Wellek and A. Warren, Theory of Literature (New York: Harcourt, Brace and World, 1956), p. 85.

question then arises: can categories of history, novel, poetry or drama, but using the generic category of narrative which all these different forms can share in common. In technical terms narrative itself is not even a genus or category but rather a mode of discourse which can have different functions in different contexts. Even in antiquity we see that literary works, with different formal characteristics such as poetry and history, precisely as narrative can perform similar functions. Vergil's Aeneid and Livy's Histories both tell the contemporary Roman who he is in terms of the origin of his people and help him to come to terms with the world in which he lives. They both do this by telling a story, by using narrative. Therefore our task will be to see if by a study of the fact that Mark casts his version of the Christian message in the form of narrative, we can arrive at a fuller understanding of his gospel. In order to do this we will first indicate some ways in which Mark is de facto a narrative and then study the function of narrative as applied to the gospel of Mark.

Narrative is one of the concepts which is so basic that it eludes precise definition. The third edition of Webster's International Dictionary describes it as the "account of a series of events," and W. B. Gallie has written, "every story describes a sequence of actions and experiences of a number of people real or imaginary."[1] In their analysis of narrative Scholles and Kellog have noted that there are two essential characteristics of narrative: plot, the dynamic sequential element in narrative literature, and characterization, what happens

---

[1] W. B. Gallie, Philosophy and the Historical Understanding (New York: Schocken, 1968), p. 32.

to individuals in this plot.¹ In contrast to the Christian
literature which preceded it, the gospel of Mark is most ob-
biously a narrative. Its extended story of Jesus moves beyond
the kerygmatic proclamations and the small narrative units found
in Pauline paradosis.² By introducing a plot and the interac-
tion of characters, the gospel assumes a radically different
character than the Q source which contained mostly teaching of
Jesus and lacked a conclusion to the work of Jesus, the Passion
narrative. It is precisely in those areas which give the work
its formal characteristics of narrative where the Marcan redaction is strongest. The linking of separate stories by temporal
and geographical designations and the movement of Jesus toward
Jerusalem and his fate give the dynamic sequential element to
what was prior to Mark a series of unrelated pericopes. Mark
also shows a strong interest in characterization. The constant
tension between Jesus and the disciples and the movement from
imperceptivity through misconception to denial on the part of
the disciples shows Mark's concern for developing characteriza-
tion.³ The studies of Marcan structure and the recognition of
its importance for an understanding of Mark's theology show that
the flow and development of the narrative is important to Mark.
This recognition of the formal characteristics of narrative as
present in Mark, leads to a discussion of the function of narrative as an entree to understanding the trial narrative as
narrative.

In a recent study of the rise of the novel and of

---

[1] R. Scholles and R. Kellog, The Nature of Narrative (New York: Oxford University Press, 1966), pp. 207, 169.

[2] 1 Cor 11:23-26; 15:3-8.

[3] Weeden, "The Heresy," pp. 145-147.

historical writing in the modern period Leo Braudy has written:

> The continuity of history, both past and present had become a problem. Both novelist and historian sought to discover its plot. . . . Both novelist and historian tried to present a plausible world, complete in itself, yet directly relevant to the reader's actual life.[1]

This statement is much like Wilder's description of biblical narrative:

> The narrative mode in the Bible provided not only orientation in the mysteries of time and existence, but therewith the structures of a human order against chaos, and of meaningfulness against unreason.[2]

Therefore, one function of narrative is to create an ordered world. This ordered world of the narrative confirms to the reader the triumph of meaningful sequential events over the power of chaos, and, by showing how events flow one from another, it gives an explanation against the unreason of life. In the case of the suffering and death of Jesus, Mark creates an ordered world by putting together the events which lead up to the death of Jesus in the dynamic order of a plot. These events culminate in the trial narrative. Mark is anxious to tell a story of Jesus which is "directly relevant to the reader's actual life." One way in which this is done is to emphasize the role of human decisions in the Passion narrative. In contrast to Paul who says that Jesus was put to death by the "powers of the age" (1 Cor 2:8), what immediately strikes one about the Marcan passion narrative is its "secular" character. In Mark the dramatic action is explained in terms of human causality and

---

[1] Leo Braudy, *Narrative Form in History and Fiction* (Princeton, N.J.: University of Princeton Press, 1970), p. 3.

[2] Amos Wilder, *The New Voice* (New York: Herder and Herder, 1969), p. 58; Beardslee, *Literary Criticism of the New Testament*, p. 17, writes in a similar vein: "By creating its own ordered world, wherein, through struggle or action an end is achieved, the story expresses faith in the ultimate reality of order and life."

human decisions. It is true that the fulfillment of scripture is a motif in the Passion narrative, but this Marcan dei functions much like the tragic necessity or moira of Greek tragedy. The people who succeed or fail in the Passion narrative are not portrayed as privy to any special revelation or the object of any manifestation of Jesus' power as in the miracle stories. Mark has therefore created for his readers an ordered world in which free human decisions about Jesus make a difference. Writing as he did in close connection with the turmoil, chaos and world dissolution caused by the Jewish War, Mark creates in effect a surrogate center for the people's religious needs. With the cult center and the traditions of the Jerusalem church destroyed, Mark creates a story of Jesus to which the people can attach their hopes and aspirations. Mark speaks in a concrete way to people in this situation. The Marcan church must have experienced the phenomenon of faithful disciples denying Jesus, faith found in unexpected places (cf. 15:39, the centurion), and the malice of men in bringing faithful followers of Jesus before judges and synagogues (13:9-13). By presenting similar events in a structured sequence of the life of Jesus, Mark makes the world in which his readers live intelligible and bearable because it is an imitation of the world their master experienced.

The second major function of narrative is classified under different rubrics. Aristotle has called it in the case of tragic narrative catharsis where, by engaging itself in the emotions of the tragic characters, the audience experiences a release of pity and fear. Wilder has used the concept of "identification" where narrative becomes the mode par excellence for expressing the Christian message since "the life of a Christian is itself a pilgrimage, a race, in short, a history," so that any Christian identifies his "history" with the narrative presented to him.[1] W. K. Wimsatt has spoken of the "concrete universal" in literature whereby a particular incident or narrative speaks to the universal longings and struggles of man.[2]

All these descriptions suggest that one function of narrative is to so engage the reader or hearer that he experiences himself an experience similar to the one narrated and that he identifies with the characters. In philosophical terms the experience of imitation becomes a way by which an individual moves beyond the confines and structures of his own existence and participates in ways of existing previously closed to him. Therefore the readers of Mark's Passion narrative and the trial narrative not only are presented with an ordered world, they become part of that world. The actions and destinies of the characters in the narrative become their actions and destinies. The world of narrative is re-presented to them. In the Passion narrative Mark himself suggests this function when in 14:9 he says that wherever the gospel story is told the deed of the woman will be recounted in remembrance, mnēmosunon, of her. Marxsen says that the meaning here is that where the act is proclaimed, the act is present, so that the past of Jesus becomes part of the present of the reader.[3] Therefore in this respect the literary critic's concepts of engagement and identification converge with the biblical critic's idea of re-praesentatio. Thus one function of narrative in Mark is to create a time scheme where the past of Jesus becomes the present of his reader.

---

[1] Wilder, Language of the Gospel, pp. 64-65.

[2] Verbal Icon, pp. 69-83; also Erich Auerbach, Mimesis (Princeton, N.J.: University of Princeton Press, 1968), p. 43.

[3] Mark, p. 101.

Narrative and Apocalyptic

It is not adequate to discuss the gospel of Mark simply as narrative and study its role simply in relation to the past and the present. There are elements of the gospel of Mark which make of it a special kind of narrative and orient it to the future as well as to the past and present. It is therefore necessary to make a few brief remarks about the function of the apocalyptic elements of Mark. The motifs which have long been recognized as characteristic of apocalyptic are found in Mark and give a definite tenor to it.[1] The Kingdom is proclaimed as the definitive irruption of God into history (1:14) and at the same time an object of future hope.[2] We have noted that Mark re-apocalypticizes the tradition by creating full blown future Son of Man sayings using an apocalyptic scenario.[3] The discourse of ch. 13 has long been recognized to be part of the gospel most influenced by the imagery of Jewish apocalyptic. This orients the whole gospel to an expectation of the future definitive action of God in terminating history (13:24-27).[4] The Passion narrative becomes the final act or the turmoil which appears before the arrival of the end time.[5] The struggle

---

[1] H. H. Rowley, *The Relevance of Apocalyptic*, pp. 166-194, and C. K. Barrett, *The New Testament Background: Selected Documents* (New York: Harper and Brothers, 1961), pp. 227-255, give summaries of the principal apocalyptic motifs.

[2] Werner G. Kümmel, *Promise and Fulfillment* (Studies in Biblical Theology, Vol. XXIII; London: S. C. M. Press, 1966), pp. 1-87 (kingdom as future); pp. 105-140 (kingdom as present).

[3] *Supra*, pp. 150-162.

[4] Rowley, *Relevance*, p. 170, on historical understanding of apocalyptic.

[5] H. W. Bartsch, "Die Bedeutung des Sterbens Jesu nach den Synoptikern," *TZ*, XX (1965), 102; Strobel, *Kerygma*, pp. 145-154.

in Mark, though played out in human terms of opposition to
Jesus, assumes a cosmic dimension since the outcome of the
struggle (the return of the Son of Man, Mk 14:62) is determined
in a sphere other than that of this earth.[1] The community which
Jesus will found is one which will appear only in the future.
The present community exists in a state of expectation.

Therefore Mark uses apocalyptic motifs to give a radically future orientation to his gospel. These elements enable him to complete his time scheme by integrating past, present, and future into one unity.[2] The past of Jesus is relived in the present experience of the community, but, as in the case of Jesus, so too is the case of the believer the ultimate meaning of his existence is determined by future hope. The use of apocalyptic enables Mark to create an eschatology which is in accord with his Christology and his view of the nature of Christian discipleship and the role of the Christian community. In this sense the trial narrative of Mark is a gospel in miniature. In the previous section of this chapter we have seen how Mark uses it to unite the past of Jesus to the present of the reader by giving him the example of the confession he must make in his own time of trial. The Son of Man saying in 14:62, which is the high point of the narrative, gives the apocalyptic tone to the narrative and moves the reader's expectation to the future. Therefore the gospel as a whole and the trial narrative are both narrative and apocalypse, or better, a narrative apocalypse.[3]

---

[1] On this aspect of apocalyptic, Rowley, *Relevance*, p. 172.

[2] Norman Perrin, "The Literary *Gattung* 'Gospel'--Some Observations," *ExpT*, LXXII (1970), 7.

[3] This latter description was suggested to me in conversation by Professor Perrin.

There is another function of apocalyptic which must be mentioned to complete our attempt to understand the relation of form and content in the gospel of Mark. Apocalyptic literature is fundamentally "persecution literature."[1] The book of Daniel took root in a community experiencing the horrors of the excesses of Antiochus IV.[2] The Christian Apocalypse of John is preoccupied with persecutions which affect the community.[3] This setting for apocalyptic literature explains much of its cryptic quality. It is coded encouragement to the believer and a veiled judgment on the unbeliever or opponent of the persecuted community. In the case of Mark, written as it was in a time of persecution and turmoil, the apocalyptic elements serve this function. They encourage the reader to persevere in a time of trial, endow him with the assurance of victory and orient his hope, past the present turmoil to the future.

The function of the apocalyptic elements in Mark enables us to see why the gospel of Mark was both imitated and rejected by his immediate followers Matthew and Luke. While following his order and accepting his use of narrative, they reject his apocalyptic orientation. By prefacing the life of Jesus with birth stories, they take away the sudden irruption of the divine into the human sphere, and provide an explanation for the origin of Jesus. They also de-eschatologize his work; Matthew, by providing a doctrinal book for his expanding church and Luke by making the gospel into the first part of a two-part work, the theme of which is the growth and expansion of the church. They

---

[1] Rowley, *Relevance*, p. 173.

[2] Otto Eissfeldt, *The Old Testament: An Introduction*, trans. Peter R. Ackroyd (New York: Harper and Row, 1964), p. 520.

[3] Feine, Behm, and Kümmel, *Introduction*, p. 329.

also write, as was noted, in a period when the church is not faced with the immediacy of persecution as it was in Mark. Therefore apocalyptic is no longer needed to provide encouragement to a community which felt itself experiencing the turmoil of the last days.

In this section we have attempted to show how redaction criticism has a point of contact with secular literary criticism by raising the question of the relation of form and content in a literary work. The analysis of the form used, in the case of Mark the narrative form, and of the way in which narrative functions, leads to a deeper understanding of the content of Mark. Study of narrative in Mark reveals that his work creates an ordered world for a people experiencing the crisis of the dissolution of their world through the Jewish wars. The narrative mode also allows him to integrate the past of Jesus into the reader's own experience. Finally we saw that a particular manifestation of narrative, the narrative apocalypse, allowed us to see the further dimension of Mark's work whereby he is able to integrate past, present, and future into one time scheme and at the same time is able to give a message of hope to a persecuted community.

Conclusion

The aspects of Mark's gospel which were treated in this chapter arose out of the demands of the questions raised by redaction criticism. While in the earlier chapters of the present work (II-IV), the emphasis was on the individual parts of the trial narrative, their origin and relation to each other, and their contact with other parts of the gospel, the emphasis in this chapter was on the narrative as a whole. In the first section of this chapter we noted that the trial narrative served not only as a compendium of Mark's theology by bringing together strands from previous sections of the gospel, but it also prepared the reader for what was to follow and became, in effect, a commentary on the crucifixion narrative. In the second section of the chapter, we directed our attention to the _trial_ aspect of the trial narrative to see if a study of form and content could tell us anything about the community for whom the gospel was intended. Here it was suggested that Mark wrote for a community which had experienced real trials as a result of the Jewish wars. The trial narrative provided them with both a paradigm of how they should act and gave them an ideology or theology with which they could understand their sufferings. In the final section we devoted our attention to the _narrative_ aspect of the trial narrative and saw that a study of the function of narrative yielded information about the function of both the gospel and the trial before the Sanhedrin as narrative. The gospel narrative creates an ordered world of which the reader becomes part, and which enables him to come to terms with the world in which he lives. Since this world was for the Marcan community a world of the dissolution of structures and of eschatological expectation, the Marcan narrative has many of the qualities of apocalyptic literature which flourishes in time of persecution and crisis. There is, then, in Mark a balance between what internal literary criticism reveals of the form and theological concerns of the gospel and between what historical criticism tells us of the situation in which the first of our gospels arose.

CONCLUSION

At the termination of each chapter we have attempted to summarize the major results achieved in the particular chapter so repetition of these results is unnecessary at this point. What will be attempted here is a brief statement of our results and a suggestion of their implications for further research. The trial narrative of the gospel of Mark is a section of the Marcan Passion narrative which in its present form did not belong to the earliest traditions of the Passion narrative. Its present form is due to the evangelist Mark who has created the narrative out of traditions available to him and left his own imprint and shape on the narrative. The initial contribution of Mark is to give it the formality of trial, as our analysis of the introductory verses indicated. The traditions available to Mark were primarily exegetical traditions which reflected on the Old Testament to proclaim the innocence of the suffering Jesus before unjust accusers. Mark has historicized these traditions and added to the narrative two other sets of traditional material which he in turn alters in terms of his purpose. One set consisted of a traditional saying of Jesus against the temple and an early church reflection on the community as the new temple. Mark combines these traditions in the trial narrative to bring to a culmination the anti-temple theme which is itself redactional in his gospel. The other set of traditions consisted of Christological traditions which looked to the return of Jesus. Mark has worked these traditions into full blown apocalyptic Son of Man sayings which themselves become part of a

Son of Man Christology which gives shape and direction to the Christology of his gospel. Again the trial narrative becomes the culmination of Mark's Christology and all the titles used of Jesus receive their definitive meaning here. The final elements of Marcan literary activity in the trial narrative concern the narrative as a whole. He has intercalated it within the story of the denial of Peter to bring to a culmination the tension between the revelation of Jesus and the misunderstanding of the disciples which permeates the gospel. In the context of the Passion narrative and the gospel as a whole, Mark has given the trial narrative a twofold function. On the one hand it summarizes what has gone before; on the other it prepares the reader for, and serves as a commentary to the crucifixion narrative. Finally, by writing a trial narrative Mark speaks to a community which itself is undergoing trials and serves to encourage them by giving them an example in their own suffering while at the same time giving them an ideology or theology by which they can understand their present situation.

One major implication of our view of the trial narrative touches on the area of the historicity of the trial narrative which we observed earlier did not enter directly into our discussion. Despite the almost endless research given to the historical problems surrounding the trial narrative, the most recent works on the narrative shed little light on the unsolved problems, so much so that in one of these works Samuel Sandmel has said simply, "In short, I give up on the problem."[1] To say

---

[1] "The Trial of Jesus: Reservations," _Judaism_, XX (1971), p. 74. This issue of _Judaism_ contains articles by Blinzer, Brandon, H. Cohn, Enslin, Flusser, R. M. Grant, Sandmell and Sloyan. See also, _The Trial of Jesus_, ed. Ernest Bammel (Studies in Biblical Theology, Second Series, Vol. XIII; London: S.C.M. Press, 1970). This is mainly a restatement of traditional historical problems and the traditional solutions to

this is not, however, to give up on the trial narrative. What Sandmel gives up on, in effect, is the attempt to find history where history is not intended. Our research suggests that continually to pose the historical question of the trial narrative is to pose the wrong question. Mark did not write history, but a gospel. Any attempt to find the historicity of the events surrounding the death of Jesus must, in the future, renounce the Marcan trial narrative as its principal source.

The second major implication of our research is that since the trial narrative exists in the context of the Passion narrative whatever success we have achieved in showing that the

---

them. Certain recent studies which have investigated the historicity of the trial from the viewpoint of historical criticism support the reserve which our literary and theological analyses yield. David R. Catchpole, The Trial of Jesus: A Study in the Gospels and Jewish Historiography from 1770 to the Present Day (Studia Post-Biblica, Vol. XVIII; Leiden: E. J. Brill, 1971). Catchpole's work contains an excellent summary of Jewish writing on the trial over the past two centuries. In his own constructive treatment of the trial, while bypassing the Marcan account as the basis for historical reconstruction, he builds his own reconstruction on the Lucan account, and the traditions behind it. Here, however, he is too little concerned with the theological motivation at work in the Lucan tradition. Haim H. Cohn, The Trial and Death of Jesus (New York: Harper and Row, 1971). Cohn is a Justice of the Supreme Court of Israel and his book represents an expansion of an earlier article published in the Israel Law Review, II (1967), 332-379. Cohn's work is interesting since he writes from the perspective of the legal expert but at the same time has a very traditional view of the gospel material. He adduces massive erudition to show that there was no Jewish involvement in a trial of Jesus, and that the Romans were the sole agents of Jesus' death. His positive suggestion that the "trial" before the Sanhedrin was an attempt on the Sanhedrin's part to save Jesus, a teacher beloved by the people, by dissuading him from holding to his claims during the impending trial by Pilate, while ingenious, is not supported by Christian or Jewish historical sources. His evidence against the formal involvement of the Sanhedrin in the condemnation of Jesus is excellent. His reconstruction of what actually happened is dubious. Finally, Jeffrey G. Sobosan, "The Trial of Jesus," Journal of Ecumenical Studies, X (1973), 70-93. Sobosan's work is a good summary of select recent studies questioning the historicity of the trial of Jesus and, like Cohn's work, a plea against the anti-Semitism which naive acceptance of the historicity of the trial engenders.

trial narrative in its final form is a Marcan composition and due to his theological concerns has implications for the rest of the Passion narrative. The present work was initiated with a paradoxical relationship to the work of Martin Dibelius. On the one hand the authority of his view that the Passion narrative was the largest block of connected pre-Marcan tradition made scholars hesitate to look for Marcan activity in the narrative. Our research suggests that this hesitancy is not justified in the case of the trial narrative and therefore urges that other parts of the Passion narrative be studied as an entree to Mark's theology. On the other hand, Dibelius' observation that the theological concerns of Mark are evident by studying the Marcan additions to this original narrative, and his statement that the trial narrative and the crucifixion narrative are the high points of the Passion narrative, provided the stimulus for the present detailed study of the trial narrative. Future work on the Passion narrative must, therefore, continue in this double direction of criticism of one aspect of Dibelius' work and acceptance of his insights on the other. Our hope is that the present work is a contribution to the task begun.

APPENDIX

THE MARCAN INSERTIONS

Listed below are the places in Mark which meet the criteria established for an insertion: (a) close verbal agreement, (b) a superfluous or tautological quality to one of the phrases, and (c) synoptic alteration. Only the key words in the framing verses will be listed, not the inserted material. Continued study of this phenomenon in Mark has convinced me that it is a very important compositional technique used by Mark for a variety of functions, and not simply to call attention to the "inserted" material. I hope to examine this technique in detail and expand on its significance in a subsequent publication.

I.	2:6 2:8b	dialogizomenoi en tais kardiais autōn dialogizesthe en tais kardiais hymōn (Mt 9:3-4; Lk 5:21-23)
II.	2:9b 2:11a	egeire kai aron ton krabbaton sou egeire, aron ton krabbaton sou (Mt 9:5b-6; Lk 5:23b-24)
III.	3:7 3:8	poly plēthos plēthos poly (Mt 4:25; Lk 6:17-18)
IV.	3:14 3:16	kai epoiēsen dōdeka kai epoiēsen tous dōdeka (Mt 5:1-2; Lk 6:12-13)
V.	4:31 4:32	hos hotan sparē kai hotan sparē (Mt 13:31-32; Lk 13:19)
VI.	5:10 5:23	kai parekalei auton polla kai parakalei auton polla (Mt 8:31; 9:19; Lk 8:32; 8:40)
VII.	5:29 5:34	hoti iatai apo tēs mastigos isthi hugiēs apo tēs mastigos sou (Mt 9:21-22; Lk 8:45-48)
VIII.	6:14 6:16	kai ēkousen ho basileus hērodēs akousas de ho hērodēs elegen (Mt 14:1-3; Lk 9:7-9)
IX.	6:31b 6:32b	kat' idian eis erēmon topon eis erēmon topon kat' idian (Mt 14:12-13; Lk 9:10)

X.	7:20	ekeino koinoi ton anthrōpon
	7:23	kai koinoi ton anthrōpon
		(Mt 15:16-20; absent in Luke)
XI.	8:17	oupō noeite oude syniete
	8:21	oupō syniete
		(Mt 16:8-11; absent in Luke)
XII.	8:29	apokritheis ho pētros legei autō
	9:5	kai apokritheis ho pētros legei tō Iēsou
		(Mt 16:16; 17:4; Lk 9:20; 9:33)
XIII.	9:12	<u>kai pōs gegraptai</u> epi ton huion tou anthrōpou <u>hina polla pathē</u> kai exoudenēthē
	9:13b	kai epoiēsen autō hosa ēthelen <u>kathōs gegraptai ep' auton</u>
		(Mt 17:10-13 omits the reference to scripture; Lk omits the pericope)
XIV.	10:23b	pōs dyskolōs hoi ta chrēmata echontes eis tēn basileian tou theou eiseleusontai
	10:24b	pōs dyskolon estin eis tēn basileian tou theou eiselthein
		(Mt 19:23-24; Lk 18:24-25)
XV.	11:11	kai eisēlthen eis Ierosolyma
	11:15	kai erchontai eis Ierosolyma
		(Mt 21:10-12; Lk 19:45)
XVI.	13:5a	blepete mē tis hymas planēsē (Mt 24:4; Lk 21:8)
	13:9	blepete de hymeis heautous (Mt omits; Lk omit omits)
	13:23	hymeis de blepete (Mt 24:25; Lk 17:23)
	13:33	blepete (Mt 25:13; Lk 21:36)
XVII.	13:33b	ouk oidate gar pote ho kairos estin
	13:35b	ouk oidate gar pote ho kyrios tēs oikias erchetai
		(Mt 25:13-15; Lk 19:12-13)
XVIII.	13:35	grēgoreite
	13:37	grēgoreite
		(Mt 25:42; Lk 12:40)
XIX.	14:18	kai anakeimenōn autōn kai esthiontōn
	14:22	kai esthiontōn
		(Mt 26:21-26; Lk 22:19)
XX.	14:56	kai isai hai martyria ouk ēsan
	14:59	kai oude houtōs isē ēn hē martyria autōn
		(Mt 26:60-61; Lk omits pericope)
XXI.	15:2	kai epērōta auton ho pilatos
	15:4	ho de pilatos palin epērōta auton
		(Mt 27:11-12; Lk 23:3)

XXII. 15:24   kai staurousin auton
       15:25   kai estaurōsan auton
                              (Mt 27:34-36; Lk 23:33-34)

In addition to these places which meet the criteria for an "insertion" and seem to indicate Marcan editorial activity and intent, there are many other places where a similar repetition in language occurs:[1] 1:22 and 1:27; 1:29, 1:30; 1:35, 1:45; 1:33, 2:2; 2:14b, 15b; 2:24b, 26; 3:31, 32; 5:31, 32; 6:14b, 16b; 7:3, 4; 8:1, 2; 8:11, 12; 8:16, 17; 9:9, 10; 9:14a, 16; 9:38a (in some MSS); 10:29, 30; 10:38, 42; 8:22, 10:46; 11:28, 29, 33; 4:2, 11:38; 15:30, 32; 15:34, 37; 15:40, 47; 15:44a, 44b.

---

[1] The articles of Neirynck, supra, p. 79, n. 1, contain an exhaustive list of possible duplications in Mark.

BIBLIOGRAPHY

Commentaries

Gould, Ezra P. The Gospel According to St. Mark. International Critical Commentary, Vol. VII. New York: Charles Scribner's Sons, 1913.

Grundmann, Walter. Das Evangelium nach Markus. Theologischer Handkommentar zum Neuen Testament, Vol. II. Berlin: Evangelische Verlagsanstalt, 1968.

Haenchen, Ernst. Der Weg Jesu. 2d rev. ed. Berlin: Walter de Gruyter, 1961.

Klostermann, Erich. Das Markusevangelium. Handbuch zum Neuen Testament, Vol. III. 4th rev. ed. Tübingen: J. C. B. Mohr [Paul Siebeck], 1950.

Lagrange, Marie-Joseph. Évangile selon Saint Marc. Études Bibliques. Paris: Librairie Victor Lecoffre, 1920.

Lohmeyer, Ernst. Das Evangelium des Markus. Kritisch-exegetischer Kommentar über das Neue Testament, Vol. II. 17th ed. Göttingen: Vandenhoeck und Ruprecht, 1967.

Mally, Edward J. "The Gospel of Mark." Jerome Biblical Commentary. Edited by Raymond Brown, Joseph Fitzmyer, and Roland Murphy. Englewood Cliffs, N.J.: Prentice Hall, 1968.

Nineham, Dennis Eric. The Gospel of St. Mark. Pelican Gospel Commentary. Baltimore: Penguin Books, 1967.

Schmid, Josef. The Gospel According to Mark. The Regensburg New Testament. Translated by Kevin Condon. Staten Island, N.Y.: Alba House, 1968.

Schniewind, Julius. Das Evangelium nach Markus. Das Neue Testament Deutsch, Vol. I. Göttingen: Vandenhoeck und Ruprecht, 1952.

Schweizer, Eduard. The Good News According to Mark. Translated by Donald H. Madvig. Richmond: John Knox Press, 1970.

Swete, Henry Barclay. The Gospel According to St. Mark. London: Macmillan and Co., 1908.

Taylor, Vincent. The Gospel According to St. Mark. 2d ed. London: Macmillan and Co., 1966.

Wellhausen, Julius. Das Evangelium Marci. Berlin: Georg Reimer, 1909.

General Works

Achtemeier, Paul J. "Toward the Isolation of Pre-Markan Miracle Catenae." Journal of Biblical Literature, LXXXIX (1970), 265-291.

_____. "The Origin and Function of the Pre-Markan Miracle Catenae." Journal of Biblical Literature, XCI (1972), 198-221.

Albertz, Martin. Die Synoptischen Streitsgespräche. Berlin: Trowitsch und Sohn, 1921.

Arndt, William F., and Gingrich, F. Wilbur. A Greek-English Lexicon of the New Testament and Other Early Christian Literature. 4th rev. ed. Chicago: University of Chicago Press, 1952.

Auerbach, Erich. Mimesis. Princeton, N.J.: Princeton University Press, 1968.

Bacon, Benjamin W. The Gospel of Mark: Its Composition and Date. New Haven: Yale University Press, 1925.

Balz, Horst R. Methodische Probleme der Neutestamentlichen Christologie. Wissenschaftliche Monographien zum Alten und Neuen Testament, Vol. XXV. Neukirchen-Vluyn: Neukirchener Verlag, 1967.

Bammel, Ernst, ed. The Trial of Jesus. Studies in Biblical Theology, Second Series, Vol. XIII. London: S. C. M. Press, 1970.

Barrett, Charles Kingsley. The New Testament Background: Selected Documents. New York: Harper and Brothers, 1961.

Bartsch, Hans-Werner. "Die Bedeutung des Sterbens Jesu nach den Synoptikern." Theologische Zeitschrift, XX (1965), 87-102.

_____. "Early Christian Eschatology in the Synoptic Gospels." New Testament Studies, XI (1964-1965), 387-397.

_____. "Historische Erwägungen zur Leidensgeschichte." Evangelische Theologie, XXII (1962), 444-459.

Beardslee, William A. Literary Criticism of the New Testament. Philadelphia: Fortress Press, 1970.

Beasley-Murray, George Raymond. A Commentary on Mark Thirteen. London: Macmillan and Co., 1957.

_____. Jesus and the Future. London: Macmillan and Co., 1954.

Benoit, P. "Jésus devant le Sanhedrin." Angelicum, XX (1943), 143-165.

Bertram, Georg. Die Leidensgeschichte Jesu und der Christuskult. Forschungen zur Religion und Literature des Alten
und Neuen Testaments, N.F., Vol. XXII. Göttingen:
Vandenhoeck und Ruprecht, 1922.

Best, Ernest. The Temptation and Passion: The Marcan Soteriology. Society for New Testament Studies, Monograph
Series, Vol. II. Cambridge: University Press, 1965.

Betz, Hans Dieter. "Jesus as Divine Man." Jesus and the
Historian. Edited by Thomas Trotter. Philadelphia:
Westminster Press, 1968. Pp. 114-133.

Beyer, Hermann. "βλασφημία." Theological Dictionary of the New
Testament. Translated by Geoffrey W. Bromiley. Grand
Rapids, Mich.: Wm. B. Eerdmans, 1964. I, 621-625.

Bird, C. H. "Some γὰρ clauses in St. Mark's Gospel." Journal
of Theological Studies, N.S., IV (1953), 171-187.

Black, Matthew. An Aramaic Approach to the Gospels and Acts.
3d rev. ed. Oxford: Clarendon Press, 1967.

Blass, F., and Debrunner, A. A Greek Grammar of the New Testament and Other Early Christian Literature. Translated
and edited by Robert W. Funk. Chicago: University of
Chicago Press, 1961.

Blinzer, Josef. Der Prozess Jesu. 4th rev. ed. Regensburg:
Pustet, 1969.

Boobyer, G. H. "Galilee and Galileans in St. Mark's Gospel."
Bulletin of the John Rylands Library, XXXV (1953),
334-348.

_____. "The Redaction of Mark IV, 1-34." New Testament
Studies, VIII (1961-1962), 59-70.

_____. "The Secrecy Motif in Mark's Gospel." New Testament
Studies, VI (1959-1960), 225-235.

Booth, Wayne. The Rhetoric of Fiction. Phoenix Books.
Chicago: University of Chicago Press, 1967.

Bornkamm, Günther, Barth, Gerhard, and Held, Heinz Joachim.
Tradition and Interpretation in Matthew. Translated by
Percy Scott. Philadelphia: Westminster Press, 1963.

Bornkamm, Günther. "Die Verzögerung der Parusie." In Memoriam
Ernst Lohmeyer. Edited by W. Schmauch. Stuttgart:
Evangelisches Verlagswerk, 1951. Pp. 116-126.

Bousset, Wilhelm. Kyrios Christos. Translated by John E.
Steely. 5th ed. New York and Nashville: Abingdon
Press, 1970.

_____. Die Religion des Judentums in späthellenistischen
Zeitalter. 3d ed. Tubingen: J. C. B. Mohr [Paul
Siebeck], 1926.

Bousset, Wilhelm. "Die Religionsgeschichte und das Neue Testament." Theologische Rundschau, VII (1904), 265-277, 311-318; XV (1912), 251-278.

Brandon, S. G. F. Jesus and the Zealots. New York: Charles Scribner's Sons, 1967.

_____. The Trial of Jesus of Nazareth. Historic Trials Series. New York: Stein and Day, 1968.

Braudy, Leo. Narrative Form in History and Fiction. Princeton, N.J.: Princeton University Press, 1970.

Braumann, Georg. "Mk 15,2-5 und Mk 14,55-64." Zeitschrift für die neutestamentliche Wissenschaft, LII (1961), 273-278.

Brown, Raymond. The Gospel According to John. The Anchor Bible, Vols. XXIX and XXIXa. Garden City, N.Y.: Doubleday and Co., 1966 and 1970.

Bultmann, Rudolf. The Gospel of John. Translated by G. R. Beasley-Murray. Philadelphia: Westminster Press, 1971.

_____. The History of the Synoptic Tradition. Translated by John Marsh. Rev. ed. New York: Harper and Row, 1968.

_____. Theology of the New Testament. 2 vols. Translated by Kendrick Grobel. New York: Charles Scribner's Sons, 1951.

Burkill, T. Alec. "The Cryptology of the Parables in St. Mark's Gospel." Novum Testamentum, I (1956), 246-262.

_____. "The Hidden Son of Man in St. Mark's Gospel." Zeitschrift für die neutestamentliche Wissenschaft, LII (1961), 189-213.

_____. Mysterious Revelation. Ithaca, N.T.: Cornell University Press, 1963.

_____. "The Trial of Jesus." Vigiliae Christianae, XII (1958), 1-18.

Buse, Ivor. "St. John and the Marcan Passion Narrative." New Testament Studies, IV (1957-1958), 215-219.

Catchpole, D. R. "The Answer of Jesus to Caiaphas (Matt. xxvi. 64)." New Testament Studies, XVII (1971), 213-226.

_____. The Trial of Jesus. A Study in the Gospels and Jewish Historiography from 1770 to the Present Day. Studia Post-Biblica, Vol. XVIII. Leiden: E. J. Brill, 1971.

Charles, Robert Henry. The Apocrypha and Pseudepigrapha of the Old Testament. Vol. II, The Pseudepigrapha. Oxford: Clarendon Press, 1913.

Clemen, Carl. Religionsgeschichtliche Erklärung des Neuen Testaments. Giessen: Alfred Töpelmann, 1924.

Cohn, H. H. "Reflections on the Trial and Death of Jesus."
Israel Law Review, II (1967), 332-379.

_____. The Trial and Death of Jesus. New York: Harper and
Row, 1971.

Colpe, Carsten. Die religionsgeschichtliche Schule. Forschungen zur Religion und Literatur des Alten und Neuen Testaments, N.F., Vol. LXVIII. Göttingen: Vandenhoeck und
Ruprecht, 1961.

Conzelmann, Hans. Der Erste Brief an die Korinther. Kritisch-
exegetischer Kommentar über das Neue Testament. 11th ed.
Göttingen: Vandenhoeck und Ruprecht, 1969.

_____. "Geschichte und Eschaton nach Mc 13." Zeitschrift
für die neutestamentliche Wissenschaft, L (1959),
210-221.

_____. "History and Theology in the Passion Narratives of
the Synoptic Gospels." Interpretation, XXIV (1970),
178-197.

_____. The Theology of St. Luke. Translated by Geoffrey
Buswell. New York: Harper and Row, 1961.

Crossan, J. D. "The Parable of the Wicked Husbandmen." Journal
of Biblical Literature, XC (1971), 451-465.

Cullmann, Oscar. The Christology of the New Testament. Translated by Shirley C. Guthrie and Charles Hall. Philadelphia: Westminster Press, 1959.

Dahood, Mitchell. Psalms I. The Anchor Bible, Vol. XVI.
Garden City, N.Y.: Doubleday and Co., 1966.

Delorme, J. "Aspects doctrinaux de second Évangile. Études
récentes de la redaction de Marc." De Jesus aux Évangiles. Edited by Ignatius de la Potterie. Bibliotheca
Ephemeridum Theologicarum Lovaniensium, Vol. XLIII.
Gembloux: J. Duculot, 1967. Pp. 42-74.

Dewar, Francis. "Chapter 13 and the Passion Narrative in St.
Mark." Theology, LXIV (1961), 99-107.

Dibelius, Martin. Botschaft und Geschichte: Gesammelte Aufsätze von Martin Dibelius. Vol. I. Zur Evangelienforschung. Tübingen: J. C. B. Mohr [Paul Siebeck],
1953.

_____. "Zur Formgeschichte der Evangelien." Theologische
Rundschau, N.F., I (1929), 185-216.

_____. "Zur Formgeschichte des Neuen Testaments." Theologische Rundschau, N.F., III (1931), 207-242.

_____. From Tradition to Gospel. Translated by Bertram Lee
Woolf. The Scribner Library. New York: Charles
Scribner's Sons, n.d.

Dobschütz, Ernst von. "Zur Erzählungskunst des Markus." Zeitschrift für die neutestamentliche Wissenschaft, XXVII (1928), 193-198.

Dodd, Charles Harold. According to the Scriptures. New York: Charles Scribner's Sons, 1953.

_____. The Interpretation of the Fourth Gospel. Cambridge: University Press, 1958.

Doudna, John C. The Greek of the Gospel of Mark. Journal of Biblical Literature, Monograph Series, Vol. XII. Philadelphia: Society of Biblical Literature, 1961.

Edwards, Richard A. "The Eschatological Correlative as a Gattung in the New Testament." Zeitschrift für die neutestamentliche Wissenschaft, LX (1969), 9-20.

Eissfeldt, Otto. The Old Testament: An Introduction. Translated by Peter R. Ackroyd. New York: Harper and Row, 1964.

Evans, C. F. "I Will Go before You into Galilee." Journal of Theological Studies, N.S., V (1954), 3-18.

_____. Resurrection and the New Testament. Studies in Biblical Theology, Second Series, Vol. XII. London: S. C. M. Press, 1970.

Evans, Owen E. "Synoptic Criticism since Streeter." Expository Times, LXXII (1961), 295-299.

Farmer, William R. The Synoptic Problem: A Critical Analysis. New York: Macmillan Co., 1964.

Fascher, Erich. Die Formgeschichtliche Methode. Beihefte zur Zeitschrift für die neutestamentliche Wissenschaft, Vol. II. Giessen: A. Töpelmann, 1924.

Feine, Paul, Behm, Johannes, and Kümmel, Werner Georg. Introduction to the New Testament. Translated by A. J. Mattil, Jr. New York and Nashville: Abingdon Press, 1966.

Frye, Northrop. Anatomy of Criticism. Princeton, N.J.: Princeton University Press, 1957.

Fuller, Reginald. The Foundations of New Testament Christology. New York: Charles Scribner's Sons, 1965.

Gaertner, Bertil. The Temple and Community in Qumran and the New Testament. Cambridge: University Press, 1965.

Gallie, W. B. Philosophy and the Historical Understanding. New York: Schocken, 1968.

Gaston, Lloyd. No Stone on Another. Supplements to Novum Testamentum, Vol. XXIII. Leiden: E. J. Brill, 1970.

Glasson, T. Francis. "The Reply to Caiaphas (Mark XIV.62)." New Testament Studies, VII (1960-1961), 88-93.

Glasson, T. Francis. The Second Advent. 3d rev. ed. London: Epworth Press, 1963.

Grant, Frederick C. The Earliest Gospel. New York and Nashville: Abingdon-Cokesbury, 1943.

Grant, Robert M. Augustus to Constantine. New York: Harper and Row, 1970.

Grobel, Kendrick. Formgeschichte und Synoptische Quellenanalyse. Forschungen zur Religion und Literatur des Alten und Neuen Testaments, N.F., Vol. XXV. Göttingen: Vandenhoeck und Ruprecht, 1937.

_____. "Idiosyncracies of the Synoptists in Their Pericopae --Introductions." Journal of Biblical Literature, LIX (1940), 405-410.

Haenchen, Ernst. Die Apostelgeschichte. Kritisch-exegetischer Kommentar über das Neue Testament. 18th ed. Göttingen: Vandenhoeck und Ruprecht, 1961.

_____. "Die Komposition von Mk VIII.28-IX.1 und Par." Novum Testamentum, VI (1963), 81-110.

Hahn, Ferdinand. Mission in the New Testament. Studies in Biblical Theology, Vol. XLVII. Translated by Frank Clarke. London: S. C. M. Press, 1965.

_____. The Titles of Jesus in Christology. Translated by H. Knight and G. Ogg. London: Luterworth Press, 1969.

Hare, Douglas R. A. The Theme of Jewish Persecution of Christians in the Gospel According to St. Matthew. Society for New Testament Studies, Monograph Series, Vol. VI. Cambridge: University Press, 1967.

Hartmann, Lars. Prophecy Interpreted: The Formation of Some Jewish Apocalyptic and of the Eschatological Discourse Mark 13 par. Lund: G. W. K. Gleerup, 1966.

Hawkins, John C. Horae Synopticae. Grand Rapids, Mich.: Baker Book House, 1968.

Hempel, J. "Religionsgeschichtliche Schule." Religion in Geschichte und Gegenwart. 3d ed. V, 991-994.

Hengel, Martin. Die Zeloten. Arbeiten zur Geschichte des Spätjudentums und Urchristentums, Vol. I. Leiden: E. J. Brill, 1961.

Higgins, A. J. B. Jesus and the Son of Man. Philadelphia: Fortress Press, 1964.

Hirsch, Emanuel. Frügeschichte des Evangelium. Vol. I: Das Werden des Markusevangeliums. 2d rev. ed. Tübingen: J. C. B. Mohr [Paul Siebeck], 1951.

Horstmann, Maria. Studien zur Markinischen Christologie. Neutestamentliche Abhandlungen, N.F., Vol. VI. Münster: Verlag Aschendorf, 1969.

Jeremias, Joachim. "Eckstein--Schlusstein." Zeitschrift für die neutestamentliche Wissenschaft, XXXVI (1937), 154-157.

_____. The Eucharistic Words of Jesus. Translated by Norman Perrin. 3d rev. ed. London: S. C. M. Press, 1966.

_____. "γωνία." Theological Dictionary of the New Testament. I, 791-793.

_____. Jesus als Weltvollender. Beiträge für die Förderung Christlicher Theologie, Vol. XXXIII. Gutersloh: Verlag C. Bertelsmann, 1930.

_____. "κεφαλὴ γωνίας--ἀκρωγωνιαῖος." Zeitschrift fur die neutestamentliche Wissenschaft, XXIX (1930), 264-280.

_____. The Parables of Jesus. Translated by S. H. Hooke. 6th ed. New York: Charles Scribner's Sons, 1963.

Jeremias, Joachim, and Zimmerli, Walther. The Servant of God. Studies in Biblical Theology, Vol. XX. Rev. ed. London: S. C. M. Press, 1965.

Jonge, M. de. Testamenta XII Patriarcharum. Leiden: E. J. Brill, 1964.

Kähler, Martin. The So-Called Historical Jesus and the Historic Biblical Christ. Translated, edited and with an introduction by Carl E. Braaten. Seminar Editions. Philadelphia: Fortress Press, 1964.

Käsemann, Ernst. New Testament Questions Today. Translated by W. J. Montague. Philadelphia: Fortress Press, 1969.

Keck, Leander E. "The Introduction to Mark's Gospel." New Testament Studies, XII (1965-1966), 352-370.

_____. "Mark 3:7-12 and Mark's Christology." Journal of Biblical Literature, LXXXIV (1965), 341-358.

Kelber, Werner. "Kingdom and Parousia in the Gospel of Mark." Unpublished Ph.D. dissertation, University of Chicago, 1970.

Kertlege, K. Die Wunder Jesu im Markusevangelium. Studien zum Alten und Neuen Testament, Vol. XXIII. Munich: Kösel Verlag, 1970.

Klausner, Joseph. Jesus of Nazareth. London: Allen and Unwin, 1925.

Klein, Günther. "Die Verleugnung des Petrus: Eine traditionsgeschichtliche Untersuchung." Zeitschrift für Theologie und Kirche, LVIII (1961), 286-328.

Knigge, Hans-Dieter. "The Meaning of Mark." Interpretation, XXII (1958), 53-70.

Knox, John. "A Note on Mark 14, 51-52." The Joy of Study. Edited by Sherman E. Johnson. New York: Macmillan Co., 1951.

Knox, Wilfred. The Sources of the Synoptic Gospels. Vol. I: St. Mark. Cambridge: University Press, 1953.

Kuby, Alfred. "Zur Konzeption des Markus-Evangelium." Zeitschrift für die neutestamentliche Wissenschaft, XLIX (1958), 52-64.

Kümmel, Werner G. "Das Gleichnis von den bösen Weingärtnern." Aux Sources de la Tradition Chrétienne. Mélanges à Maurice Goguel. Paris: Delachaux et Niestle, 1950.

_____. Das Neue Testament: Geschichte der Erforschung seiner Probleme. 2d rev. ed. Munich: Verlag Karl Alber, 1970.

_____. Promise and Fulfillment. Studies in Biblical Theology, Vol. XXIII. London: S. C. M. Press, 1966.

Kuhn, Karl Georg, and Gutbrod, Walter. "Ισραήλ." Theological Dictionary of the New Testament. III, 359-375.

Kuhn, Karl Georg. "Jesus in Gethsemane." Evangelische Theologie, XII (1952-1953), 260-285.

Lambrecht, Jan. Die Redaktion des Markus-Apocalypse. Analecta Biblica, Vol. XXVIII. Rome: Biblical Institute Press, 1967.

Langevin, Paul-Émile. Jésus Seigneur et L'Eschatologie: Exégèse de Textes Prepauliniens. Studia, Vol. XXI. Paris: Desclée de Brouwer, 1967.

Léon-Dufour, Xavier. "Passion [Récits de la]," Dictionnaire de la Bible, Supplement VI, Cols. 1419-1492.

Lightfoot, Robert Henry. History and Interpretation in the Gospels. New York: Harper and Brothers, 1934.

_____. The Gospel Message of St. Mark. Oxford Paperbacks. London: Oxford University Press, 1962.

_____. Locality and Doctrine in the Gospels. New York: Harper and Brothers, 1938.

Lindars, Barnabas. New Testament Apologetic. Philadelphia: Westminster Press, 1961.

Linnemann, Eta. Studien zur Passionsgeschichte. Forschungen zur Religion und Literatur des Alten und Neuen Testaments, Vol. CII. Göttingen: Vandenhoeck und Ruprecht, 1970.

Lohmeyer, Ernst. "Das Gleichnis von den bösen Weingärtnern." Zeitschrift für systematische Theologie, XVIII (1941), 242-259.

Lohmeyer, Ernst. Lord of the Temple: A Study of the Relation between Cult and Gospel. Translated by Stewart Todd. London and Edinburgh: Oliver and Boyd, 1961.

_____. Galiläa und Jerusalem. Forschungen zur Religion und Literatur des Alten und Neuen Testaments, N.F., Vol. XXIV. Göttingen: Vandenhoeck und Ruprecht, 1936.

Lohr, Charles. "Oral Techniques in the Gospel of Matthew." Catholic Biblical Quarterly, XXIII (1961), 403-435.

Lövestam, E. "Die Frage des Hohenpriesters," Svensk exegetisk Årsbok, XXVI (1961), 93-107.

Lund, Nils W. Chiasmus in the New Testament. Chapel Hill, N.C.: University of North Carolina Press, 1942.

Luz, Ulrich. "Das Geheimnismotiv und die Markinische Christologie." Zeitschrift für die neutestamentliche Wissenschaft, LVI (1965), 45-74.

McArthur, Harvey K. "Mark XIV.62." New Testament Studies, IV (1957-1958), 156-158.

McKelvey, R. J. "Christ the Cornerstone." New Testament Studies, VIII (1961-1962), 352-359.

_____. The New Temple. Oxford: University Press, 1969.

McKenzie, John L. Second Isaiah. The Anchor Bible, Vol. XX. Garden City, N.Y.: Doubleday and Co., 1968.

Manson, T. W. The Teaching of Jesus. Cambridge: University Press, 1963.

Marxsen, Willi. Introduction to the New Testament. Translated by Geoffrey Buswell. Philadelphia: Fortress Press, 1968.

_____. Mark the Evangelist. Translated by James Boyce et al. New York and Nashville: Abingdon Press, 1969.

_____. "Redaktionsgeschichtliche Erklärung der sogennanten Parabeltheorie des Markus." Zeitschrift für Theologie und Kirche, LII (1955), 255-271.

Matera, F. J. "Interpreting Mark--Some Recent Theories of Redaction Criticism." Louvain Studies, II (1968), 113-131.

Maurer, Christian. "Knecht Gottes und Sohn Gottes im Passionsbericht des Markus." Zeitschrift für Theologie und Kirche, L (1953), 1-51.

_____. "Das Messiasgeheimnis des Markusevangeliums." New Testament Studies, XIV (1967-1968), 515-528.

Meyer, Eduard. Ursprung und Anfänge des Christentums. 3 vols. Stuttgart: J. G. Gotta'sche Buchhandlung, 1923.

Michaelis, Wilhelm. "ὁδός." Theological Dictionary of the New Testament. V, 42-96.

Michel, Otto. "ναός." Theological Dictionary of the New Testament. IV, 880-890.

Mollat, D. L'Évangile de saint Jean. Bible de Jérusalem. Paris: Cerf, 1953.

Moore, A. L. The Parousia in the New Testament. Supplements to Novum Testamentum, Vol. XIII. Leiden: E. J. Brill, 1966.

Morgenthaler, Robert. Statistik des Neutestamentlichen Wortschatzes. Zürich und Frankfurt: Gotthelf-Verlag, 1958.

Moule, Charles F. "Sanctuary and Sacrifice in the Church of the New Testament." Journal of Theological Studies, N.S., I (1950), 29-41.

Moulton, James Hope. A Grammar of New Testament Greek. Vol. I. Edinburgh: T. and T. Clarke, 1908.

Mowinckel, Sigmund. The Psalms in Israel's Worship. Translated by D. R. Ap-Thomas. New York and Nashville: Abingdon Press, 1967.

Münderlein, Gerhard. "Die Verfluchung des Feigenbaumes." New Testament Studies, X (1963-1964), 89-104.

Neirynck, F. "Mark in Greek." Ephemerides Theologicae Lovanienses, XLVII (1971), 144-198.

_____. "Duality in Mark." Ephemerides Theologicae Lovanienses, XLVII (1971), 394-463.

_____. "Duplicate Expressions in the Gospel of Mark." Ephemerides Theologicae Lovanienses, XLVIII (1972), 150-209.

Norden, Eduard. Agnostos Theos. Leipzig: Teubner Verlag, 1913.

North, Christopher R. The Second Isaiah. Oxford: Clarendon Press, 1964.

Pedersen, Johannes. Israel: Its Life and Culture. Vol. I. London: Oxford University Press, 1926.

Perrin, Norman. "The Christology of Mark: A Study in Methodology." Journal of Religion, LI (1971), 173-187.

_____. "The Creative Use of the Son of Man Traditions by Mark." Union Seminary Quarterly Review, XXIII (1968), 357-365.

_____. The Kingdom of God in the Teaching of Jesus. London: S. C. M. Press, 1963.

Perrin, Norman. "The Literary Gattung 'Gospel'--Some Observations." Expository Times, LXXXII (1970), 4-7.

_____. "Mark XIV.62: The End Product of a Christian Pesher Tradition?" New Testament Studies, XII (1965-1966), 150-155.

_____. Rediscovering the Teaching of Jesus. New York: Harper and Row, 1967.

_____. "The Son of Man in Ancient Judaism and Primitive Christianity: A Suggestion." Biblical Research, XIII (1968), 1-23.

_____. "The Use of (παρα)διδόναι in Connection with the Passion of Jesus in the New Testament." Der Ruf Jesu und die Antwort der Gemeinde. Festschrift für Joachim Jeremias zum 70 Geburtstag. Edited by Eduard Lohse. Göttingen: Vandenhoeck und Ruprecht, 1970. Pp. 204-212.

_____. What is Redaction Criticism? Guides to Biblical Scholarship. Philadelphia: Fortress Press, 1969.

Pesch, Rudolph. Naherwartungen: Tradition und Redaktion in Mk 13. Düsseldorf: Patmos Verlag, 1968.

Philonenko, Marc. Les interpolations chrétiennes des Testaments des Douze Patriarches et les manuscrits de Qoumrân. Cahiers de la Revue d'histoire et de philosophie religieuses, Vol. XXXV. Paris: Presses Universitaires de France, 1960.

Rad, Gerhard von. Old Testament Theology. 2 vols. Translated by D. M. G. Stalker. New York: Harper and Row, 1962, 1965.

Rigaux, Beda. Saint Paul, Les Épitres Aux Thessaloniciens. Études Bibliques. Paris: Librairie Lecoffre, 1956.

Ringgren, Helmer. The Faith of Qumran. Fortress Press Paperback. Philadelphia: Fortress Press, 1963.

Robbins, Vernon K. "The Christology of Mark." Unpublished Ph.D. dissertation, University of Chicago, 1969.

Robert, A., and Feuillet, A., eds. Introduction à la Bible. Paris: Desclée, 1959.

Robinson, James M. The Problem of History in Mark. Studies in Biblical Theology, Vol. XXI. London: S. C. M. Press, 1957.

_____. "The Problem of History in Mark Reconsidered." Union Seminary Quarterly Review, XXX (1965), 131-147.

Robinson, John A. T. Jesus and His Coming. London: S. C. M. Press, 1957.

_____. Twelve New Testament Studies. Studies in Biblical Theology, Vol. XXXIV. London: S. C. M. Press, 1962.

Rohde, Joachim. Rediscovering the Teaching of the Evangelists. Translated by Dorothea M. Barton. Philadelphia: Westminster Press, 1969.

Roloff, Jürgen. "Das Markusevangelium als Geschichtsdarstellung." Evangelische Theologie, XXIX (1969), 73-93.

Rose, A, "L'influence des psaumes sur les annonces et les récits de la Passion et de la Resurrection dans les Évangiles." Orientalia et Biblica Lovaniensia, Vol. IV. Louvain: Publications Universitaires, 1962.

Rowley, H. H. The Relevance of Apocalyptic. 3d rev. ed. London: Lutterworth Press, 1963.

Sacks, Sheldon. Fiction and the Shape of Belief. Berkeley: University of California Press, 1967.

Schille, Gottfried. "Bemerkungen zur Formgeschichte des Evangeliums." New Testament Studies, IV (1957-1958), 1-31.

_____. "Das Leiden des Herrn: Die evangelische Passionstradition und ihr Sitz im Leben." Zeitschrift für Theologie und Kirche, LII (1955), 161-205.

Schmidt, Karl Ludwig. Der Rahmen der Geschichte Jesu. Berlin: Trowitzsch und Sohn, 1919.

Schnackenburg, Rudolf. God's Rule and Kingdom. Translated by John Murray. New York: Herder and Herder, 1968.

_____. Das Johannesevangelium, I. Herder Theologischer Kommentar zum Neuen Testament. Freiburg: Herder, 1965.

Schneider, Gerhard. "Gab es eine vorsynoptische Szene 'Jesus vor dem Synedrium?'" Novum Testamentum, XII (1970), 22-39.

_____. "Jesus vor dem Synedrium." Bibel und Leben, XI (1970), 1-15.

_____. Verleugnung, Verspottung und Verhör Jesu nach Lukas 22, 54-71. Studien zum Alten und Neuen Testament. Munich: Kösel Verlag, 1970.

Scholles, R., and Kellog, R. The Nature of Narrative. New York: Oxford University Press, 1966.

Schreiber, Johannes. "Die Christologie des Markusevangeliums." Zeitschrift für Theologie und Kirche, LVIII (1961), 154-183.

_____. Die Theologie des Vertrauens. Hamburg: Furche Verlag, 1969.

Schrenk, Gottlob. "τὸ ἱερόν." Theological Dictionary of the New Testament, III, 230-247.

Schweizer, Eduard. "Anmerkungen zur Theologie des Markus." Neotestamentica. Zurich: Zwingli Verlag, 1963. Pp. 93-104.

Schweizer, Eduard. "Der Menschensohn." Neotestamentica. Stuttgart: Zwingli Verlag, 1963. Pp. 56-84.

_____. "Die theologische Leistung des Markus." Evangelische Theologie, XXIV (1964), 337-355.

Schweitzer, Albert. The Quest of the Historical Jesus. Translated by W. Montgomery. Macmillan Paperbacks. New York: Macmillan Co., 1961.

Simon, Ulrich. "The Problem of Biblical Narrative." Theology, LXXII (1969), 243-253.

Spicq, C. "Le philonisme de l'épitre aux Hebreux." Revue Biblique, LVII (1950), 212-242.

Stauffer, Ethelbert. Jesus and His Story. Translated by Richard and Clara Winston. New York: Knopf, 1963.

Stein, Robert H. "The 'Redaktionsgeschichtlich' Investigation of a Markan Seam (Mc 1:21f.)." Zeitschrift für die neutestamentliche Wissenschaft, LXI (1970), 70-94.

_____. "What Is Redaktionsgeschichte?" Journal of Biblical Literature, LXXXVIII (1969), 45-56.

Strack, Hermann L., and Billerbeck, Paul. Kommentar zum Neuen Testament aus Talmud und Midrasch. 4 vols. Munich: C. H. Beck, 1922-1956.

Strecker, Georg. "Zur Messiasgeheimnistheorie im Markusevangelium." Studia Evangelica. Edited by Frank L. Cross. Texte und Untersuchungen, Vol. LXXXVII. Berlin: Akademie Verlag, 1964. Pp. 87-104.

_____. "The Passion-and-Resurrection Predictions in Mark's Gospel." Interpretation, XXII (1968), 421-442.

Strobel, August. Kerygma und Apokalyptik. Göttingen: Vandenhoeck und Ruprecht, 1967.

Suhl, Alfred. Die Funktion der alttestamentlichen Zitate und Anspielungen im Markusevangelium. Güttersloh: Gerd Mohn, 1965.

Thackery, Henry St. John, ed. Josephus: The Jewish War. Loeb Classical Library. New York: G. P. Putnam's Sons, 1927.

Tillesse, G. Minette de. Le Secret messianique dans l'Évangile de Marc. Lectio Divina, Vol. XLVII. Paris: Cerf, 1968.

Tödt, Heinz E. The Son of Man in the Synoptic Tradition. Translated by Dorothea M. Barton. Philadelphia: Westminster Press, 1965.

Turner, C. H. "Marcan Usage: Notes, Critical and Exegetical on the Second Gospel." Journal of Theological Studies, XXV (1924), 377-386; XXVI (1925), 12-20, 145-156, 225-240; XXVII (1926), 58-62; XXVIII (1927), 9-30, 349=362; XXIX (1928), 275-289, 346-361.

Tyson, Joseph. "The Blindness of the Disciples." Journal of Biblical Literature, LXXX (1961), 261-268.

Vanhoye, A. "Structure et théologie des récits de la passion." Nouvelle Revue Théologique, XCIX (1967), 135-163. [English translation by Homer Giblin, Structure and Theology of the Accounts of the Passion in the Synoptic Gospels. Collegeville, Minn.: The Liturgical Press, 1967]

Vielhauer, Philipp. Aufsätze zum Neuen Testament. Theologische Bücherei, Vol. XXI. Munich: Kaiser Verlag, 1965.

_____. "Zur Frage der Christologischen Hoheitstitel." Theologische Literaturzeitung, XC (1965), 569-588.

Volz, Paul. Die Eschatologie der Jüdischen Gemeinde in neutestamentlicher Zeitalter. Tübingen: J. C. B. Mohr [Paul Siebeck], 1934.

Waetjen, Herman. "The Ending of Mark and the Gospel's Shift in Eschatology." Annual of the Swedish Theological Institute, Vol. VI. Leiden: E. J. Brill, 1965. Pp. 114-131.

Walter, Nikolaus. "Tempelzerstörung und synoptische Apokalypse." Zeitschrift für die neutestamentliche Wissenschaft, LVII (1966), 38-49.

Weeden, Theodore J. "The Heresy that Necessitated Mark's Gospel." Zeitschrift fur die neutestamentliche Wissenschaft, LIX (1958), 145-158.

_____. Mark--Traditions in Conflict. Philadelphia: Fortress Press, 1971.

Wellek, R., and Warren, A. Theory of Literature. New York: Harcourt, Brace and World, 1956.

Wellhausen, Julius. Einleitung in Die Drei Ersten Evangelien. 2d ed. Berlin: Verlag Georg Reimer, 1911.

Wending, Emil. Die Entstehung des Marcus-Evangeliums. Tübingen: J. C. B. Mohr [Paul Siebeck], 1908.

Weiss, H. "History and a Gospel." Novum Testamentum, X (1968), 81-94.

Wilcox, Max. "The Denial Sequence in Mark XIV.26-31, 66-72." New Testament Studies, XVII (1969-1970), 426-436.

Wilder, Amos. The Language of the Gospel. New York: Harper and Row, 1964.

_____. The New Voice. New York: Herder and Herder, 1969.

Wilson, W. R. The Execution of Jesus. New York: Charles Scribner's Sons, 1970.

Wimsatt, William K. The Verbal Icon. New York: Noonday Press, 1953.

Winer, G. B. Grammar of New Testament Greek. Translated by W. F. Moulton. Edinburgh: T. and T. Clarke, 1882.

Wink, Walter. John the Baptist in the Gospel Tradition. Society for New Testament Studies, Monograph Series, Vol. VII. Cambridge: University Press, 1968.

Winter, Paul. "The Marcan Account of Jesus' Trial by the Sanhedrin." Journal of Theological Studies, N.S., XIV (1963), 94-102.

_____. "Marginal Notes on the Trial of Jesus." Zeitschrift für die neutestamentliche Wissenschaft, LIII (1962), 260-263.

_____. On the Trial of Jesus. Studia Judaica. Berlin: Walter de Gruyter, 1961.

Wrede, William. Das Messiasgeheimnis in den Evangelien. Göttingen: Vandenhoeck und Ruprecht, 1901. [The Messianic Secret. Translated by J.C.C. Grieg. The Library of Theological Translations. Cambridge and London: James Clarke and Co. Ltd., 1971]

Zimmermann, Heinrich. "Das absolute Ego eimi als die neutestamentliche Offenbarungsformel." Biblische Zeitschrift, N.F., IV (1960), 54-69, 266-276.

_____. "Das absolute 'Ich bin' in der Redeweise Jesu." Trierer Theologische Zeitschrift, LXIX (1960), 1-20.

INDEX OF SCRIPTURAL CITATIONS

GENESIS

17:1	88
28:13	88

EXODUS

3:6	88
20:2	88
20:16	88

LEVITICUS

26:1	106

DEUTERONOMY

19:11	76
22:26	76

JUDGES

6:31	76
22:2-3	200

1 KINGS

6:7	202
6:16	202
6:19	202
6:21-23	202
6:31	202
22:24	98
26:33ff	202

PSALMS

2:7	88
3:1	76
22	193
22:1	193
22:7	193
22:18	193
27:3	76
27:12	24,74,75,76,100
35:4	75
35:7	75
35:11	74-76,100
38:13-16	22-23
44:5	76
109:2	24
110	173-174,182,186
110:1	93,94,143,145,147,161,173,175,177
118:22-23	122-126
118:25-26	125-126

PROVERBS

6:19	75
19:5,9	75

ISAIAH

5:1	123
8:14	125,127
13:9-10	133
19:1	106
21:9	106
27:2	123
28:16	125,126
31:7	106
50:5-6	21
50:6	21,98
50:8-9	100
53	99-100
53:3-5	98
53:7	22,23,87
53:8	100
56:7	66
58:2-3	14,15

JEREMIAH

12:10	123

EZEKIEL

17:6-8	123
41:3	202

DANIEL

5:12-13	200
6:6	200
7:13	93,94,142,143,145,147,158,159,160,161,169,173,177,182,183
7:14	169
9:27	130
11:31	130
12:11	130

JOEL

2:10-11	133
2:31	133

MICAH

5:1	98

ZECHARIAH
12:10ff.   90

MALACHI
3:1   121

MATTHEW
3:16-17   89
4:25   241
5:1-2   241
8:16   66
8:31   241
9:3-4   241
9:5-6   241
9:7   66
9:19   241
9:21-22   241
10:18   214
10:23   155
10:32   153
12:40   153,154
13:26   155
13:31-32   241
13:41   155
14:12-13   241
14:13   66
15:16-20   242
16:8-11   242
16:16   242
16:27-28   155
17:4   242
17:10-13   242
17:14   66
19:23-24   242
19:28   155,156,200
21:10-12   242
21:13   66
22:69   142
23:38   108
23:39   125
24:2   108
24:4   242
24:9-10   214
24:14   214
24:15   130
24:25   242
24:27   153,154
24:30   155
24:34ff.   154
24:37-39   153,154
24:39   155
24:44   153
25:13   242
25:13-15   242
25:31   155,156
25:42   242
26:21-26   242
26:60-61   72,242
26:61   104,186

26:64   88,91,142,186
26:66   58
27:5   105,108
27:11-12   242
27:28-31   98
27:34-36   243
27:39   104
27:42   198
27:57-68   55
27:60-61   78

MARK
Ch. 1
1:1   89,90,121,163,
               177,205
1:2-9   207
1:5   67
1:6   56
1:8   121
1:9   64
1:11   88,123,124,
               148,179,181
1:12   64
1:13   56
1:14   61,64,212,232
1:14-15   37,206,207
1:15   66,119
1:16   64,74
1:18   68
1:21   36,64,114
1:22   56,119,243
1:24   57
1:25-27   78,119,243
1:28   56
1:29   64,114,243
1:30   243
1:31   208
1:32   56,66,168,208
1:33   56,243
1:34   208
1:35   56,64,114,
               168,207,243
1:37   66,70
1:38   56,74,114,165
1:39   37,56
1:41-44   208
1:42   56
1:44   56,70,208
1:45   56,114,243

Ch. 2
2:1   64,114,208
2:1-5   82
2:1-11   81,82
2:1-12   208
2:1-13   37
2:2   56,243
2:5-10   37,82
2:6   56,57,78,241

2:6-11	119	4:13	165
2:7-8	81	4:21	165
2:8	78,119,241	4:24	165
2:9	241	4:31-32	241
2:10	81,120,163	4:31-34	78
2:10-11	82	4:34	129,207
2:11	241	4:35	165
2:12	66,67	4:38	56,57
2:13	37,64,66,67, 88,114,208	4:39	86
2:13-3:8	78	Ch. 5	
2:14	57,68,243	5:1	64
2:15	68,74,243	5:1-43	208
2:17	95	5:2	114
2:18	56	5:3	56
2:23	56,207	5:5	56
2:24	243	5:7	90,179
2:25	56,95,243	5:9	86
2:27	78,165	5:10	241
2:28	107,163	5:11	56
Ch. 3		5:15	56,57
3:1	64,113	5:17	56
3:1-6	208	5:20	56,66,67
3:2	107	5:21	37
3:4	57,86,165	5:21	64
3:6	57,69,71, 113,114,206	5:21	208
3:7	64,68,207	5:21-43	42,59
3:7-8	78,80,207	5:23	241
3:7-12	37,38,207	5:24	68,208
3:8-9	208	5:29	241
3:10	208	5:30-34	81
3:11	88,89,90, 178,179,208	5:31	243
3:12	208	5:32	243
3:13	64	5:34	241
3:13	207	5:37	56
3:14-15	81,83	5:39	114
3:14-16	241	5:43	208
3:15	119	Ch. 6	
3:20	56,64,66, 88,208	6:1	64,114,207
3:20-35	42,58	6:2	56,119
3:22	57,62	6:4	56,165,208
3:26	56	6:6	37,64
3:27	56	6:7	56,119
3:31	243	6:7-13	208
3:32	243	6:7-32	42,59
3:34	57	6:10	165
3:35	60	6:11	70
Ch. 4		6:12	114
4:1	56,57,64, 66,208	6:12-13	37
4:1-34	38	6:14	243
4:2	56,74,165,243	6:14-15	61,83
4:7	67	6:14-16	61
4:10	64,207	6:14-29	61
4:12	83	6:16	243
		6:17-29	61
		6:19	57
		6:30	64
		6:30-33	37,207,208
		6:30-8:21	83
		6:31	74,129,165

6:31-32	241
6:33	66,67
6:34	56,114
6:41	66
6:45	64
6:50	66,67,92
6:52	56
6:53	64
6:53-56	37
6:54	114
6:55	66

Ch. 7

7:3	66,67,243
7:4	243
7:9	165
7:12	56
7:14	88,107
7:15	56
7:17	114
7:18	165
7:20-23	242
7:21	56
7:23	119
7:24	64,114
7:30	70
7:31	64,88,114
7:32-36	78
7:33	56,129

Ch. 8

8:1	88,243
8:2	243
8:3	212
8:11	56,243
8:12	243
8:16	243
8:17	242,243
8:18	83
8:21	165,242
8:22	64,243
8:22-26	59,78
8:27	62,64,86,114, 163,166,181
8:29-9:1	162,163, 165,169
8:27-10:45	59
8:27-10:52	11,43
8:28	61,83,212
8:28-9:1	163
8:29	88,89,163, 177,178,181,242
8:30	178
8:30-9:4	81
8:31	11,43,56,57, 64,110,163,164, 166,170,172, 178,206
8:32	56
8:34-38	163,212

8:35	213
8:38	149,152, 162-168,165, 171,175,183
8:38-9:1	155

Ch. 9

9:1	94,133,163,164, 165,166,171,175
9:2	56,64,129
9:4	56,242
9:6	74
9:7	90,123,148, 179,181
9:8	56
9:9	167,243
9:10	243
9:11	86
9:12-13	81,242
9:14	243
9:15	66,67
9:16	243
9:22	57
9:28	114,129
9:30	64,114
9:31	43,57,110, 167,206
9:33	64,212
9:34	86
9:41	89,177
9:43	114
9:45	114
9:47	114,166

Ch. 10

10:1	37,64,88
10:5	107
10:11	165
10:15	114
10:17	114,214
10:20	119
10:23	64,114
10:23-24	80,242
10:23-25	166
10:24	81,114
10:25	114
10:27-31	167
10:28	56
10:29	213,243
10:30	168,243
10:32	56,64,212
10:33	11,43,64,96, 110,172,206
10:34	57,165,167
10:38	243
10:41	56
10:42	243
10:45-52	59
10:46	57,64,114,243
10:47	56

10:48	86	12:1-12	122-128,136
10:52	68,212	12:5	57
		12:6	90,123,124
Ch. 11		12:7	57
11:1	64,115,127,	12:8	57
	129,203	12:9	57,127
11:1ff.	185	12:10	125,126
11:1-3	129	12:10-11	122-125,134
11:1-6	78	12:12	69,113,124,
11:1-12	115		127,206
11:1-18	113-117	12:13	116
11:1-27	115-117,120	12:13-17	115,117
11:1-12:44	115,116,	12:13-44	116,117
	120,128	12:14	56
11:3	95	12:16	165
11:4	70	12:17	118
11:9	125,126	12:18	86,116
11:9-11	114	12:18-27	115,117,167
11:10	114,125,126,166	12:28	116
11:11	104,113,114,	12:28-33	115
	115,242	12:28-34	117
11:12	129	12:30	165
11:12-16	60	12:32	165
11:12-25	42	12:34	118,165
11:12-26	42,59	12:35	64,89,104,
11:13	70,74		116,177
11:14	56	12:35-37	115
11:15	56,64,104,	12:36	57,165
	113,242	12:37	165
11:15-18	114	12:38-40	116,135
11:15	115	12:41-44	116,135
11:15-17	115		
11:16	104	Ch. 13	
11:17	66,114	13:1	64,104,128,129
11:18	57,62,64,66,	13:1-2	78,135
	69,113,114,	13:1-4	128
	127,206	13:1-5	128
11:19	115	13:2	64,72,108,
11:20	115		133,136
11:20-27	115	13:3	57,104,128,
11:26	115		129,135
11:27	64,104,113,	13:4	119,129
	115,117,127	13:5	56,131-132,242
11:27-33	115,<u>117</u>,	13:5-37	135
	118,120,<u>121</u>,	13:6	92,130,221
	122,136	13:6-8	213
11:27-12:12	116,117	13:7	130,132,134,198
11:28	117,119,243	13:7-20	130
11:28-12:44	116	13:8	119
11:29	243	13:9	70,97,170,
11:30	118		<u>212-215</u>,218,242
11:31-32	118,120,121	13:9-13	170,
11:33	118,165,243		<u>212-222</u>,230
11:38	243	13:10	66,<u>213,221</u>,222
		13:11	97,170,212,
Ch. 12			213,215,222
12:1	56	13:12	57,70,120,
12:1ff.	125		212,213-215
12:1-9	122,124	13:14	94,130,133,168

13:14-19	213
13:21	177
13:21-23	130
13:22	168,221
13:23	66,242
13:24	94,132
13:24-25	132,169,170
13:24-27	133,168, 172,232,149
13:26	94,137,143,149, 152,155,160,165, 168-172,183,200
13:26-27	130,175
13:27	134,166,171
13:29	119
13:30	165
13:32-37	134
13:33	242
13:33-35	242
13:34	81
13:35	134
13:35-37	80,242
13:36	70
13:36	81
13:37	66,67

Ch. 14

14:1	17,56,57,69, 113,128,135,206
14:1-11	59
14:1-25	42
14:2-10	17
14:3	64
14:3-9	60
14:4	56
14:8	62
14:9	231
14:10	17,64
14:10-25	59
14:12-16	17,129
14:13-16	78
14:13	129
14:16	70
14:17	134
14:18	242
14:19	56
14:22	242
14:25	56,62,166
14:26	114,129
14:26-31	222
14:27	64,206
14:28	167,205
14:30	168
14:32	64
14:32-42	17
14:33	56
14:40	56,70
14:43	56,64,168
14:43-50	134
14:48	56
14:49	104
14:50	11,68
14:51	55,206
14:51-52	191
14:53	9,55,57,63-66, 68,87,101,117, 164,172
14:53-55	63-67
14:53-65	1,9,22,224
14:54	9,11,42,55,56, 57,67-68,87
14:54-72	42,59
14:55	3,9,23,57,64, 67,68-71,75, 87,97,101,113
14:55-61	9
14:55-64	65,211
14:56	9,50,70,73,74, 77,78,79,83,87, 101,103,242
14:56-57	74,75,79
14:56-59	71-84
14:57	9,23,55,74
14:57-58	74
14:57-59	21
14:58	2,11,18,19,21, 23,27,29,30,34, 50,71,72,77,78, 83,101,103,104-113, 108,109,112,120, 132,134,136,139, 166,175,176, 190,196
14:59	9,23,55,60,70, 73,77,78,79,83, 101,103,242
14:60	22,23,55,56, 57,71,74,101
14:60-61	85,86,99
14:60-62	21,23,84-95
14:60-64	71
14:61	10,23,27,55,56, 57,85,86,88,89, 90,177,179,196, 222,233
14:61-62	2,11,21,29, 30,44,50,87, 88-95,120, 138-142,146,149, 164,190,196
14:61-63	19
14:62	10,22,27,57,84, 85,86,87,89,90, 92,93,94,95,97, 101,102,133,142, 143,145,147,148, 149,158,161,164, 165,169,172, 172-177,173,175, 176,178,182,183, 184,185,200,233

14:63	55,56,57,84
14:63-64	95-98
14:64	66,67,96,97,101
14:65	19,21,26,55,56, 71,73,98,99,172
14:66	42,55,68
14:66-72	9,11,222
14:69	56
14:71	56
14:72	134

Ch. 15

15:1	19,21,64,65, 117,134
15:1-5	22,23,24, 29,211
15:2	88,89,199
15:2-4	211,242
15:2-5	65
15:3	64
15:4	22,56,86
15:5	27,56
15:7	56
15:8	56
15:11	64
15:12	199
15:15	64
15:16-20	25
15:17-20	98
15:18	199
15:20-22	192
15:20-24	194
15:20-41	189,190
15:22	192,195
15:23	81,192
15:24	64,193,195,243
15:24-27	192
15:25	192,195
15:26	56,192,194, 195,199
15:27	194,196
15:27-29	192,205
15:29	72,104,192, 193,194,195,198
15:29-30	196,197
15:29-32	190,192,194, 195,196
15:30	243
15:30-31	192
15:31	64,194
15:31-32	194,196
15:32	75,177,192,193, 194,196,200,243
15:33	192,195
15:34	192,193,195,243
15:34-36	192
15:34-37	192
15:36	194
15:37	194,195,201,243
15:37-38	192
15:38	108,194,195, 201,203
15:38-39	190,192,194, 196,201,205
15:39	90,148,178,185, 192,193,196,201, 204,223,230
15:39-41	192
15:40	56,176,196,205, 209,243
15:41	205
15:42	168
15:43	56,166
15:44	243
15:46	56
15:47	243

Ch. 16

16:1	176
16:1-8	113
16:2	168
16:5	57,206
16:7	133,171,176, 205,209
16:8	17,56,74,114

LUKE

1:6	57
1:68	90
4:40	66
5:21-23	241
5:23-24	241
5:25	66
6:12-13	241
6:17-18	241
8:32	241
8:40	241
8:45-48	241
9:10	241
9:11	66
9:20	242
9:33	242
9:37	66
11:30	153,154
12:8	153,154,164,166
12:40	153,154,242
13:19	241
13:34-35	108
13:35	125
17:22	155
17:23	242
17:24	153,154
17:26	153
17:28ff.	155
17:28-30	154
18:8	155
18:24-25	242
19:12-13	242
19:45	242

19:46	60
21:6	108
21:8	242
21:13	215
21:15	215
21:21-23	215
21:36	155,242
22:19	242
22:63-64	98
22:66	21,65
22:67	88
22:71	70,96
23:3	242
23:9	87
23:33-34	243

JOHN

1:14	107
2:19	104,105
2:19-22	72
2:20	108
2:21	107,110
4:21	107
10:33	96
10:36	96
18:13	65
18:18	57,67
18:23-24	96
18:25	57,67
19:2-3	98
19:7	96
19:9	87
19:13	14,15
19:19	199
19:21	199

ACTS

1:6	200
4:11	124,125
6:14	104,105,106
7:1-55	107
7:48	106
7:55-56	158
17:24	106
18:12ff.	218
22	218

ROMANS

1:25	57,90
8:33-34	174
9:5	57,90

1 CORINTHIANS

2:8	229
3:16-17	108
4:13	97
11:23-26	228
15:3-8	228
15:4	110
15:24-25	174,175
16:13	158

2 CORINTHIANS

1:3	57,90
5:2	158
6:16	108
11:31	57,90

GALATIANS

1:4	159
1:8	158
2:18	106
2:20	159
6:16	200

EPHESIANS

1:3	57,90
2:11	106
2:20-21	108

COLOSSIANS

4:2	158

1 THESSALONIANS

1:3	158
1:9-10	147,157-159
1:13	160
3:13	159
4:15-17	147,159
4:16	158
5:6	158
5:8	158

2 THESSALONIANS

1:7	158
1:7	160
2:4	108

1 PETER

1:3	57,90
2:1-10	125
2:5	125
2:6-9	126
4:4	97

HEBREWS

6:19	203
9:3	203
9:24	106
10:19	203

REVELATION

1:5-7	160
1:13	160
2:9	97
6:12-13	133
6:16-17	133
8:12	133
11:19	108
14:14	160
14:15-17	108

www.ingramcontent.com/pod-product-compliance
Lightning Source LLC
Chambersburg PA
CBHW031251230426
43670CB00005B/139